The Third Miracle

✠

Also by Bill Briggs

Amped: A Soldier's Race for Gold in the Shadow of War
(coauthor)

The Third Miracle

An Ordinary Man,
a Medical Mystery, and
a Trial of Faith

✠

Bill Briggs

Broadway Paperbacks
New York

BROADWAY

Library of Congress Cataloging-in-Publication Data
Briggs, Bill.
The third miracle : an ordinary man, a medical mystery,
and a trial of faith / Bill Briggs.
p. cm.
1. Guérin, Theodore, Saint, 1798–1856.   2. McCord, Phil, 1946–   I. Title.
BX4651.3.B75 2010
282.092'2—dc22
[B]
2010014599

ISBN 978-0-767-93271-4
eISBN 978-0-767-93270-7

Book design by Leonard Henderson
Cover design by David Tran
Cover photograph: Michael Duva/Getty Images

First Paperback Edition

146122990

For Margaret and Robert

For Helen and Bill

For your wisdom. For your love.

And for Nancy

My beautiful muse.

There are two ways to live:

you can live as if nothing is a miracle;

you can live as if everything is a miracle.

—*Albert Einstein*

Contents

Prologue

The convent's caretaker was an ordinary man. Quiet and industrious. Good with his hands. Good with people. And while he rarely spoke of himself, if pressed, the caretaker would say he was diligent, clever, and careful about protecting precious things—such as his family and his planet. He wasn't Catholic. Of course, that never stopped the nuns from liking Phil McCord. He always fixed what was broken.

In his fifty-plus years, the caretaker had pondered and solved many conundrums—like snarled plumbing and leaky roofs, like who he was and why he was here. But after his baffling overnight cure, McCord faced new questions. And some of those questions bothered him deeply.

Had he really deserved God's help?

Would he ever receive a bill for his divine favor?

If that bill came due, how much would it cost him?

The caretaker was shaped by an endless appetite to see and to grasp the intricate machinery of this world and beyond. He peered past the obvious surface, past accepted explanations. He ripped apart riddles, busted them down to better comprehend their complexities. How did electricity work? How did a biomass furnace function? How much of our paths were forged by self-determination and how much by a higher power? By McCord's estimation, people generally made their own choices and their own way in this life, and rarely—very rarely—did God step in. He compared his own vision of faith to the massive web of National Security Agency supercomputers that simultaneously eavesdropped on millions of e-mail chats and phone conversations.

"They listen to everything and occasionally they pick up one snippet of something. I look at it like that: God doesn't micromanage but when something pops up, when there's an opportunity to do something with meaning, there will be an intervention."

That was one of the lessons he had learned after he beat the incalculable odds and suddenly got better.

In blue jeans and a gray beard, the caretaker mirrored his humble, homey surroundings. Indiana was his land, and the place had branded him with certain essential values: Earn your keep, mend your own problems, and hash out your big decisions at the supper table. That was where he spent the better part of each evening, sitting across from his wife. She once had been a farm girl. Now she was a nurse. A touch sarcastic, she had seen a lot of blood and a lot of death. She kept him grounded.

"I wonder what all this means?" he posed one night as they shared another steaming meal at the circular wooden table nestled just off their kitchen, next to a bay window.

She usually just listened quietly for a while, letting him vent, letting him search.

"Was I just at the right place, at the right time? Am I worthy? How did this happen? How did that work? What caused it? It wasn't like there was a bolt of lightning or something. I don't understand."

"I've seen people walk away from so much worse," she finally answered. "It is what it is. Deal with it. It happens. I've seen it. In fact, I've seen a lot of it. Accept it."

If only I could, he thought.

If only it was that easy.

Looking back at his trial in 2003, he had done just as the priests had asked. He had told the truth. Yet long after he had watched the priests smile at his miraculous tale, the caretaker fought to find some context in which he could understand those facts, some universe in which that truth made sense.

Before his swift recovery, he had been so frightened. So anxious and desperate. At least now he was healthy. He had found new vision. But he had not yet found peace. He still could not answer his own immense questions. He still had not cracked the most perplexing mystery of all.

The Third Miracle

✝

The Woods

The sisters simply called it "the crypt." Smelling of cold stone and old dampness, the underground chapel felt like a secret sanctuary. Between numerous brick pillars stood life-size statues of saints, their smooth features bathed in candlelight. Beneath the snug ceiling, rows of neatly lined pews faced a raised altar. In a narrow chamber near the altar, concrete drawers encased the corpses of three nuns.

The crypt had only two ways in or out. One dark corner offered a wooden ladder that led to a trapdoor in the main floor of the motherhouse. In another nook, fifteen wooden steps—barely wider than an old woman's shoulders—linked the chapel to the convent above. On a frosty Friday evening, October 30, 1908, that stairwell thundered with a solemn, steady parade of sisters. Draped in full black habits, they descended to the catacomb to recite communal prayers and confess private sins. Near the end of the procession, one hunched nun gripped the railing with a quivering left hand that had gone cold and numb. She staggered on unsteady feet. Her bloated belly throbbed. Her head whirled in a dizzying grayness. She was forty-eight years old.

Her body was dying.

Sister Mary Theodosia Mug was a meticulous woman with deep-set eyes hardened by pain. She had spent almost half her life in the rural enclave—Saint Mary-of-the-Woods—an academy and college for young women and a community of nuns. In the classrooms she taught English to young girls. At night she composed music and wrote poetry. Slight and sickly since her teenage years,

Sister Mary Theodosia nonetheless blazed with a fierce creative energy. Her literary achievements filled entire bookshelves: dozens of magazine articles, a compilation of hymns, and a 500-page book published nationally. Yet her litany of ailments was equally extensive: neuritis in her right hand and arm, lung trouble, heart disease, rheumatism, and then, in 1906, breast cancer followed by a mastectomy that had destroyed the nerves and muscles in her left shoulder, leaving her left arm rigid and useless. Despite the surgery, the cancer had spread, sprouting in her abdomen, eventually forcing her to loosen her belt one notch at a time—four inches in all—just to ease the growing pressure of the tumor.

Eventually the disease turned her stride into a hobble. What puny morsels of food she could chew, she was forced to swallow while standing. Even so, she vomited almost continuously, sometimes unable to keep down even a slurp of water. But each day and night, Sister Mary Theodosia planned her classroom lessons, penned her melodies, played the organ at morning Mass, authored her articles, and tried to live while her insides rotted. Each day and night, she also prayed. And that crisp October evening would be no different.

Like the other nuns clustered in the basement chapel, Mary Theodosia first would step into a slender wooden booth. As a priest listened on the opposite side of a mesh partition, she would offer her confession—one of the Catholic sacraments and a convent ritual. After Mass, she would wait for the other sisters to exit the chapel, climb the stairs, and return to their bedrooms in the motherhouse high above. Finally, in the empty stillness, Mary Theodosia would stand alone and ask for some healing.

But not for herself.

†   †   †

Five miles northwest of Terre Haute, Indiana, tucked into a thicket of pin oak and black walnut trees, Saint Mary-of-the-Woods was

established on October 22, 1840, as a rustic Roman Catholic outpost in ardently anti-Catholic country. Its feisty founder, Mother
Théodore Guérin, had been handpicked by her French religious
order, the Sisters of Providence, to lead five young nuns from
Ruillé-sur-Loir, France, across the hurricane-battered Atlantic on
a sailing ship to New York City, then westward via trains, river-
boats, and horse-drawn carriages to the rough-and-tumble Upper
Midwest. Out there, from the woodlands and lime-green meadows
of western Indiana to the shores of Lake Michigan 180 miles to
the north, Catholicism already was proliferating as French, Irish,
and German immigrants surged into the region. The bishop of Vincennes, Indiana (a diocese that then included Chicago), had sought
the French nuns to run Catholic schools, to treat the sick, and to
convert more souls.

After reaching New York and trekking nearly eight hundred
miles through the eastern United States, the six women crossed the
swollen Wabash River on a stagecoach and, minutes later, finally
arrived at their destination—a lone farmhouse in the trees. With
a loose grasp of English and a few trunks full of clothing, Mother
Théodore and her French missionaries went to work, building a
self-sufficient farm, a religious colony, and, fairly quickly, some
potent adversaries. Then again, bedlam was nothing new to Mother
Théodore, a woman who had often stared down turmoil with her
"bright, luminous, and serene eyes," as a fellow sister once said.
Throughout her life she had been neck-deep in illness, rough waters,
and even a family murder.

She was born Anne-Thérèse Guérin on October 2, 1798, in the
last days of the French Revolution. She grew up in a beachfront
cottage perched on the northwest French peninsula of Brittany,
overlooking the English Channel. She was raised by a devoutly
Catholic mother, and for a time she attended a small school in her
village, Étables. But the decade-long revolution had transformed

France from an aristocratic monarchy where the Catholic clergy held sway to a nation beset with antireligious uprisings. Churches were closed, clerics were executed, and public worship was temporarily banned. In hushed tones, behind the rock walls of her modest home, Anne-Thérèse learned the Catholic catechism from her mother, Isabelle Lefevre Guérin. The little girl found courage in her outlawed faith. One biographer described her as "buoyant, mischievous [and] commanding." In womanhood, the same biographer wrote, Anne-Thérèse "had a fine appearance and an attractive personality and, as might be expected, there were many offers for her hand. She promptly declined all." The reason: during her first communion at age ten, Anne-Thérèse had promised God to someday become a nun. And that vow, she believed, was sacred.

Anne-Thérèse was the second of four Guérin children. But an older brother had died of burns after his fireside cot caught a spark from the hearth, engulfing the boy and his blankets in flames. A younger brother had died in infancy, leaving only Anne-Thérèse and her sister, Marie-Jeanne. Their mother somehow endured the losses of her sons, but her emotional resolve soon would crumble.

Isabelle Guérin came from royalist bloodlines. Her relatives were part of the French nobility that supported the overthrown monarchy. The girls' father, Laurent Guérin, had Italian roots and served as a ship's captain in the French navy. Captain Guérin was loyal to his military commander, Napoleon Bonaparte. Following Napoleon's bloody invasion of Russia in 1812 and the French Army's subsequent retreat, Captain Guérin steered his vessel back to France, docking in the south. He disembarked and immediately began journeying north—alone—to reunite with his wife and daughters. Shortly into his trip, however, a band of thieves attacked the naval officer. They snatched the money he was bringing home and left him dead on the road.

The violent ambush nearly destroyed the Guérin family. At the time, Anne-Thérèse was fourteen years old and her sister eight. After receiving word of her husband's death, Isabelle lapsed into a deep ten-year depression, forcing Anne-Thérèse to care for both her mother and little sister. Anne-Thérèse took a job as a seamstress to buy basic provisions for the cottage. She tended a small vegetable garden outside their cottage to help keep the family fed. But in those gloomy, grueling years, Anne-Thérèse began to flash hints of her late father's soldierly nerve and his head for business. The teenager pulled her remaining family through the crisis with her grit and her prayers.

By age twenty, over her mother's objections, Anne-Thérèse decided to fully devote her life to Catholicism, keeping her promise to become a nun. She entered the Sisters of Providence convent at Ruillé-sur-Loir, a small river town located 132 miles southwest of Paris. She took the vows of poverty, chastity, and obedience, and she was given the name Sister Saint Théodore; then, as now, it is common for nuns to rename themselves in honor of saints, regardless of the saint's gender. *Théodore* was derived from a Greek word that meant "gift of God." Convent life, however, could not shield the young nun from additional torment. Soon she contracted smallpox, and the blistery rash spread inside to her esophagus and stomach, ravaging her digestive system. She barely survived the illness. For the rest of her days, her meals consisted of only mild broth and bland, soft foods such as porridge.

After her recovery, at age twenty-six, her superiors appointed Sister Théodore superintendent of a troubled, six-hundred-pupil school in Rennes, a town at the confluence of two rivers in northwestern France, and the capital of Britanny. The school was notorious for its unruly children, but Sister Théodore firmly restored order in the classrooms and even managed to lure some of the students' parents into the Catholic faith. She spent nine years in Rennes before being redeployed about ninety miles south to

Soulaines, a country village, where she divided her time among teaching, studying medicine under a local doctor, and ministering to the sick. Not long after her transfer, the bishop of Vincennes, Simon Bruté, sent his top priest to Ruillé-sur-Loir to request a cadre of the congregation's hardiest nuns for a risky assignment in the American frontier. The bishop had recently purchased about an acre of land from a local farmer, Joseph Thralls, in a clearing just outside Terre Haute, Indiana. There, Bruté had overseen construction of the first church in Vigo County. He dubbed the tiny Catholic compound "Saint Mary-of-the-Woods." Now he needed some nuns to create a convent on his patch of Indiana wilderness. Having taken command of her own failing family and the rowdy schoolchildren in Rennes, Sister Théodore emerged as the first candidate to shepherd the small band of nuns across the ocean. "We have only one sister here who could lead a mission like that," one of her superiors told Bruté's representative. "If she volunteers, we will accept." But, still weak from her bout with smallpox, Sister Théodore initially declined the offer. Her superiors countered Sister Théodore's hesitation with an ultimatum: If she chose to stay in France, the entire American undertaking would be scrapped. Reluctantly—not wanting to leave her beloved France or her mother and sister—she agreed to go.

On July 27, 1840, Sister Théodore and five other French sisters set sail from the port at Le Havre aboard a sailing ship called the *Cincinnati*. Their stormy, forty-day voyage would test their faith and their stomachs. "When I felt the vessel beginning to move and I realized I was no longer in France, it seemed as if my soul were being torn from my body," Sister Théodore later wrote in her diary. All six sisters were sobbing. Even worse, before exiting their homeland, the nuns learned that Bishop Bruté had died unexpectedly in Vincennes at the age of sixty. His replacement would be Father Célestine de La Hailandière, the emissary Bruté had dispatched to France in search of recruits. In Indiana, Bishop La Hailandière would become Sister Théodore's most ferocious adversary.

The *Cincinnati* was buffeted during the ensuing weeks by four separate storms during which "waves appeared like mountains," gales bent the masts "like reeds," and the creaking ship "seemed on the verge of sinking," Sister Théodore recounted in her diary. During the tempests, the nuns became either so nauseated they couldn't leave their beds or so frightened they told God they were ready to sacrifice their lives "should it please Him." When calmer days dawned, the sisters prayed on deck in a corner or watched from the rails as whales surfaced and spouted plumes of water. On September 7 they finally spotted the rooftops of New York City. Because the *Cincinnati* could not maneuver to port, the passengers were asked to climb down a rope ladder and step into boats to reach the docks. When several nuns nervously balked at descending over the side of the ship, Sister Théodore barked: "Come, sisters, if we must die, let us die and say nothing about it."

Their subsequent overland journey on rails, canals, and rock-strewn buggy trails took almost as long as their ocean crossing. On October 22, a Thursday, they stepped off a horse-drawn carriage into a seemingly empty forest. They hiked down a deep ravine and trudged up the leafy opposite bank before they finally viewed a simple farmhouse — the home of Joseph and Sarah Thralls and six of their twelve children. Also waiting there were four young American girls who hoped to join Sister Théodore's religious community. After introductions, the newcomers were shown to their temporary accommodations: the farmhouse attic, where the six sisters and four prospective nuns would sleep on straw mats. The dormitory was so crowded, the women dressed in their beds. As wintery weather fell, snow blew into their room through cracks in the roof. "It is bitterly cold. Everything is frozen, even our bread," Sister Théodore noted in her journal. In November, Bishop La Hailandière purchased the

Thralls' house outright along with the family's fifty-five acres of land and some farm equipment and animals. The plot, which had cost the diocese $1,345, instantly became the first convent for the Indiana branch of the Sisters of Providence. (The Thralls family moved only about a mile south.) As was customary in those years, the head of the tiny new religious institution was given a title to match her authority. Sister Théodore became Mother Théodore.

The nuns cleared some land to prepare vegetable gardens for the spring. Their first church altar consisted of two planks driven into the mud, with a third plank placed across them. In the American outback, the initially tentative Mother Théodore blossomed into a willful leader, defeating her own self-doubts and defending her new turf against attacks from both people and nature. In their shady notch — "this remote solitude," as she called it — Mother Théodore took barely a year to erect a boarding school and academy for young women (later Saint Mary-of-the-Woods College). The first student enrolled on July 4, 1841. Over the next fifteen years, traveling throughout Indiana by stagecoach, riverboat, and buggy, she established parish schools in eleven towns, including Fort Wayne and Evansville, as well as three orphanages, two pharmacies and, at Saint Mary-of-the-Woods, a brick motherhouse for the sisters. Amid that rapid expansion, however, Mother Théodore and her nuns often ran low on funds and food, battling crop failures, biting bugs, and snake infestations. Worse, they feared that their isolated settlement was "surrounded by enemies," as she once wrote in her journal.

They had their reasons.

In October 1842, a suspicious fire tore through the barns and granary that held the nuns' winter supply of flour and other freshly harvested provisions as well as their entire store of animal feed and all their farming implements. Their survival stash was turned overnight into a pile of black ash and charred metal. Because they lived in a region rife with anti-Catholic sentiment, the nuns believed the inferno had been set intentionally in an effort to frighten them back to France.

Meanwhile, the emotional flames also raged in the hottest war of Mother Théodore's life—a savage feud with her immediate church superior, Bishop La Hailandière. The French cleric and the French nun, each forty-two years old when their paths clashed, wrestled for almost a decade over who should control the community of nuns and who should own the land where the sisters lived. Mother Théodore wanted possession of the deed to their property, noting that she and the sisters already had paid more than $4,000 for the plot. The bishop wouldn't yield. By 1845 the frustrated founder wrote a desperate letter to the bishop of Detroit, asking that she and her sisters be allowed to uproot from their compound and restart their community in Michigan. The request was not approved. La Hailandière saw the mother superior as insubordinate. She saw him as overbearing and chauvinistic—a theme that would color Mother Théodore's legacy decades after her death, and shape the sisters' worldview well into the twenty-first century. Ultimately, during an 1847 showdown between the nun and the bishop at his home in Vincennes, La Hailandière locked Mother Théodore in a room alone for the better part of a day as punishment for what he saw as her insolent behavior. Soon he stripped her of her vows and ordered her to leave the diocese "and go elsewhere to hide in her disgrace," according to one of her journals. Once she was in exile, La Hailandière also mandated that she be forbidden to write letters to her fellow sisters. But immediately after receiving La Hailandière's decision on May 20, 1847, the mother superior contracted pleurisy and spiked a high fever, sending her to a sickbed. She became, she wrote, "occupied only in preparing myself for death, which I believed was not far away. But I was mistaken." She rallied. La Hailandière, also unhappy after all the years of bickering, had asked to resign his office in 1845 and again in 1846. During Mother Théodore's 1847 sickness, Pope Pius IX finally granted La Hailandière's request and he was transferred back to France. That war was over, yet its causes remained murky. Historians later speculated that La Hailandière was mentally unbalanced, or overwhelmed by the culture shock of living in America, or secretly in love with the mother superior, or perhaps all three.

Once more, Mother Théodore regained her strength and dashed off a letter to the archbishop of Baltimore, with whom she had been corresponding. In her note she revealed that her nemesis had left the nuns with some curt words: "He would have nothing more to do with us."

With the clash put to rest, the congregation's schools continued to attract more pupils, and Mother Théodore forged a reputation from Indiana to Illinois as an independent pioneer with a backbone for business, a heart for deep faith, and eyes that crackled with dry humor—which she often flashed during the storms of her life. She once wrote in her journal, "We were to find a multitude of enemies athirst for the blood of the French. Until then we had not fought unto the shedding of blood, but this was a night of slaughter. I may say without boasting too much that several of my enemies perished in my hands." In that entry she was referring to mosquitoes.

Her Catholic commune near the river soon adopted a shortened nickname that echoed their founder's robust exterior and softer charms: "the Woods."

But as her thriving ministry was winning new souls and new sisters, Mother Théodore's body began to deteriorate following decades of chronic digestive trouble. A heart condition further weakened her and forced Mother Théodore back to a sickbed in March 1856. She had cheated death a half dozen times during her life—surviving cholera, arsenic poisoning, and a near drowning in the Wabash River. Yet she always had pulled through, usually after

saying a prayer. That spring, however, she grew uncharacteristi-
cally quiet and withdrawn in her convent room. The other sisters
worried their founder might be in a fatal tailspin. Mother Théodore
scrawled her final diary entry on March 17, six days before Easter:
"I am obliged to remain in bed. What a beautiful week to be upon
the Cross!" She died eight weeks later, at 4:00 a.m. on May 14,
1856. She was fifty-seven.

Following her funeral, all of the nuns escorted her coffin as
pallbearers carried it to a shady spot on the east side of the convent grounds. The Woods' first cemetery, which then contained the
remains of four other Sisters of Providence, was nestled next to a
small log chapel named for Saint Anne, the patroness of sailors and
someone to whom Mother Théodore had often prayed during her
harrowing ocean travels. Under Mother Théodore's instruction,
some of the nuns later decorated the chapel's interior walls with the
iridescent shells of mussels and oysters plucked from the Wabash
River. Her plot was marked by a simple, small wooden cross etched
in Latin: "I sleep but my heart watches over this home that I have
built."

At the time, the Woods housed eighty-three nuns who pledged
to sustain Mother Théodore's vision of Catholic activism and self-
reliance. They taught their classes, offered their faith, and tended
to the apple orchards and horse pastures that spilled across their
now sixty-seven-acre property. And the sisters kept on building.
By 1890 they had completed construction on Providence Hall, a
redbrick convent deemed a technological marvel because it boasted
running water and electricity. When the power was first switched
on, three stories of windows suddenly glowed with six hundred
incandescent lamps, bathing the lawn outside in yellowish warmth.
The sisters who gathered to watch the occasion forever referred to
that night as "the illumination." Next door to their plush living quarters, they also erected a new shrine, the Church of the Immaculate

Conception—a towering Italian Renaissance–style basilica adorned with marble columns, Bavarian stained glass, and Stations of the Cross cut from alabaster. Beneath the massive church they installed their own basement chapel and a twelve-drawer burial chamber accessible via a trapdoor in the floor and a slim wooden staircase that led down from Providence Hall.

Their elegant campus—along with Mother Théodore's enduring celebrity and the sisters' earthy values—helped attract hundreds of other young women to study in the tall trees. Many of those students later professed their vows and joined the Sisters of Providence. Among these was a teenager named Nellie Mug.

She was born in 1860—four years after Mother Théodore's death—christened Helen, and raised seventy miles upriver in Lafayette, Indiana, a former French military outpost that gave rise to Purdue University. Her mother, Ellen Phillips, was a native of Fort Wayne and her family had come from Ireland. Ellen had attended the Woods academy during Mother Théodore's final months, taking a religious class from the founder herself. When Mother Théodore died, Ellen was among the line of students who had viewed the body, placing her rosary beads against Mother Théodore's remains. After completing school, Ellen married John Theodore Mug, a Dutch immigrant and an affluent retailer. She gave birth to two daughters and nicknamed her oldest "Nellie." In Lafayette, Ellen nurtured Nellie's skills on the piano and with the pen, eventually enrolling both of her daughters at her beloved alma mater. Nellie graduated from the Woods academy in June 1877, but decided to stay at the convent. She loved academics and she loved God. She wanted to become a Sister of Providence, and she wanted to teach children. The following January she was accepted as a novice—a nun in her first year of training. And she took a new name, Sister Mary Theodosia.

Four years later, at twenty-one, she took her vows as a nun

and donned the traditional habit: a black veil draped over a white headband, a white neckpiece worn from chin to chest, a black woolen cape with long sleeves and matching floor-length skirt, and a small white cross that dangled from a black neck cord. Now Sister Mary Theodosia had to learn how to instruct children. She embarked on a ten-year circuit through Catholic schools in Ypsilanti, Michigan; Galesburg, Illinois; Kansas City, Missouri; and Boston, Massachusetts, working her way up to the rank of local superior, or principal. But Mary Theodosia's body already was showing hints of catastrophic failure.

To ease the neuritis attacks that weakened her right arm, doctors sent Mary Theodosia to soak in mineral baths in Mount Clemens, Michigan. Later they tried to zap her arm nerves back to health with electrical impulses. Neither treatment worked. Then Mary Theodosia contracted heart and breathing troubles—possibly resulting from fibromyalgia. She was forced to take a one-year leave from her school job in Michigan. Frequent gastritis left her visibly thin. She wore thick eyeglasses with noticeable magnification to help correct her poor vision, but they only accentuated the young nun's frail appearance. Finally, in 1891, she was reassigned back to the Woods to teach English and philosophy to academy students and the novices.

After her daytime classes and the evening meal, alone in her Providence Hall bedroom, Mary Theodosia often poured her faith into her writing. She crafted dozens of religious poems, many of which were published in magazines. Some of her compositions— for example, "The Will May Approve But the Heart Must Bleed"— seemed to hint at her lingering sickness. Still, she wrote. And her superiors noticed. Soon they allowed Mary Theodosia to pursue a second career. She began authoring religious articles for publications like the *Catholic Encyclopedia*, the *New York Catholic News*, and the *Indianapolis Journal*.

Many nights, she wrote until long after nine thirty, when the electric lights in Providence Hall were shut off. Some midnights passed with Mary Theodosia crouched over candlelight, scrawling words onto paper at a wooden desk in her room. As a journalist, she was thorough and painstakingly precise, lacing her articles with solid reporting, injecting her prose with a confident voice. In a piece she penned about Mother Théodore, Mary Theodosia described the founder's relaxed charisma and her relentless teaching style: "Absence of formality gave a charm to Mother Théodore's counsels that insured for them a readier acceptance than any studied discourse could have done. . . . Every duty was an opportunity to her for imparting a lesson which places in evidence her constant zeal."

The speed and literary skill with which Mary Theodosia churned out articles deeply impressed Mother Mary Cleophas Foley, the community's general superior at the dawn of the twentieth century. In fact, Mother Mary Cleophas soon would come to see her in-house wordsmith as the perfect choice to undertake the convent's boldest, most audacious mission: building the case for Mother Théodore's sainthood.

With her pen, Mary Theodosia could help the Sisters of Providence launch a historic crusade.

That is, if her body didn't give out first.

CHAPTER TWO

The Quest

The Woods hummed with heavenly whispers in 1900. Behind the stained glass of the chapels, along the pathways that linked the dormitories and classrooms, the nuns were taught to believe their founder carried serious clout in the hereafter. And in the first days of the new century, they were not shy about gazing skyward and soliciting her help.

When the sisters struggled to quell boisterous students in their classrooms, they were encouraged to openly invoke Mother Théodore's name. On warm days, Mother Mary Cleophas Foley, then general superior, sometimes led packs of young nuns across campus and into the cemetery. Standing at the foot of their most famous grave, the sisters prayed for personal favors through Mother Théodore's "intercession"—her ability to hear their solemn pleas from heaven and to, in turn, ask God to intervene in their lives below.

Intercession, Roman Catholics believed, was made possible by a saint's proximity to God. But if an intercessory prayer seemed to induce something wondrous, something that seemed to defy the maxims of science—like the spontaneous cure of a terminal disease—Catholics stamped that brand of divine aid with a rare name: *miracle.* The Catholic Church specifically defined a miracle as a work of God—a temporary suspension of nature's laws, delivered directly from God or through the intercession of a saint.

When intercessory prayers allegedly prompted such supernatural favors, the Church conducted special investigations to vet the facts and question the witnesses. Only the pope could ultimately affirm miracles. But according to Catholic doctrine, a pope-approved miracle was proof that the deceased holy person invoked in the original prayer was indeed a saint.

In Catholicism, achieving sainthood was the highest honor. And by 1901, Mother Mary Cleophas and her convent colleagues believed the moment was drawing near to make their intercessory prayers more official. They foresaw a hardy crusade to deliver Mother Théodore to sainthood—in Catholic terms, to canonize her.

The fiftieth anniversary of her death would arrive in 1906. Under Roman Catholic edicts at the time, no canonization cause could be formally initiated until a candidate had been dead for fifty years, the original idea being that if a person was truly worthy of saintly devotion, her fame and cult following would still shine five decades after her final breath. At the Woods, 1906 loomed as a bright landmark. But before any sanctification campaign could begin, some preparatory work had to be done—and most of those duties would fall on the increasingly ill Sister Mary Theodosia Mug.

The mandated half-century waiting period was just one of many stringent guidelines decreed by the Vatican and tucked into the Catholic canonization rulebook since 1234. In that year, Pope Gregory IX took the first tentative steps toward formalizing Catholic saint-naming, establishing the protocol for investigating the lives of candidates. During the preceding thousand years, the practice of picking and classifying saints had been little more than a chaotic, jumbled popularity contest. Local churches kept their own individual lists or "calendars" of venerated dead and martyrs—those killed in the name of the religion. As a result, the roster of Catholic saints had exploded into a disorganized, bloated catalog of more than ten thousand holy names, including many who had never existed and some whose glorified deeds were mere fables.

Consider, for example, the curious case of Saint Philomena. On May 5, 1802, inside a Roman tomb painted with second-century frescoes of Madonna and Child, and long thought to have been a burial place for early Christian martyrs, the ancient bones of a teen-aged girl were discovered in the dirt. Archaeologists determined that her skull had been crushed. Tiles near her tomb indicated the girl's name might have been Philomena. A small bottle filled with a dark liquid was found with the body. Church lore held that martyrs were often interred with vials of their blood to signify their sacrifice. Shortly after the corpse was unearthed, a nun in Naples, Italy, announced that she had received a wave of religious visions about the mysterious young victim. According to those visions, the Roman emperor Diocletian had demanded to marry Philomena. But when she refused and pledged her virginity to Jesus, Philomena was tortured and killed like other Christians of the day. The nun's revelation seemed to explain everything. The story spread among the Catholic faithful.

By 1837 Saint Philomena had a Vatican-certified feast day — part of the Catholic calendar of saints — plus a papally approved shrine near Naples. She also had global cult following. In the early 1960s, however, scientists began to unravel the real story behind that body from the tomb. Archaeologists were given permission to test the bones. They determined that the remains came from a woman who had lived in the fourth century CE — specifically, in a time when the wholesale persecution of Christians had ceased. And that vial of liquid found with the body? Analysis showed it was funeral perfume, not blood. In 1961 the Vatican stripped Philomena of her feast day. The Vatican's reversal did not, however, deter her most devoted followers, who chose to trust that the mythical martyr's indomitable tale was valid. As of 2009, at least a half dozen Saint Philomena churches and schools still existed in the United States, scattered from Portsmouth, Rhode Island, to Carson, California. Philomena fans maintained their pilgrimages to the Sanctuary of Saint Philomena, an ornate gold church near Naples, flanked by twin four-story clock towers. And a website created to celebrate "Saint Philomena, Virgin & Martyr" continued to offer Philomena statuettes at a price of $59.95 each.

But the Vatican's about-face on Philomena proved that, if presented with fresh evidence, Catholic leaders would react and step in to preserve their saint-naming operation—an ancient custom they believed to be airtight and pristine. Centralized to the Vatican, the canonization process remained a largely secretive enterprise built on the collection of hard evidence, sworn testimonies, and mounds of medical records. And although the system had been overseen by the pope since the thirteenth century, it often was described as the most democratic process within the Church simply because causes never were started at the top; they had to begin in the would-be saint's home diocese, with the people on the ground. Since the first canonization reforms of 1234, fewer than one thousand new saints had been recognized by the Catholic Church as of 2009.

Called by some historians the Western world's oldest legal system, the route to canonization included Church trials that, in many ways, mirrored criminal court trials. All cases of alleged miracles—typically medical cures—were first tested by local Catholic tribunals, and always heard behind closed doors. The trials were held in the same dioceses in which the prospective saints lived, or in the places the purported miracles were performed in the name of the would-be saints. Priests trained in canon law—the internal, ecclesiastical codes that guided the Catholic Church—were appointed by local archbishops to serve in the traditional roles of judge, prosecutor, and defense attorney. Further, the priests were assigned to pepper alleged miracle witnesses with a series of blunt questions. The priests were expected to weed through, pluck out, and document all the pertinent theological and medical facts. Ultimately these facts were sent to Rome for judgment.

At the Vatican, alleged miracles were first evaluated by a

group of doctors appointed by the Holy See—a special task force called the Consulta Medica. If the Vatican's doctors could not find a scientific explanation for a purported miracle, the case was next passed to a panel of Vatican theologians. If the theologians voted to approve the alleged miracle, the case was presented to the final jury: a consistory of cardinals and bishops and, ultimately, the pope himself.

The allegedly supernatural cures that flowed through that web of Vatican ductwork were the fuel for Catholic sainthood. Under canon law, no person—no matter how piously he lived or how selflessly he served—could be canonized as a saint unless and until two miracles were attributed to him *following* his death. This was the price of saintly admission. Approved miracles were the lifeblood of the Church's heavenly hierarchy, the bricks and mortar that built much of the modern roster of saints—from Joan of Arc to Mother Cabrini. And this was the stuff of exhaustive inquests.

Miracles, in fact, dominated two of the three fundamental steps needed to reach Catholic sainthood. Initially, Church examiners dissected the candidate's living deeds, even her words, verifying that she displayed seven specific qualities: faith, hope, and charity along with prudence, justice, fortitude, and temperance. If these characteristics were confirmed, the pope then decreed that the candidate had lived a life that was "heroic in virtue." Upon that proclamation, the candidate received the title "Venerable." Then things moved into a more mystical realm. Church investigators next had to validate two instances in which living people facing apparently incurable illnesses or impossible hardships conquered those troubles after praying to and invoking the name of the deceased "virtuous" person. The evidence had to show that the laws of nature, medicine, and science were inexplicably lifted. One pope-approved miracle allowed a candidate to reach an intermediate threshold called "beatification." A second sanctioned miracle led to canonization, and sainthood. Martyrs, meanwhile, required only one Vatican-verified miracle to be named saints.

In the eyes of the pope and Catholics around the world, a miracle showed that the soul who was invoked in prayer had God's ear and, thus, the power to intercede in earthly troubles. This was a core concept of Catholic theology. For the faithful, this was where the inexplicable resided, and where science surrendered to God's will. For skeptics, this was the front line for an epic confrontation between belief and reason.

During the local Church tribunals—and, later, inside the Vatican panels that ultimately ruled on these alleged miracles—medical doctors were summoned by Catholic officials to help decipher the MRI scans, biopsy results, and hospital records of the alleged miracle recipients. In a rare alliance of religion and science, clerics and doctors worked together to declare whether certain spontaneous healings fell into one of two categories: explainable medical anomalies or the works of God. For a miracle to be endorsed, Church investigators had to certify that the event under their scrutiny transcended not only their expert appraisal but all natural laws. An alleged miracle was a paradox: the only way to verify one, according to the Church, was to show it defied scientific verification.

But long before all that analysis and reasoning was applied by the doctors and theologians in Rome, saintly pursuits encountered a far more mortal buildup—a necessity of modern business and a chore essential to any grand crusade or small campaign: public relations. Whether the would-be saint was a pope or a backwoods nun, his followers first had to sell his candidacy to the masses in the pews and the Church brass in Italy. They had to enthusiastically make the case for eternal admiration. In the computer era, that typically translated into splashy websites, grassroots glad-handing, souvenir shops, phone banks, and, by some estimates, about $1 million in expenses for legal fees and, ultimately, for staging massive celebratory ceremonies in St. Peter's Square.

In 1901, when the Sisters of Providence began mulling over Mother Théodore's potential sainthood, they faced the mountainous job of globally publicizing her cause from their remote outpost in the Indiana trees. It was a tall order. She was a French immigrant known mainly within the confines of the American Midwest. Moreover, when it came to judging saintly candidacies, Rome didn't often look beyond the borders of Europe. In that era there still were no American saints.

The founder's dramatic tale, the nuns understood, had to be spread to the Catholic faithful via the written word. Her words. The tedious job of translating Mother Théodore's massive collection of letters and journals from French to English originally fell to Sister Mary Eudoxie Marshall, who had arrived at the Woods from England in 1852. By 1900 she was pushing eighty and still had not finished the work. So Mother Mary Cleophas Foley assigned her budding scribe, Sister Mary Theodosia Mug, to the vital project.

Mary Theodosia immediately saw that the journals were merely multiple sheets of large, thin paper, each folded in half to form six individual books, spanning two or three years apiece. Mother Théodore had drawn straight vertical columns on each page to organize the dates of her entries and her thoughts and observations. Filled with a flourished, cursive handwriting that alternated between black and blue ink, the journals offered colorful albeit businesslike snippets about her hostile drama with Bishop La Hailandière, her near-death illnesses, and those faced by the other nuns. She chronicled her perils on the high seas and referenced farm life: penning the hogs, buying butter in Terre Haute, wearing heavy underwear in winter, and enjoying "little boiled squirrels," a favorite convent meal. Some of the pages also carried scorch marks and tiny spark holes from an 1889 fire that had erupted inside the building where the journals were being stored.

Not long after Mary Theodosia began translating the last stack of journals, the new bishop in Indianapolis, Francis Silas Chatard, decided that Mother Théodore's legacy—not to mention her possible canonization campaign—needed a lift, and some polish. Roman Catholic edicts required that all beatification and canonization causes be formally launched by local bishops in the candidate's home diocese. In 1901 Chatard formally instructed Mother Mary Cleophas to choose one of her nuns to write an exhaustive biography of the Woods founder. In part, Chatard sought to clear up some of the misconceptions that a number of priests and bishops, both at home and abroad, held about the tough-minded French missionary. Many of those familiar with Mother Théodore's name had only been given La Hailandière's decidedly harsh description of her. Put bluntly, she had a bad reputation among some clergymen who didn't appreciate a woman who stood up to men. But Chatard recognized that a book about Mother Théodore's sacrifices and selfless works could serve as the first sales pitch for her eventual sainthood.

The biography was assigned to the most accomplished writer on campus, Mary Theodosia. To speed the book's completion, Mother Mary Cleophas suspended the remainder of Mary Theodosia's community duties. This was job one.

Mary Theodosia plunged hard into the project in 1901, scouring the full trove of Mother Théodore's now fully translated writings, searching for gritty anecdotes and examples of her stout faith. Mary Theodosia also mined her own notes from conversations she had held years earlier with four of the six founding sisters. As a teenage student and novice, Mary Theodosia (then just Nellie Mug) had devoted hours to talking with the surviving missionaries. She had listened to their tales and jotted down their vivid memories. Now those oral histories would breathe life into her book.

The grind of reading, editing, outlining, and, finally, threading

Mother Théodore's story into twenty-four chapters consumed almost three years—a grueling stretch drawn out by the slow deterioration of the author's health. By then, the ache from her neuritis prevented Mary Theodosia from raising her right arm high enough to place it on a desk. So she wrote the entire manuscript in pencil while resting each sheet of paper at knee height.

The final version filled 499 pages. It was titled *Life and Life-work of Mother Theodore Guérin,* and was dedicated to "Mary Immaculate." Mary Theodosia never signed her name as the author, simply listing the work's creator as "a member of the congregation." In 1904 the book was published by a New York firm, Benziger Brothers, which broadly promoted the title and trumpeted its journalistic bite. Within her chapters, Mary Theodosia had exposed a controversial reality faced by many religious orders: how convent leaders had to remain accountable to their sisterly congregations while simultaneously fending off sexism in the church's male hierarchy. As ironic proof of this motif, some priests in Indianapolis hated the book because they felt it dishonored La Hailandière. But Bishop Chatard—who had originally encouraged the biography—shot down one protesting priest with a crisp reply: "We are having it read in our dining room now."

More important, Mother Théodore's story was on bookstore shelves. Her cause for sainthood would gain added steam. Reviews were positive. Although Mary Theodosia occasionally lapsed into flowery, passionate prose when portraying the woman who had shaped her own life, she more often stuck to succinct and spare sentences—a style likely influenced by her Indiana roots—as evidenced in this portrayal of Mother Théodore's dying days: "Her affability and genial manner impressed all who approached her. . . . Sickness made no change in her sentiments unless to deepen her trust, her humility, and her love."

But as a stooped Mary Theodosia scrawled that somber sentence

onto a sheet of paper, she was about to face a diagnosis that would
test those very same traits.

† † †

On a gray December day in 1907, as snow flurries caked the cluster
of gravestones on the east side of the Woods, workers slashed their
shovels into the dry, dead grass. Soon they had sliced far enough
through the chilled Indiana soil to reach the remains of the cemetery's most famous name. Finally they hoisted the body of Mother
Théodore Guérin back to daylight.

The macabre ceremony had been ordered by Bishop Chatard—
partly to inspire a new wave of public worship for Mother Théodore, but also, quite honestly, to get a glimpse of her half-century-old
corpse. As head of the Indianapolis Diocese since 1878, Chatard had
been mesmerized by stirring tales about the French missionary and
her Catholic compound near the river. He suspected that Mother
Théodore had a legitimate shot at canonization. And according to
Catholic customs, the bishop now needed to inspect her remains, to
verify that the body in the grave indeed belonged to the legendary
founder of the Woods.

What was more, a new shrine had been built for Mother Théodore beneath the freshly consecrated Church of the Immaculate
Conception in the heart of the campus. Her body would be stored
in a basement tomb, making it more accessible to the sisters and to
any visitors who wanted to stand close and offer prayers for her
intercession or for her canonization. The shrine, supporters reasoned, would further stoke her cause.

At the time of the exhumation, Chatard was well into his second
professional career. A Baltimore native with graying hair, bound-
less energy, and the intellectual muscle to win almost any argument, Chatard originally had studied medicine at the University

of Maryland, graduating as a physician. At age twenty-three, however, he experienced a "revelation," according to several historical accounts. The divine message told Chatard to go to Rome and join the priesthood. Later, as he climbed through the ranks of the Catholic Church, Chatard maintained his sharp interest in medicine—and in medical miracles.

In 1885 he had personally investigated the puzzling cure of an eastern Indiana girl named Rosa Warren, who had fallen ill with meningitis-like symptoms: chills, fever, severe neck swelling, partial paralysis in her legs, and an odd tightening of her back muscles that had caused her head to be drawn so far back that her eyes were fixed upward. Rosa, raised as a Methodist, wasn't known as a particularly devout girl. But the night before she was scheduled to make a seventy-mile journey to Indianapolis for medical treatment, she entered Our Lady of Lourdes chapel in her hometown of Oldenburg and prayed to the Virgin Mary for healing. At dawn she was taken to Indianapolis as planned. Three weeks after her symptoms first appeared, they abruptly vanished. When she returned to Oldenburg the day after her recovery, Chatard was waiting. He interviewed Rosa, jotting notes as they talked. She insisted it was her prayer—not her Indianapolis doctor—that had restored her health. According to an article published on June 28, 1885, in the *New York Times*, Chatard openly "vouched for" what the newspaper called an "extraordinary faith cure." The bishop ruled that Rosa had not suffered from meningitis after all, but from a spinal "concussion" caused by a recent roller-skating fall. Yet her injury, he said, had spontaneously and inexplicably healed following the girl's prayer.

Twenty-two years after that medical anomaly, Chatard, the ex-doctor, was similarly mystified after he received a report from the Woods describing what the sisters saw when they opened the coffin of their beloved founder.

†   †   †

Mother Théodore's exhumation on that snowy day marked a grisly but solemn step common to sainthood campaigns. During the first phase of a canonization bid, a candidate's remains often were unearthed and placed within or beneath a new temple. The disem-tombment tradition had two purposes: to reignite awareness for the would-be saint's cause and to allow local Church officials to inspect the remains in order to certify their authenticity.

Since the earliest days of Catholic saint-naming rituals, exhu-mations also allowed supporters a chance to pluck relics from the corpse—pieces of the deceased person's clothing, strands of their hair, even their bones. The worship of holy relics spanned multiple faiths—Buddhism, Hinduism, Islam, and Christianity—as well as much of secular history. The word "relic" itself is derived from the ancient Latin expression for "remainder." The Bible describes the healing of several people who grasped relics, including Elisha's bones and Paul's handkerchief. During the Middle Ages, this belief raged more fervently: many thought holy relics were packed with heavenly influence that could offer a medical cure or divine protec-tion, and the hunt for relics sometimes sparked wars. For centuries, Catholics had embedded saintly relics—often tiny bone chips—in the stone slabs that made up their church altars. While many among the faithful still believed that touching a relic could bring miracles, modern Catholic doctrine stated there was no inherent magic in these sacred pieces, nor were they lucky charms; they were merely stored as public mementos, reminders of the person, and tangible pieces to petition for intercession.

In Mother Théodore's case, assorted relics also were collected from her body, including four of her fingers, a rib bone, and some-thing else: her brain.

After saintly candidates were exhumed, the subsequent examinations sometimes provided an eerie windfall. If local Catholic officials saw that the body was not "corrupt"—had not naturally deteriorated—that evidence could help support the canonization cause. One example involved Philadelphia bishop John Neumann, who died in 1860. Never embalmed, he was buried in a wooden casket beneath the floor of St. Peter of the Apostle Church. His tomb was lined with bricks. Despite dampness in and around the grave, Bishop Neumann's remains were fully intact when he was exhumed in 1902 for a pre-canonization inspection. In 1977 he became the fifth American saint.

If an exhumed body had decomposed as nature intended, the Catholic Church didn't rule out that candidate for sainthood. Any inexplicable preservation, however, was seen as a boost to the cause. That notion dated back to a time, centuries ago, when Catholics believed the corpses of their saints emitted a pleasant, flowery smell. They called it "the odor of sanctity." And they took that scent to mean that the person had been chosen by God.

After Mother Théodore's body was disinterred, the sisters placed her remains in a cedar box lined with soft linen. They inventoried her remains. They gazed at her bones. They took note that the flesh that once surrounded her skeleton had naturally decayed and vanished. Then they spotted something they had not expected. Inside the skull, they saw what appeared to be her brain—"as fresh and entire as if death had just occurred," according to exhumation records in the Saint Mary-of-the-Woods archives. Bishop Chatard—the ex-physician—immediately understood that this discovery defied the laws of science. He told Mother Mary Cleophas to bring in three independent doctors to conduct their own analyses—and one of the three, he urged, had to be a non-Catholic to give the process extra credibility. The physicians would each survey the remains, Chatard instructed, and then fully document their findings.

On December 10, 1907, Dr. Leon J. Willien came to the Woods

to begin this strange series of examinations. Sixty-six years old and a native of France, Dr. Willien was well known to the sisters: he was a Terre Haute gynecologist, the nuns' community physician, and he had been trying to treat Mary Theodosia's worsening illness. Now he was studying the brain of the woman whom Mary Theodosia had spent years researching and profiling.

Following a few moments of analysis, Dr. Willien declared that the brain seemed fully preserved. In addition, he stated that brain tissue, laden with water during life, was the most fragile material in the human body and the first organ to dissolve after death— usually within six hours. The next day, a Wednesday, Dr. Willien returned to the Woods accompanied by two more physicians. They too probed Mother Théodore's brain and then, according to convent records, they stood before a notary public and gave sworn affidavits in which they "marveled" at the brain's condition.

Amid the grim inspections, however, the sisters stole a moment to dabble in the supernatural. They borrowed the brain for a bit of relic alchemy. Although Catholic tenets stated that the remains of saints and saintly candidates possessed no special healing force, nuns at the Woods—in 1907—believed otherwise. On December 20, the brain was "applied" to the burned foot of Sister Mary Alma Ryan, according to convent archives. A high-ranking nun, Sister Mary Alma had recently accompanied Mother Mary Cleophas to Europe, where they visited Catholic basilicas to gather internal décor ideas for their new Church of the Immaculate Conception. After returning to Terre Haute, Sister Mary Alma had undergone an operation, the details of which were not clear. But while she was under sedation, a medical aide had rested a hot water bottle on Mary Alma's foot, severely scalding her skin and preventing her from walking. After the founder's brain was touched to Mary Alma's foot, however, she suddenly was able to walk with crutches and with the help of a special shoe, according to convent records. The sisters characterized her healing as "miraculous."

The final test of the brain's authenticity came on Christmas Eve 1907. Dr. Willien brought to the Woods a fourth doctor, Frank Barbour Wynn, an anatomy expert and ranking member of the American Medical Association from Indianapolis. Dr. Wynn also was a Methodist. At first Dr. Wynn thought the lump inside the skull might have been merely clay or mineral deposits somehow trapped from the surrounding soil. But when he placed thin slices of the tissue under a microscope, Dr. Wynn saw many of the delicate fibers and "neuroglial" cells that comprised the brain, he noted. While the nuclei of the brain cells had disappeared, what remained on the slide led Dr. Wynn to write, "It does indeed seem very remarkable that there should not have been complete disintegration of the brain. I have no satisfactory scientific explanation to offer for this strange phenomenon." While convent records did not show the depth of Mother Théodore's original grave, they confirmed that it was prone to flooding—during her exhumation, fifteen buckets of clear, odorless water were dredged from the hole. Still, Dr. Wynn believed the moisture in no way aided in the preservation of the brain tissue. In a letter to Mother Mary Cleophas dated January 4, 1908, he added, "If one allege that it is due to sulphor [*sic*] of the water in the ground, acting as a preservative, the staggering reply can be made, why have not the other tissues been preserved?"

The discovery further convinced Bishop Chatard that Mother Théodore had a stout a case for canonization.

Soon after, he formally opened that sacred campaign, launching what the Vatican called "the informative process"—a gathering of oral testimonies from surviving friends, former students, and fellow sisters on how she had lived and what she had accomplished from her backwoods compound. With that single step, Mother Théodore had achieved a new status. She was now considered by the Catholic Church a "Servant of God"—which is how the Church referred to saintly contenders at that early stage. Meanwhile, the Sisters of Providence also appointed Monsignor Pietro Fumasoni Biondi as their first "postulator"—the Church official designated to present to the Vatican a formal plea for beatification and, later, canonization. Biondi was a thirty-seven-year-old Italian aristocrat by birth with an affinity for the work of nuns: his own sister had joined the order formed by Mother Francis Xavier Cabrini. In Rome, Biondi would essentially become the top cheerleader for the cause.

Somewhere in the distance loomed the next milestone in Mother Théodore's potential path to sainthood, and still another title— "blessed." That was how Catholics referred to anyone who had been formally beatified.

But in 1907 that righteous frontier seemed almost unreachable.

Quite literally, getting there would take a miracle.

CHAPTER THREE

The Voice

As she staggered past the crypt's ground-level windows on Halloween eve 1908, Sister Mary Theodosia looked out on brown lawns, leafless trees, and the cold grip of autumn darkness.

Around her, filling the cozy pews of the basement chapel, the other nuns silently genuflected toward the altar. Many dangled rosaries from their palms. All had just confessed their sins to a visiting priest. Lifelike representations of sainthood watched the hushed scene from the chapel's stone alcoves: statues of Saint Joseph, Saint Anthony—even Saint Philomena, whose legendary tale of martyrdom would someday be expunged from the Vatican rolls.

While her fellow sisters bowed and prayed, Mary Theodosia was forced to stand. The bulging tumor inside her abdomen now prevented her from kneeling. As her lifeless left arm hung at her side, she slowly circled the church, trudging about one hundred fifty yards around the white and maroon terrazzo floor, making "the way of the cross." The Catholic ritual contained fourteen stops or "stations," each marked by a painting or statuette portraying a scene from "the passion" of Jesus Christ, his final hours: the condemnation, bearing the cross, his crucifixion, his death. At each station, a few set prayers were meant to be recited, followed by some meditation on Christ's suffering. By that night, Mary Theodosia could almost relate. No stranger to anguish, she fully felt the prospect of her imminent death.

Dr. Leon J. Willien—the first physician to analyze Mother

Théodore's brain—had diagnosed Mary Theodosia with breast cancer in 1906. He'd told the nun that without a mastectomy, she would be dead in a month. He had removed her diseased left breast, but decided not to operate on her abdominal tumor because, he felt, her body was too weak to survive two major surgeries. During a follow-up exam three months after the mastectomy, Dr. Willien recognized that Mary Theodosia's cancer was back and spreading fast. In her medical chart, he noted that some of her tissue was "becoming necrosed," or was dying, and that she appeared emaciated. The tumor in her belly was indeed malignant. The physician wrote that he expected "a fatal result."

Twenty months after her terminal prognosis—far weaker and much thinner—Mary Theodosia watched the other nuns stand and exit their basement chapel. She waited for the last sister to disappear up the tiny stairwell and climb to her convent quarters three floors above. The only sound in the room was the scuffling of Mary Theodosia's shoes as she walked feebly toward the altar. There she turned right, climbed a few stone steps and wandered toward a side chamber. She heaved open a heavy metal door and entered the burial vault. As she did so, she thought of an ill friend—another sister who was bedridden upstairs.

In the tomb, three ceiling lights burned, reflecting a dull sheen off the room's glazed white tiles. To Mary Theodosia's left, inside concrete drawers, three bodies rested: Sister Mary Joseph Lefer and Sister Saint Francis Lefer—siblings from France—and the corpse of the recently exhumed founder. In all, the crypt contained twelve drawers, built into a single wall and stacked in four columns of three. Each was sealed by a three-inch-thick marble cover affixed with a pair of brass handles. Brass plaques were etched with the names of the dead women inside. A top drawer—second from the right and about chest high—held a simple wooden box. Mary Theodosia paused there. Its name plate read MOTHER THEODORE.

When the founder was buried in the cemetery, the sisters had routinely visited her plot to pray for her intercession. And though Mary Theodosia had probed and plumbed the founder's life while authoring her biography, she herself had only once—listlessly—asked Mother Théodore to help cure her cancer. She had made that request in 1907, on the snowy day when the founder's casket was unearthed. Following the exhumation, Mother Mary Cleophas had quietly urged the sickly sister to pray to Mother Théodore for healing.

"At your bidding, I prayed," Mary Theodosia later revealed in the letter to her superior. "[But] rather half-heartedly though, as I had no desire to live."

In the silent gloom of the burial vault, Mary Theodosia once more passed up a chance to pray for her own rejuvenation. Instead she recited several psalms, including *De Profundis,* which is often used in liturgical prayers for the dead. It begins, "Out of the depths I cry to You, O Lord . . . hear my voice." Then she prayed for her friend, Sister Joseph Therese O'Connell, who was in the convent infirmary a few floors above, debilitated by rheumatoid arthritis. Mary Theodosia badly wanted to see Sister Joseph Therese walk again without pain. While worrying about her friend and simultaneously staring at Mother Théodore's name, she pondered a simple yet potent question about the founder.

I wonder, she thought, *if she has any power with Almighty God.*

Instantly, Mary Theodosia's head crackled with three clear words, so distinct and booming they seemed almost audible to her, almost palpable, but certainly real, she later recalled.

"Yes . . . she . . . has."

Terrified by the sharpness of the words, fearing she might even see something spectral, the sickly nun spun her body and broke into a sprint toward the stairwell. Feeble legs, rigid arms, throbbing belly and all, she dashed out of the tomb and lunged up five steps to the landing. There she whirled to her right and raced up ten remaining steps, skidding to a stop on the convent's first floor, breathing harder than she had in years.

No question, the "experience at the vault"—as she would dub it—was deeply spooky. On the night before Halloween, standing alone next to three bodies, Mary Theodosia had asked a question of the dead and had received a reply, she later claimed. Then again, the Woods was thought, by some, to be a place of spirits and ghostly tales. Many students and teachers claimed they often glimpsed an apparition they nicknamed "the Faceless Nun" throughout the corridors of Foley Hall, four stories of campus classrooms erected in the late 1800s and named after Mother Mary Cleophas Foley. The reported sightings even scared some people away from entering Foley Hall. Others had sworn that they heard swishing sounds beneath the floors of Foley. Finally, in the 1930s, the sisters had a special Mass said inside the hall—complete with a sprinkling of holy water. While the nuns were careful not to use the word "exorcism," the Mass carried one mission, "to quiet the ghosts in Foley," according to a 1974 interview with Sister Esther Newport, an art teacher who worked in Foley Hall at that time. Reports of "Faceless Nun" sightings ceased immediately after that Mass. Foley Hall was razed in 1989.

Ghost stories, however, were not part of Mary Theodosia's world. She was spiritual, yes, but also businesslike and bookish. Even more, as she later revealed in writing about that October 30 night: "I am never afraid of the dead; why should I fear now?" As she stood atop the stairwell, regaining her composure, she scolded herself for what she considered her silly excitement. But she could not shake the sound of the voice or those three words—"Yes . . . she . . . has." And as she climbed to her Providence Hall bedroom, she pondered again whether Mother Théodore really had some divine influence.

"If she has," Mary Theodosia said to herself, "I wish she would show it."

† † †

In her room that night, several floors above the crypt, Mary Theodosia buried herself in an upcoming issue of *The Child of Mary*, the community magazine she edited. Packed with poems and articles by Mary Theodosia and the other sisters—mainly pieces written about the Virgin Mary and Immaculate Conception dogma—the periodical was published on a fine grade of paper and sprinkled with lavish illustrations. The proofs were due the next day to a printer in Terre Haute. According to her clock, the time was seven thirty. She plowed through the pages until nine thirty, when all of Providence Hall's electric lights automatically clicked off. Then she struck a match, lit a candle, and lost track of the hours, correcting and rewriting the proofs until twelve forty-five in the morning, when she slipped into bed and fell immediately asleep.

When the convent lights came on again at four a.m., Mary Theodosia sat up in bed with a fresh energy she hadn't known in years. Though she had only snoozed for three hours, her body buzzed with pep and strength. She felt so good, in fact, she momentarily feared she had badly overslept. She stood and began smoothing her blankets only to abruptly stop the task. Her eyes widened with awe. Once again she started tugging and tucking the coverlets, but now she watched her own hands work in tandem as if they belonged to another woman. In the twenty months since her mastectomy and the loss of function in her left arm, Mary Theodosia had been forced to make her bed each morning with just her right arm.

Still, there was more.

After her cancer surgery, she had been forced to invent a creative, one-armed way to roll up her long hair by resting her head on her knees—until, that is, the abdominal tumor eventually blocked her from bending. Now, as a new dexterity flowed through the fingers in her left hand, she sat upright on her bed and quickly fixed her hair for the coming day.

And still there was more.

She began to dress. She immediately realized, however, the waistband on her habit was loose. Puzzled, she examined the extra cloth in her fingers. As she pinned the sash in place near her hip, the reason for her baggy clothing became suddenly, stunningly clear: the lump in her belly was gone. So was the pain. Meanwhile, her long-dormant appetite was raging. Even her chronically weak eyes seemed to soak in the world with a fresh clarity, she later noted.

Jubilant though confused, she nonetheless didn't say a word. She celebrated in private silence by going to Halloween morning Mass an hour early, knowing only that something wondrous had happened as she slept in her small, one-window room.

Sister Mary Theodosia Mug—diagnosed with aggressive cancer—had gone to bed a terminally sick, broken woman and had awakened feeling completely healthy.

The other nuns noticed the physical changes straightaway. They saw her kneel at Mass. They saw her lug two sloshing buckets of water—one in each hand—from a pump in the Providence Hall courtyard to the first-floor dining hall where the sisters had their meals. They saw her eat—with gusto—the same food the rest of the community was served. Three days later, word of Mary Theodosia's overnight healing reached Bishop Chatard. The ex-doctor instantly understood two things: first, if the nun's widespread cancer had spontaneously vanished over the course of just a few hours, her recovery transcended all known laws of medicine; and second, because she had prayed for intercession—the night before, no less—her rejuvenation could someday be decreed, by definition, a miracle.

In human terms, a forty-eight-year-old woman seemed to have

cheated death—with divine help. In theological terms, Mother Théodore Guérin's cause for sainthood—which would require two proven miracles—was alive and booming. Chatard also realized, however, that the facts behind the alleged miracle would have to be painstakingly assembled. And like any good piece of detective work, the first step was to collect evidence and document the event.

Chatard instructed Mary Theodosia to put the details of her experience in writing. She followed his orders by penning a one-page letter to Mother Mary Cleophas, dated November 21, 1908. In it, she depicted her prayer, her fright in the tomb, her late-night magazine editing, and her awakening with a robust feeling. She even joked about her food revival: "I can eat anything that comes to the table and in such quantities as to amuse everyone."

Yet Mary Theodosia began her letter with an earnest and impossible question—one that would be echoed a century later on the same ground by a man basking in the same miraculous glow and tussling with the same unshakable doubts: Why me?

"Why should I be favored above the many that have so fervently sought grace through the intercession of our revered and holy Foundress?" she asked.

That enigma would stay with Mary Theodosia for the rest of her life. Even more perplexing to her: Sister Joseph Therese—the nun with rheumatoid arthritis for whom she had actually prayed—never got better.

Meanwhile, a parade of physicians attempted to crack Mary Theodosia's medical mystery. On November 15, 1908, she was examined yet again by Dr. Willien. He was impressed by her newfound fitness but not totally convinced she was healthy to stay. He pronounced her "apparently cured." Several years would need to elapse before any doctor could declare her cancer in remission. By November 1912, she was under the care of another Terre Haute physician, Dr. Wilbur O. Jenkins, who stated in her medical charts that he found no evidence of tumors in her body. That same year, Dr. Willien made another assessment of Mary Theodosia, noting that her muscles and nerves were in excellent condition. This time, Willien stamped her rally as "a complete and supernatural cure."

The final say would come from one of the ultimate medical authorities in the United States. On February 18, 1913, Mary Theodosia traveled to the Mayo Brothers Clinic (later just called the Mayo Clinic) in Rochester, Minnesota. Doctors there performed the most rigorous tests available. They issued a clinical report confirming both her healthy blood chemistry and the absence of any disease.

Back at the Woods, there were only quiet whispers about Mary Theodosia's crypt prayer and swift healing. Mother Mary Cleophas made it a point not to bring up the topic with her nuns, fearing that open commentary about a potential miracle could jeopardize the founder's possible canonization. The Vatican frowned on Church personnel publicly discussing miracle investigations—like the search to explain Mary Theodosia's cure. The tactic was not unlike judicial gag orders placed on defense attorneys, prosecutors, and witnesses before a trial to keep potential juries untainted by sensational media reports. The jury for an alleged miracle consisted of Italian doctors and theologians, along with a consistory of cardinals and the pope himself. And they didn't tolerate meddling or coercion.

At the same time, however, the sisters saw no real need to promote Mary Theodosia's story. It spoke for itself. Her prayerful plea already had been chronicled. Her mended body had been exhaustively probed by outside doctors. She was living evidence, the sisters felt, of something wondrous. In their view, Rome certainly, inevitably, would brand it a miracle—the first miracle to bolster Mother Théodore's potential canonization cause. What they didn't know then: none of them would live to see it happen.

Despite its brisk start, the cause slowed and eventually lan-
guished in the Vatican pipeline, its progress sporadically beset by
the difficulties of long-distance communications, the Great Depression, two world wars, and the deaths or reassignments of its various
postulators, its champions in Rome. The campaign's next milestone
came in 1926 when the Holy See approved all of Mother Théodore's
writings — meaning every line of her diaries and communications
had been checked and were found to support her virtuousness. By
then her cause had been moved to a second postulator (following
the Vatican's 1916 transfer of Monsignor Biondi to the East Indies),
and in 1927 it would be transferred to a third and still a fourth postulator. In all, nine postulators would handle the cause — three of
them would die on the job, and three more would fall so ill they were
forced to resign. With each change, the cause lost continuity, sap-
ping its momentum and creating an agonizing, ninety-seven-year
slog through Vatican channels.

In the midst of that long wait, Sister Mary Theodosia became
an old woman.

Her final work as a writer was to compile and edit a collection
of Mother Théodore's journals and letters. The book was published
in 1937 with a cover bearing black-and-white photos of a sailing
ship on rough seas and one of the community's farm buildings. Her
last duties of any kind came in 1940 — the community's centennial.
She secured monuments to mark historical "memory spots," as she
called them, including the grassy hillside where Mother Théodore
and her five French traveling companions had stepped out of a
stagecoach and taken their first peek at Saint Mary-of-the-Woods.
In 2009 that "arrival stone" — a gray, two-foot-high rock speckled
with green moss — rested above a grotto built to replicate the famous
shrine in Lourdes, France, where millions of pilgrims flocked to ask
for miracles.

While the sisters were discouraged from mentioning Mary

Theodosia's apparent miracle, some of the newest members of the order—the novices—couldn't help but treat the aging nun as a secret celebrity by the early 1940s. The novices rarely interacted with the fully professed sisters, whom they called "the black veils." For the novices, that forced separation from the black veils only heightened Mary Theodosia's mystique. When they would spot her at Mass or in the dining hall, some would cover their mouths and quietly say to one another, "There she is! There she is! That's the sister that Mother Théodore healed!"

The youngest Woods residents during that pre–World War II span were the girls in the academy who worked toward earning high school diplomas. Many of those girls hoped someday to join the Sisters of Providence as nuns, including a teenager with lively blue eyes, a fondness for strawberry shortcake, and a deep affection for Mother Théodore's rural fortitude. She even shared the founder's birth name. Anna Therese Tighe (pronounced *Tie*) was the baby of her family, the youngest of six sisters, born August 23, 1924, in New Albany, Indiana—a small city on the Ohio River, just across the state line from Louisville, Kentucky. New Albany was known for its veneer factories. Anna Therese was named after her stay-at-home mother, Anna Therese Buche. Her father, Edward John Tighe, began his career as an accounting officer at a Louisville law firm. He later launched his own insurance agency. His brother, a lawyer, then persuaded Edward to establish the Floyd County Savings and Loan in New Albany, which later became First Federal Savings and Loan.

At her Catholic elementary school, nuns imbued Anna Therese with tales of Mother Théodore's dangerous deeds and devout ways. She was captivated by their accounts. And she felt the first pangs of a spiritual calling. One schoolhouse moment reinforced her respect for the nuns. On Valentine's Day 1937, during her eighth-grade year, several boys left the school playground—a major rules infraction—to go buy boxes of candy, which they subsequently placed on their girlfriends' desks. Anna Therese fully expected that when their classroom teacher—a Sister of Providence—saw the candy and realized the boys had stepped off school property, she would explode in anger. But when the nun returned to the classroom and surveyed the half-eaten boxes, she merely smiled and said, "Isn't love grand?"

Soon her parents enrolled Anna Therese at Presentation Academy, a Catholic preparatory high school for girls in downtown Louisville. Founded in 1831 by the Sisters of Charity of Nazareth, the academy was the oldest continually operating high school in that city. During her freshman year, Anna Therese's homeroom teacher quietly suggested to the teenager that perhaps she had been divinely called to become a nun. Anna Therese, in turn, mentioned this to her parish priest, adding, "Maybe I do want to be a sister." The priest paused. "Don't tell anyone about this for a year," he said. "Not even your mother or father. In a year we'll talk again." She complied. Twelve months later, Anna Therese told the priest she still sought the life of a nun. Moreover, she ached to join the Indiana convent founded by Mother Théodore. She was drawn by what she saw as the legendary nun's resilient yet compassionate example, her lingering magnetism and enduring charisma. The Catholic Church used its own word for that type of aura—*charism,* defined as a special power of influence conferred by God. After she finally revealed her plans to her parents, Edward Tighe approved but told his daughter she had to wait until her junior year before transferring to the Saint Mary-of-the-Woods Academy. She waited. In 1940—one hundred years after Mother Théodore had first stood among the groves of walnut trees and the clusters of white violets near the Wabash banks, Anna Therese enrolled at the Woods.

Two years later, after earning her high school diploma, she prepared to enter the Sisters of Providence school for nuns, its "novitiate"—the rigorous classes and training required to formally join the order. The night before she enlisted in the novitiate, Anna Therese and her five sisters gathered at the family house in New Albany. To mark the occasion, the Tighe girls all donned their formal dresses and had a group photo taken. The next day, Anna Therese switched from formal wear to a postulant's black uniform. In time, she was a professed nun with a new name that she picked after much thought—Sister Marie Kevin. "Marie" is the French variant of "Mary." Saint Kevin was a sixth-century Irish abbot, a lover of animals and a determined vegetarian, who lived to be 120 years old; the name Kevin was said to mean "fair begotten."

Though she shared the campus with Mary Theodosia for almost three years, Sister Marie Kevin never met the woman who claimed to have been cured by the founder. That was due, in part, to the natural separation between the young sisters and the professed nuns. What's more, by 1943 Mary Theodosia had again fallen ill—this time to old age. She was moved from her room in Providence Hall to a bed in the convent infirmary. There, "her mind became a blank," according to one caretaker. On March 23, 1943, Sister Mary Theodosia Mug died. She was eighty-two years and eight months old. Her listed cause of death: arteriosclerosis, or hardening of the arteries. Meanwhile, Sister Marie Kevin, who was by then settling into the community's ways and rhythms, still had not heard the full story of Mary Theodosia's chilling prayer at the crypt and her overnight resurgence. In fact, she wouldn't learn those details for many more years as the congregation's leaders maintained their dutiful silence on the matter.

In time, however, Marie Kevin would not only soak up every morsel of that otherworldly tale, but would become its chief publicist, offering vivid accounts of the alleged miracle to investigators in Rome—and to anyone else who would listen. She became intoxicated with Mother Théodore's cause for sainthood and her legacy as a battle-hardened leader, a compassionate soldier for the sick, and a woman who never lost her French passion or her female spirit, confronting convent crises and personal illnesses with occasional tears yet never with a complaint. From the 1940s through the 1960s, while working as a teacher and a principal at Catholic schools throughout Indiana and Illinois, Marie Kevin preached the gospel of Mother Théodore to hundreds of children, hoping to ignite a new generation to shed their middle-class comforts and pursue gritty missions of faith.

In the 1990s, Marie Kevin continued speaking about Mother Théodore to church groups and to other gatherings. She became, in a sense, a modern version of Mary Theodosia, a pitchwoman for the founder's achievements. She was outgoing and effervescent, and by 1994, the convent's general superior saw Marie Kevin as an obvious choice to become the congregation's next point person to head the local campaign for sainthood — officially known as "the promoter of the cause." A promoter's chief responsibilities were to sell the candidate's sanctification to the masses and to gather reports of mysterious healings performed in his or her name. This was a sacred role to Marie Kevin, a job she had seemed destined to fill.

Then she, too, fell gravely ill.

Some of the darkest, most disappointing hours of Mother Théodore's cause came in 1977. Having never appointed one of their own to the role of "promoter," the congregation had for eight decades relied solely on a series of Roman postulators to try to press the Vatican for her sanctification. Most of those seven postulators — all priests — had eventually become enfeebled by sickness or had died on the job, repeatedly bottlenecking progress. The man appointed postulator in 1977, Father Andrea Quemard, would similarly resign due to illness in 1980.

By 1977 the sainthood campaign was mired in forgotten memories. Every sister who had known Mary Theodosia was dead. There were no surviving "witnesses" to testify about the nun's cancer recovery. That year, Quemard regretfully informed the convent that the cause was being returned to a "historical commission" at the Archdiocese of Indianapolis—a clear step backward. Such panels, appointed by a local archbishop, were assigned to collect and examine all documents pertaining to the candidate. In 1949 the cause had likewise been mothballed at a "historical commission" where it remained for five years.

Despite the latest setback, the nuns did not surrender. In 1978 the convent dispatched Sister Joseph Eleanor Ryan to Rome to begin fresh research to resurrect some momentum. During the next ten years, Sister Joseph Eleanor repeatedly flew back and forth between Indiana and Italy, poring over the founder's exploits from France to America, leafing through stacks of French journals and letters, and perusing the pages of medical documentation on Mary Theodosia's cancer comeback. For the first time she organized all those stories and facts into a massive thesis—the bible for any sainthood cause: the *positio* (Latin for "statement"). The exhaustive volume—essentially the arguments for her beatification and, eventually, her canonization—had two parts and two goals: The first was the *Positio Super Virtutibus* (or statement on heroic virtues), a summary of Mother Théodore's life, work, and writings, meant to substantiate her holiness. The second, the *Positio Super Miraculo* (or statement on the miracle), consisted of the doctors' reports and hospital records of Mary Theodosia's disease, operation, and recovery; Mary Theodosia's 1908 letter describing her illness, prayer, and physical revival; and a transcript of the 1958 testimony of Sister Dorothy Eileen Howard, one of Mary Theodosia's nurses during her final days in the infirmary. The latter compendium aimed to defend the alleged supernatural cure. When the final page of the *positio* was typed, Sister Joseph Eleanor stacked all the sheets loosely in front of her on a desk. Wearing her black habit, slightly hunched, and meekly smiling, she gazed down at the tome. Someone snapped a black-and-white photo to capture the moment. The written case for Mother Théodore's sainthood stood more than a foot tall.

Originally written in French by Sister Joseph Eleanor, the *positio* was translated into English and Italian, and printed in 1987. The next year, historical consultants were appointed by the Holy See to read the opus. They voted unanimously that the *positio*'s facts were sufficient, meaning the work could eventually be used to judge Mother Théodore's sanctity. Next, the bulging report would be handed to Vatican theologians for their judgment—potentially opening the way for the pope to declare Mother Théodore "Venerable."

New hope surged at the Woods. And the sisters had a new champion to toast. In 1989 Sister Joseph Eleanor was formally appointed vice-postulator of the cause in recognition of her Vatican success. A quiet woman from Joliet, Illinois, and a poet in her spare time, Sister Joseph Eleanor desperately hoped to remain the vice-postulator until—and if—Mother Théodore was beatified and ultimately canonized. By 1989, however, she was in her eightieth year. She mentioned to a friend that perhaps if she prayed to Mother Théodore, the founder might cure her age-related infirmities, thus supplying the Sisters of Providence with a necessary second miracle. Her prayers would prompt no cure, nor an elongated life. Sister Joseph Eleanor died on May 7, 1991.

The nun's good work, however, rolled through the Vatican machinery. In February 1992 a panel of eight Vatican theologians perused the 1,300-page *positio* and voted unanimously that Mother Théodore had lived a life of heroic virtue. In written opinions that accompanied their votes, three of the theologians specifically called out how Mother Théodore had shown grace and toughness during her noxious clashes with Bishop La Hailandière. "The test the . . . foundress and first Superior General had to confront, did not come from within, but rather from the circle of the clergy, particularly the local Bishop, whom sources describe as a man of impossible character, convinced of his role as bishop-master, incapable of constructive dialogue, as much with his clergy as with religious communities," one of the seven theologians wrote. "This was the test, long-lived and harsh, which the Servant of God had to face. According to witnesses and sources—she bore this with patience and humility, but also with maternal firmness, showing thus the measure of her spiritual maturity and the strength of her character."

The theologians' united approval prompted Pope John Paul II to issue a decree on July 11, 1992, granting Mother Théodore a new title, "Venerable." The next question looming at the Vatican: Was the healing of Mary Theodosia truly inexplicable to science? Was it a miracle?

While waiting for that answer, Sister Marie Kevin abruptly found herself in need of her own miraculous cure. At age seventy, she was diagnosed with gastroesophageal cancer. Her oncologist never had known a patient to beat her level of disease. Surgeons removed half of Marie Kevin's stomach, half of her esophagus, her spleen, and part of her diaphragm. They rebuilt her entire food-absorption system. And though the cancer was apparently out, her internal incisions would not mend. She grew steadily weaker, wasting away. For seventy-two days, she stared at a ceiling from a bed at Methodist Hospital in Indianapolis. The medical staff did not expect her to leave the facility alive. Her bedside visitors harbored similar fears, including the congregation's general superior at that time, Sister Nancy Nolan.

"She was really at death's door, hooked up to more things, and I thought, 'Oh dear God, this woman is a goner,'" recalled Sister

Nancy, then in her eighth year as the community's leader. "I didn't see how she could survive."

The image was as tragic as it was disappointing. With the cause teetering in a make-or-break phase in Rome, the convent needed a theological whiz with both public charm and a firm grip on history to become the new face of the cause. They needed one of their own to help close the deal and to, eventually, find a second possible miracle. They needed someone like Marie Kevin. As a school principal, she had preached and peddled Mother Théodore's cause and charism. In the 1970s she was tapped to serve on a special team of sisters charged with leading a congregation renewal—a return to Mother Théodore's civic-minded mission. In that task, Marie Kevin had soared, finding her voice and her life's larger pursuit. Later she was named to run the Office of Pastoral Councils at the Indianapolis Archdiocese, guiding Catholics throughout central and southern Indiana to reinvigorate their local faith communities. But Marie Kevin's various ministries—not to mention her time—appeared to be near an end. In desperation, her doctor decided to try one more high-risk operation to save her.

The thoracic surgeon planned to cut into her upper back in order to reach her new digestive connections and then, he hoped, to pull them tighter and patch her lingering internal wounds. At the same time, a plastic surgeon planned to graft skin from her legs to her lower back, where bedsores had turned into ulcers.

"I must tell you," her doctor warned beforehand, "this surgery could go this way or that."

"Do what you have to do," Marie Kevin responded.

As the medical staff prepared for their intricate series of cuts and maneuvers, a nurse wheeled Marie Kevin into a diagnostic lab to peer once more inside her body and check on her two-month-old lesions.

After a careful exam by the hushed team, the nurse stood next to Marie Kevin's gurney and leaned her face close.

"We don't have to do the surgery!" the nurse whispered. "It is healed!"

Her doctors were mystified and amazed at what they saw on the scans. She had somehow, finally, recovered. She was cured.

Fifteen years later, Marie Kevin recounted that day while sitting in a soft but formal chair in a Providence Hall parlor adorned with a fireplace, dark-stained windowsills, and a painting of Mother Théodore. Outside, plump snowflakes fell. She had just finished a lunch of fresh bass, wild rice, steamed vegetables, iced tea, and lemon pie. Her voice was weaker than it once had been, but her words were clear, her mind sharp. Atop her head was a soft puff of white hair. She wore a silver cross over her red sweater. And her blue eyes still danced behind wire-rimmed glasses. She closed them and smiled as she remembered that morning in the hospital. The relief and wonder she had felt upon receiving the good news were still visible in her face.

"Then the plastic surgeon came in and told me we didn't have to do the skin graft either. He said he had never seen wounds like that heal so fast."

In the hospital, had she prayed to Mother Théodore for healing?

"People ask me that all the time. I was flat on my back. The closest I got to praying is that I would say, over and over, 'I know God loves me.' That's about as far as I could get."

Was your recovery, by definition, a miracle?

"To me, it was. But I don't really care. I'm not pushing to have it examined or tested. I feel that . . . I don't know how to explain this. It just was a great gift and a grace to me. Because I could now work on the cause. As I was recuperating, I was asked to take over that work."

Marie Kevin had endured, she believed, to complete her life's mission: to try to secure Mother Théodore's sainthood.

Indeed, once released from the hospital, she quickly regained her strength and her appetite. Flashing her old, bubbly personality, she told friends she pined to get back to work. Sister Nancy Nolan, the Woods' top nun at the time, watched her closely. The general superior still believed that Marie Kevin's gregarious ways, gentle style, and gift for storytelling all would serve as perfect traits for the crusade's new local leader. And she felt that such responsibilities would give Marie Kevin new purpose, new life. They did. In June 1996, Sister Nancy appointed Marie Kevin as the promoter of the cause.

She shone immediately. During the summer and fall of 1996, the Vatican's special panel of doctors—its Consulta Medica—dug through the old medical records describing Mary Theodosia's disease and her overnight improvement, and they researched known medical practices in Indiana in 1908. Ultimately the Italian doctors could not find a single logical medical reason to explain Mary Theodosia's survival. In November the Consulta Medica unanimously ruled that Mary Theodosia's return to good health had defied science. In March 1997 the Holy See's panel of theologians unanimously concurred.

And on July 7, 1997, in a cramped, tapestry-draped Vatican room—barely large enough to hold four rows of seats—Pope John Paul II read aloud an official proclamation. In the small audience, three Sisters of Providence sat and smiled.

It was, the pope ruled, a miracle.

The papal endorsement led to a massive beatification ceremony in St. Peter's Square on October 25, 1998, which drew about a hundred nuns from the Indiana compound and more than forty thousand people from Rome and around the world. During the service, Sister Diane Ris, the Woods' new general superior, carried a glass-and-brass box called a reliquary up a long, sheer flight of stairs toward the pope. At the top of her climb, she placed the container near John Paul II. The box held one of Mother Théodore's rib bones.

Papal gifts were an age-old tradition at beatifications and canonizations, hinting at both the monetary inducements ingrained in the process and the exorbitant costs associated with the business of sainthood. In other words, a pope usually received much more than a few bones for green-lighting a cause. As was often the custom, the Sisters of Providence also furnished John Paul with a check—albeit a unique one: a $50,000 banknote shellacked onto a slice of wood cut from a downed campus tree. The wood also bore the image of Mother Théodore as well as one of the pope's quotes about helping the poor. Then the sisters did something almost unheard of—they asked John Paul to return the funds. They promised to use the money to build low-income homes and apartments in West Terre Haute for struggling families and the elderly. The pope consented. In 1999 the sisters opened Providence Place on a twenty-acre tract a few miles away from their campus.

During the beatification service, John Paul subtly referenced Mother Théodore's acerbic relationship with La Hailandière.

"Her love embraced even those who caused her pain and anguish. She transformed the hardest hearts by her inspired words," John Paul said. "She is a model of the best of womanhood."

As the sun set on St. Peter's Square that day, the founder of the Woods was now known as Blessed Mother Théodore.

But her journey to sainthood was only halfway home.

Her cause for canonization required a second miracle—another event that would evade the laws of science, a phenomenon that would withstand an intense Church tribunal in Indianapolis and a fresh round of Vatican scrutiny. And there was an important stipulation: under Church doctrine, the second miracle could only occur after Mother Théodore's beatification.

At the Woods, Marie Kevin launched still one more quest in 1998 to find something wondrous. By then she was nearing her mid-seventies. Some of the other nuns were pushing into their eighties and nineties. They knew it had taken a lifetime for Mother Théodore's cause to reach the edge of saintly glory. How long until the payoff? Many convent residents wondered aloud if that moment would be savored by another generation of sisters. A new pressure built. A new rush was felt. What they needed was a bolt of heavenly luck, or a dash of a supernatural coincidence. Or, perhaps, a timely dose of their own divine creed: providence.

CHAPTER FOUR

The Malady

In the spring of 1997, just as the first miracle was inching toward papal acceptance, a legally blind non-Catholic with bottle-thick glasses and little use for organized religion arrived at the convent. Phil McCord had been hired by the sisters as their new director of facilities management. He would care for the community's ancient boilers, crusty roofs, and century-old plumbing. Whatever the quandary, he was the man to repair, rebuild, or restore it.

On a whim, McCord had answered the nuns' newspaper ad about the position. After his job interview, he stayed overnight in a guesthouse tucked a few hundred feet beyond the Woods' main gate. Upon waking, he saw pristine snow coating the stately lawns, the calm waters of La Fer Lake nestled in a southwestern corner of campus, and the arched footbridge spanning that tiny lake. In a northwestern corner of the property, horses stood in a pasture, steam puffing from their nostrils. The primary entrance road—dubbed "The Avenue" by the nuns and students—sliced north through campus. Immediately to the east and west of that driveway sat classroom buildings and dormitories, a library, and a music conservatory. The Avenue ultimately wrapped around a mid-campus fountain nestled near the Church of the Immaculate Conception and Providence Hall. McCord quickly fell in love with the serenity of the place, and with the sisters' affinity for earth-friendly farming.

Throughout much of his forties, McCord had been the head of engineering at Porter Hospital in Valparaiso, Indiana, where he also worked with his wife, Debbie, a nurse. But on his first visit to the convent, he felt he was home.

"This is a joyous place," he told Debbie on the phone during his stay.

He had taken the job without hesitation. The McCords bought and moved into a two-story, suburban-style house—green with black shutters. Located on East Blinn Court in a cul-de-sac eleven miles southeast of Terre Haute, the spacious home boasted a three-car garage, a fenced backyard, a basketball hoop in the driveway, and a front porch adorned with an American flag and a white spindle railing.

Shy and sharply intelligent, McCord quickly earned a reputation at the Woods as a rock-solid, self-reliant guy, an inquisitive thinker, a dreamer of inventive projects, and a finisher of jobs. He was easy to be around, self-deprecating and sometimes laughably klutzy. He occasionally could be quick-tempered, although he recognized his short fuse and typically apologized if his passions erupted on the job. He built scores of close ties on campus. After work, he helped coach the Saint Mary-of-the-Woods College softball team. On many weekends he took his twenty-eight-foot motorboat onto Lake Michigan. He was private and guarded with his emotions—a good friend and a good worker, yet not the kind of man who willingly sought help from others. Not from his colleagues. Not from the nuns. And certainly not from God or Mother Théodore.

Born and raised in Anderson, Indiana—a General Motors town—McCord grew up on the rural fringe of the Indianapolis metroplex. That's where he met Debbie, who became his high school sweetheart. He was raised by a father who also served as a Baptist lay minister, a mother who practiced Christian Science, and a grandmother who had once warned young Phil that the Catholics were arming themselves and plotting to take over the world.

McCord's own religion, however, was science.

Soft-spoken and balding, with a close-cropped gray beard, he had a measured IQ of 170 and the methodical soul of an engineer. For anything to be truly understood it first had to be dismantled and analyzed; it had to be touched, sniffed, and inspected against the light of day. He adored his moments of "creative destruction" as he called them—taking a sledgehammer and a power saw to a so-called piece of junk, slashing away its vital parts, and reassembling those bits for rebirth in another machine, another structure, another way. He was a recycling fanatic, once nicknamed "Sanford" by hospital coworkers because of his scrounging skills.

For McCord, one of the Woods' great allures was that the sisters shared his zest for resurrecting the planet's various forms of refuse. From a revamped laundry facility on the north end of campus, the sisters ran the ambitious White Violet Center for Eco-Justice. Launched in 1996, the program included a wetlands restoration project; 343 acres of certified organic farmland plus orchards laced with plum, peach, apple, pear, and cherry trees; a straw-bale retreat house; a trail of bluebird houses; a population of wild bees; and a huge composting site. In addition, the sisters raised and grazed a herd of fifty alpacas—animals that returned important nutrients to the soil and offered coats of fleece later used for spinning and weaving. Soon, with McCord's help, the community would convert the aging boiler furnaces in many buildings from gas to biomass fuels—lumber scraps, unwanted branches, lawn trimmings, and old Christmas trees collected from Terre Haute. "His mind never rests," said Sister Denise Wilkinson, one of McCord's friends among the nuns. "In his vision, he saw that we would be a complete circle, that anything produced on campus wouldn't get thrown away, that we could always make use of it for the next thing." McCord felt that his priorities meshed beautifully with the sisters' Earth-first interests. He abhorred waste, whether of material or of time. And he believed that the solution to almost any dilemma could be found in its smallest pieces, that the answer to almost any mystery rested somewhere in the plain, cold facts.

In short, he was a solver of problems.

But by late 2000, something inside McCord's head was severely broken. In fact, it was getting worse by the day.

And what bothered him most of all: he could not fix it.

For more than two months his right eye had glowed with a nuclear shade of red, like the last ember in a midnight campfire. The swollen lid sagged. The skin around the eye had assumed a brownish tint. Half of his face seemed drawn. Half of his vision had become a yellowish blur of odd shapes and shadows. Tears trickled. Sometimes the entire monstrous mess felt even worse than it looked.

But the dull throb in his eye socket only reminded McCord of the real nastiness that loomed: A surgeon planned to slice out a blistered sliver of his eye and stitch in a strand of replacement tissue freshly harvested from a "donor"—that is, from a corpse. That was the macabre repair for McCord's diagnosed condition: a chronically inflamed cornea. His eye was dying, and had been ever since a routine cataract operation that produced dire and unexplained complications. But although the transplant itself sounded downright ghoulish, his surgeon had, in frightening detail, listed the operation's potential dangers: rejection, infection, a horrible eye-socket hemorrhage, permanent blindness, and even, possibly, death. Left untreated, the eye would remain a gruesome, achy, useless wreck. And if the transplant actually worked, he faced months, maybe years, of recovery until his right eye saw the clear light of day.

So, on a harsh, gray Wednesday morning, January 3, 2001, beneath the big trees just outside Terre Haute, McCord's head buzzed with a secret mix of fear and funk. In fact, his mood pretty well matched the frosty landscape. A steady wind out of

the southwestern sky lashed the empty limbs and made the outside air feel like it was three degrees below zero. The convent's
lawns were matted with five inches of crusty snow left over from a
pre-Christmas storm.

McCord had started his workday with a mundane business
meeting at the Providence Center—the community's one-story,
white-brick welcoming post, located where Foley Hall once stood.
He spent about an hour in the office of Brother Barry Donaghue,
director of the Providence Center and a member of the Congregation of Christian Brothers, a group of laymen who profess poverty
and chastity and who commit to a life of ministry. Brother Barry
still carried an Australian accent from his Melbourne upbringing.
That morning they discussed buying new carpet for the center.
Just down the hall from their meeting was the Heritage Room, a
mini-museum teeming with Mother Théodore's possessions: the
scratched wooden writing desk on which she penned nearly five
thousand letters, her calfskin wallet, the wicker market basket she
carried into Terre Haute to buy supplies (the sight of a woman conducting business often drew stares from townsfolk), a worn book of
psalms, her watch, her penknife, and the blue porridge bowl from
which she ate mashed meals to soothe her damaged stomach. In
small ways, each item hinted of Mother Théodore's daily struggles
and scrambles, a sickly woman leading other women to survive in
an unkind wilderness. As the two men talked near those sacred
artifacts, Brother Barry could sense the strain of the caretaker's
own battle. From across the desk, McCord peered at him through
a flaming red eye. Yet his mind seemed miles away. That wasn't like
him at all.

When the meeting ended at eleven o'clock, McCord planned
to walk back to his office, situated just a few hundred feet east of
the Providence Center in one of the historic redbrick buildings that
dotted the campus. He opted for a route that would shield him from

the piercing, wintry breeze — a twenty-five-yard detour through an inside corridor that ran adjacent to the Church of the Immaculate Conception, or "the big church," as the sisters called it. His footsteps echoed off the hallway's terrazzo floor, which typically smelled of vinegar following the morning mopping. Above him, on the high, white ceiling, a line of hanging lights glimmered brightly. But as he strolled, McCord sank even deeper into his own darkness. He felt suffocated by anxiety, ashamed that the pending surgery had mentally whipped him.

I can't do this, he thought. *I really don't think I can do this.*

Eighty-three days earlier, while lying prone in an ophthalmologist's chair, he had been disfigured and partially blinded during a routine outpatient eye procedure. At first everything had seemed to go perfectly. Using a titanium-tipped, penlike tool, a surgeon had pulverized the cataract in McCord's right eye with ultrasonic vibrations. The doctor had then sucked out the hard bits of diseased lens through a minuscule probe. But the next morning, a Friday, McCord had awakened with a persistent pang in that eye. It felt heavy. It looked bruised. He complained to his wife, Debbie, that something seemed very wrong. He returned to the ophthalmologist that same day and was diagnosed with a swollen cornea — not completely uncommon after a cataract removal, his surgeon had said. He was prescribed drops to ease the edema — fluid buildup — and told to return four days later for a recheck. Yet after two months of additional exams, a stream of drops, and a bottle of Tylenol 3, the eye remained a sore, visionless, puffy blotch. McCord had grown increasingly frustrated and upset. Each day he lived the same optic time loop: in the mornings the white or sclera of his eye appeared pink and his lid seemed saggy; but each evening, due to fatigue, the eye scowled a bright red and the lid hung even lower, as if he had been socked with a fist. His ophthalmologist couldn't explain what had gone wrong. Even worse, after eleven weeks of chronic inflammation, he told McCord the eye had reached a state where it would never heal on its own. The only hope was a complete corneal transplant. Without it, the eye would be forever raw and blind.

The news rattled the normally placid McCord. Months of pain and distorted vision had left him physically and emotionally spent. He didn't want another doctor digging inside his head—slicing and removing a piece of the clear corneal dome that covered his eyeball, carving out his ravaged cornea, and stitching in a replacement plucked from a dead body. He didn't want to think about the operation's risks or the months, maybe years, of recuperation. As always, though, he revealed his rising anguish only to Debbie, who later recalled that her husband was "scared to death." No one who saw him on campus that wind-bitten morning—neither Brother Barry nor the nuns who smiled at him in the vinegary-smelling corridor— sensed his true turmoil. No one expected panic from steady Phil McCord.

That was when he heard the music.

Halfway down the hallway, as he passed a series of six stained-glass windows that faced into the sanctuary on his right, the soaring notes of a pipe organ began filling the corridor. His steps slowed. The instrument—similar to the type that Sister Mary Theodosia had played long ago at the Woods—had been installed in the church loft in 1954, the third organ to reside there. It had recently been cleaned and refurbished, enhancing its sweet tones. Now the keyboardist was warming her fingers for the 11:30 a.m. Mass. The melody seemed to beckon, seemed to offer an air of calm, a refuge. "A beautiful sound," he would later relate. McCord followed the hymn like a hungry man sniffing the scent of warm bread. Instead of turning left at the end of the corridor and continuing toward his office, he entered the big church through a side door, to the left of the altar.

Except for the organist, the massive space was empty and still.

Directly below him was the crypt where Mary Theodosia had prayed to Mother Théodore, and where she had heard the voice in 1908. Mother Théodore's remains had since been moved from her crypt drawer to a small box affixed to the crypt ceiling. As McCord shuffled toward a sixth-row pew, the founder's body rested just under the basilica floor, to the right of the main altar. That spot was specially outlined in the marble for church visitors and worshippers to see.

He sat down and inhaled some of the blissful tranquillity, unsure of why he was there or what he was about to do.

On the computer screen atop Sister Marie Kevin Tighe's small wooden desk, e-mails from around the world glowed in an ever-swelling cyber-stack. Fifteen to twenty new notes per day filled her inbox. And many of those spoke of otherworldly happenings.

The e-mails—along with heaps of handwritten letters and a tide of phone calls—originated in Belgium, Norway, Spain, Malaysia, Saudi Arabia, Poland, Italy, Sri Lanka, and scores of other foreign lands and various U.S. cities and towns. Many writers, citing the sisters' professed hotline to heaven via Mother Théodore, requested urgent prayers from the nuns for ill family members or sick friends, or for their own woes. Others contacted Marie Kevin to relay their own baffling, spontaneous cures from horrible sicknesses or conditions—including a priest who described holding a "friendly" chat with Mother Théodore about his paralyzed left arm, and who subsequently regained use of the appendage. These reports were among the most precious messages that poured into Marie Kevin's office. As the promoter of Mother Théodore's cause for sainthood, it was her job to surf through the desperate and breathless dispatches and find something the Sisters of Providence had been praying for since the 1998 beatification—the final piece to the community's now ninety-one-year crusade. Marie Kevin was searching for a second miracle. If needed, she would scour the entire planet.

As Phil McCord settled into an empty pew in the Church of the Immaculate Conception just next door, allowing the organ music to bathe his anxious mind, the pine limbs outside Marie Kevin's window swayed in the breezes of January. Her office in the aging Providence Hall was situated on the first floor—not far from the stairwell where a profoundly ill Sister Mary Theodosia had bounded in fright following her seemingly answered prayer in 1908. The modified Colonial-style building, which had provided living quarters for the nuns since the late nineteenth century, was covered with red bricks baked in kilns on the congregation grounds. One stone from Mother Théodore's original convent was embedded in the foundation as a sacred tie to the Woods' early years. Several tidy stacks of papers rose from Marie Kevin's wooden writing desk. A portrait of Mother Théodore hung on one wall, and a small sculpture of the founder rested on the windowsill. The surface of one file cabinet contained a statuette of Charlie Brown and other Peanuts characters in baseball uniforms, along with the slogan How can we lose when we're so sincere? Marie Kevin was equally serene about the vast task she faced. Some of her colleagues, however, were more anxious about the progress.

Pope John Paul II's 1997 declaration of Mary Theodosia's cure as something divine still infused many Woods residents with a glow of hope. The canonization seemed more a matter of when, not if. But three and a half years had passed since that momentous threshold had been reached, and the sisters had not collected a potential second miracle to offer the Vatican for consideration. Would it take another full century, some wondered, to track down a candidate? Sister Diane Ris, then the congregation's general superior, acknowledged that some of the nuns—particularly the older ones—felt a rising urgency to finish the journey, and soon. Ris also understood that the medical and theological facts constituting a second miracle claim would need to be nearly impenetrable in order to survive far more rabid analysis at the Holy See. "Because of all the unanimous voting for the first miracle, we knew [Rome] would be very careful with the second. They would examine everything so thoroughly," Ris said later. That level of intensity, she knew, could potentially lengthen the search process. And consequently, Ris recalled, "some people were saying, 'I hope I live to see it.'"

Although purported miracle cures arrived in bunches at Marie Kevin's office, by early 2001 she had not read many accounts that she considered exemplary enough that they merited further investigation by an archdiocese tribunal. However, the lack of concrete claims didn't immediately deflate her. "I received not more than ten that I felt were worthy of exploring," she would say later. Yet "I was calm, cool, and collected. Because it had already been ninety years and we had gotten used to the wait. I don't think we got overanxious. The cause was not *the* thing running our lives. [The other sisters] were otherwise occupied with their full-time ministries. Not that we didn't care. Not that we put the cause aside. But we had waited so long already. We were willing to wait a little longer."

At that time, some of the juiciest claims of Mother Théodore's intercessions were purely victims of bad timing. That is, they were cures that seemed to justify further attention based on their swift or unknown nature, but they had occurred prior to the 1998 beatification, nullifying them from consideration in the canonization stage. That technicality was one of the arcane rules of Catholic saint-making — and an example of the arbitrary essence of what many Catholic faithful believed to be an immaculate process. Simply put: a medical recovery the Church might deem a miracle had it occurred in 1999 would be rejected if it took place in 1996. Case in point: two months after Mother Théodore's beatification, Marie Kevin received a detailed letter from Charles Giesting, a father in a small town in eastern Indiana. This letter chronicled the 1987 diagnosis of a malignant brain tumor in his infant daughter, Allison. Among thirty children who were being treated for brain tumors at the same hospital at that time, Allison was the only one who survived. The miracle, Giesting believed, came in the aftermath of the illness. Doctors had used their drugs and skill to remove the cancer. But they also predicted that the operations and chemotherapy would permanently rob Allison of her balance and, as a result, her ability to walk. Charles, who had learned of Mother Théodore during his student years at a Catholic elementary school, prayed to her for his daughter's full recovery. Not long after Allison's diagnosis, a Franciscan nun gave the Giesting family a prayer card that contained Mother Théodore's image and a snippet of linen that had been laid against one of the founder's bones. According to Roman Catholic beliefs, that made the prayer card a third-class relic, which was any item that had been touched to a first-class relic, such as the bone or hair of a saint or a candidate for sainthood. (Second-class relics were considered to be anything a saint wore, owned, or often used, such as a book). Oddly enough, the nun who bestowed the Giestings with the relic hailed from Oldenburg, Indiana—the hometown of Rosa Warren, whose sudden recovery from a spinal injury in 1885 had prompted the miracle investigation by Bishop (and ex-doctor) Francis Silas Chatard. Whenever Allison Giesting received her chemo treatments or underwent surgery, her parents always tucked the prayer card into her clothing. And despite the doctors' forecasts that she would never walk due to brain damage, she not only developed normally, but became a cheerleader. All those unexpected events had occurred, however, prior to the beatification. "She once was considered not curable, and yet here she was, jumping! But we could not submit her case," Marie Kevin later lamented, "because the second miracle had to have taken place after 1998."

Catholic theologians have long maintained that a second proven miracle represented a direct nod from God that the would-be saint's beatification was valid. This was a crucial underpinning for the Church's careful sequence of events: a miracle provided, Catholics believed, a heavenly signal that the sanctification work performed by the living was proper. After succeeding the most prolific saint-maker in history—Pope John Paul II, who canonized more than four hundred people—Pope Benedict XVI made sure to reinforce this strict doctrine in a 2006 message to the Vatican wing responsible for saint naming. "Miracles constitute divine confirmation of a judgment expressed by the ecclesiastical authorities," Benedict wrote. In other words, timing was everything.

"So," Marie Kevin said, "we had to wait for one more sign from God."

Amid the modest list of supernatural claims that Marie Kevin had fielded by the first months of 2001, she believed the most compelling case involved a telephone technician who lived, appropriately enough, near the banks of the Mystic River.

† † †

Edward Mulkern was a father of four, a staunch Roman Catholic, a Red Sox fan, and a resident of Chelsea, Massachusetts—a historic nook of 30,080 people originally settled in 1624. The small city sat just north and across the river from its newcomer neighbor, Boston, which was founded in 1630.

Born in 1952, Mulkern possessed the type of long New England lineage that seemed to interlace the region, preserving its language and provincial ways. He and four generations of his family were educated by the Sisters of Providence at Saint Rose Catholic School in Chelsea. He still remembered how, during his childhood, the school nuns spoke often of Mother Théodore's possible road to sainthood. He graduated from Chelsea High School in 1971 and, two years later, joined what became his lifelong employer, then called New England Telephone and Telegraph. He survived a flurry of buyouts and mergers that ultimately reshaped his company into Verizon Wireless. In 2001 he was installing high-speed data circuits for Verizon. In his private hours he volunteered for the Chelsea Historical Society and the Chelsea Public Library. He also preferred to be called "Eddie." When Sister Marie Kevin got her first glimpse of Mulkern's story, she immediately noted his snug roots in the age-old Catholic community around Boston. Moreover, she saw that he had survived advanced cancer—with a Mother Théodore relic in his hand and a prayer for her intercession in his head.

Stage 3 squamous cell carcinoma of the larynx—Mulkern's diagnosis at age forty-five—was a malignant tumor in a part of the throat known as the "voice box." When doctors designated that disease as Stage 3, it meant the tumor had grown larger than four centimeters, about the size of a lime, and that it may have spread beyond the larynx. Inside Mulkern's neck, the mass also affected his left vocal cord and had started to erode the surrounding cartilage in his neck. Musicians George Harrison, Sammy Davis Jr., and Mary Wells all were diagnosed with laryngeal cancer. None survived. For people who had Mulkern's type and degree of cancer, the median survival time was four years, and about four in ten people with that same diagnosis didn't live beyond five years, according to medical studies.

In early 1997, Mulkern first noticed that his voice sounded raw and hoarse, and those harsh tones lingered well into the next year—as the nuns at the Woods merrily prepared for their founder's October beatification in St. Peter's Square. He had hoped he was merely suffering the chronic effects of seasonal allergies. He sensed no pain, felt no loss of energy, and had not missed any work. But at Saint Rose Church, where he attended Mass, one of the Sisters of Providence also heard his constant roughness. She urged Mulkern to see a doctor. On June 30, 1998, Mulkern began a series of diagnostic exams with three doctors at three local medical facilities. On July 8, 1998, at the Massachusetts Eye and Ear Infirmary in Boston, Dr. Gregory Ota snaked a soft, lighted probe through Mulkern's nose and down into his throat for a peek. He also snipped some tissue in the larynx for a biopsy. The test was positive for squamous cell carcinoma—a cancer of the thin, flat cells that line the organ.

Mulkern wasn't completely shocked by the news. He realized then that, subconsciously, he had suspected all along he might have something serious, but he had dreaded hearing the word "cancer." He began praying to Mother Théodore for a heavenly save—and also to Saint Jude and to Saint Peregrine, the patron saint of people with cancer.

"I'd be lying if I said I didn't ask others for intercession," Mulkern would recall eleven years later, his voice still gruff, his words punctuated by heavy breaths and flattened by his Boston accent. "I had heard great things about Saint Jude, and I let him know I was in need of help. I looked up and said, 'If anybody wants to help, here I am.' You get desperate. My oldest child was sixteen at the time, and my youngest was three. I had a lot to live for. I prayed that I'd live to see grandchildren."

Doctors mapped out an assertive plan to try to save Mulkern's life. They would bombard the cancer for six weeks with both chemotherapy drugs and radiation bursts. If the treatments were successful in shrinking the tumor, surgeons then hoped to cut out the remaining throat mass.

While listening to his doctors, Mulkern also leaned hard on his Catholic faith—and on his mother-in-law, a Mother Théodore fan who had enjoyed a long friendship with Sister Mary Eleanor Galvin, a native of nearby Malden, Massachusetts, and a Sister of Providence since 1945. Many years earlier, Sister Mary Eleanor had aided Mulkern's future mother-in-law in her quest to adopt a baby boy. In gratitude, when Mulkern's future wife was born, she was named in honor of Sister Mary Eleanor.

During the late summer of 1998, as that same Sister Mary Eleanor helped Marie Kevin prepare for the beatification in Rome, Mulkern's mother-in-law handed Eddie a relic—a laminated Mother Théodore prayer card containing the founder's image and a fragment of bone-touched linen. Mulkern drew strength from all his odd yet sacred connections to the Woods founder. He placed the relic against his throat as he prayed. He also took comfort when he heard that the sisters at Saint Rose were asking Mother Théodore to intercede on his behalf.

His treatments began at Massachusetts General Hospital on Monday, August 3—his first chemotherapy drip. He returned to the facility the next day for his first two rounds of radiation therapy. On Wednesday, Thursday, and Friday of that same week, he repeated the two-a-day radiation sessions at Mass General as technicians aimed beams of energy at the killer cells in his larynx. That pattern would become his weekly grind for much of the rest of the summer. Yet he felt an inner calm, he said, a confidence that all would be well.

With his prayer card in hand and his wife, Mary, at his side, Mulkern again strolled into Mass General on Tuesday morning, August 11, ready for his ninth—and later that day, his tenth—blast of radiation. Before lying beneath the big machine, Mulkern sat on an exam table and exchanged greetings with his radiation oncologist, Dr. C. C. Wang. Born in Canton, China, and later a resident at Mass General, Wang was by then in his mid-seventies, and radiating a few warm vibes of his own. Described by colleagues as an infectious optimist, Wang routinely told patients his initials stood for "Cure Cancer." In reality, his name was Chiu-Chen, but, indeed, he had helped thousands of bleakly ill patients regain their health. He was equally skilled in handling people and in inventing proverbs. He showed his oncology students how to decimate tumors while also protecting surrounding tissue, and then always advised, "Don't burn down the house to kill a mosquito." He often quoted his three keys to good doctoring: "ability, availability, and affability." Mulkern appreciated Wang's direct manner. Now he tried not to squirm as the Chinese doctor snaked a fiberoptic scope into his nose and then down to his damaged throat. But during the scan, Wang seemed to dawdle longer than usual. Finally he spoke.

"Where the hell did that goddamn thing go?" he asked in his Cantonese accent.

Mulkern, nearly gagging on the instrument, assumed Wang had dropped his pen and was blindly feeling around for it.

"Do what you got to do and then get this thing out of me," Mulkern rasped, fiddling with the prayer card in his hands. From a nearby chair, Mary watched the scene.

"Where did it go?" Wang asked again. "Where did it go?"

"Where did what go?" Mulkern responded with growing unease.

"Your tumor. I can't see it," Wang said, slowly retrieving the scope. "It's amazing! I can't see it! I can't find it!"

Mulkern began to cry. So did his wife. So did Wang.

"It looks like our prayers have been answered," Eddie whispered to Mary.

Wang, as stumped as he was elated, wanted another set of eyes to confirm that a Stage 3 tumor had vanished in just one week. So, later that day, Mulkern headed back to Dr. Ota's office, and the ear, nose, and throat specialist repeated the scope exam. After a long search inside Mulkern's neck, Ota agreed with Wang, noting in the medical charts that Mulkern was "doing extremely well with no evidence of persistent or recurrent cancer at this time." Instantly, Mulkern began thinking one word: *miracle*. Still, Wang and the other doctors at Mass General told Mulkern he had to continue with his six-week treatment course to ensure that the disease was gone.

He agreed. On December 16, 1998, Mulkern experienced trouble swallowing, but his doctors still saw no evidence of the tumor. On January 5, 1999, his symptoms worsened. He was losing weight and experiencing severe throat pain and, again, the swallowing difficulties. He was admitted to Massachusetts General Hospital for six days. By January 19, he told his doctor he was unable to swallow liquids without coughing, and he was readmitted to Mass General on January 31 for more observation and placed on the painkiller Roxicet. After Mulkern began to feel better, he was again sent home. Soon he returned to work. For the next three years, doctors carefully tracked any changes in his throat and thorax with a series of CT scans. On April 16, 2002, a follow-up scan on Mulkern performed at Mass General found no evidence of metastatic disease in his thorax, according to hospital records. Another scan on October 12, 2002, showed "no significant change" and no evidence of a cancer recurrence, records indicated.

Throughout his ordeal, the day that shone brightest for Mulkern was the warm Tuesday morning in August 1998 when C. C. Wang told him the thing inside was gone. Before nightfall on that same day, Mulkern had placed a phone call from Chelsea to the Indiana countryside. At Saint Mary-of-the-Woods, Sister Mary Eleanor Galvin had picked up the line and listened as Mulkern calmly but stirringly relayed the day's events. Soon, Marie Kevin had similarly been told all of the intriguing details. But with Pope John Paul II set to beatify Mother Théodore in just seventy-four days, Marie Kevin and many of her fellow nuns were feverishly finalizing their travel plans, lining up their Italian accommodations, and gathering the essential minutiae for the big event, such as the type of wooden box that would hold a few of Mother Théodore's bones—the relics they would present to the pope. Marie Kevin was so inundated, in fact, that any inspection of the Mulkern case would have to wait for many months.

In 1999 Marie Kevin took a plane ride to Boston to visit the Sisters of Providence in Chelsea and to explore the Mulkern matter. She and Mulkern met at the Saint Rose convent and talked quietly about his cure for thirty minutes. When Mulkern finished recounting his story, Marie Kevin appeared convinced that his healing was miraculous.

The nun had instantly liked Eddie Mulkern upon their introduction. (In 2008, they still traded annual Christmas cards.) And she adored the theological elements of his astounding recovery: his family's ties to the Sisters of Providence and their affection for Mother Théodore, his prayer for intercession, his placing the prayer card to his throat as well as his clasping of the relic just as Dr. Wang first noticed the absence of cancer. Medically, the cure seemed to baffle his doctors. For the next three years, Marie Kevin would rate Mulkern's healing as her top nominee for the elusive second miracle.

And yet there were flaws in the mysterious storyline that could prompt the Vatican's panels of physicians and theologians to dismiss the cure. If the sisters tapped the Mulkern case as their supernatural Exhibit A to try to complete their century-long canonization push, Marie Kevin would have to vigorously defend those soft spots.

Two questions had to be answered. First, did Mulkern's cure come as a result of his doctors' talents? Two of the country's leading oncologists had administered to Mulkern two rounds of chemotherapy and eight rounds of radiation by August 11, the first day that doctors couldn't locate his tumor, and they continued their precise doses for many weeks after that. Wasn't it possible that the medicine had simply worked faster and more effectively than the doctors had expected? Second, when did the cure technically occur? If it indeed was August 11—two months before Mother Théodore's beatification—that date would disqualify Mulkern's case. Under ancient Vatican rules, a second alleged miracle made in the name of a prospective saint could be considered only if it occurred after that saintly candidate's beatification. Still, Mulkern's symptoms had flared up again in 1999, and hospital records showed he had remained a sick man much of that year. Marie Kevin pinned the official date of the cure as April 16, 2000—when a CT scan found no new or suspicious nodules in Mulkern's body.

Long before those theological weaknesses could be addressed, however, Marie Kevin found herself slogging through other unpleasant complications in Boston. Her initial communications with some of Mulkern's key doctors were met with disregard or disdain. Although it is not uncommon for medical experts to snub nuns and priests who request their help during miracle investigations, Marie Kevin also encountered initial chilly interest in the case from the monsignor who served as the top vicar judicial for the Archdiocese of Boston—the man who would preside over any Church tribunal that might be held to assess the possible miracle. Likely fueling the lack of response to Marie Kevin was the fact that the Archdiocese of Boston—and its vicar judicial—was then embroiled in a child sex abuse scandal.

Undaunted by the tension in Boston, Marie Kevin bulldozed ahead in 2001, compiling more medical facts on Mulkern's case and hoping her patience and warmth would eventually win over the doctors and clerics there. The Mulkern cure, in her mind, had become the best hope for the founder's canonization.

Despite her honeyed demeanor, Marie Kevin could not escape one more unpleasant wave of friction. That stinging resistance, however, would occur not in Boston but back at her lifelong sanctuary, the Woods.

† † †

Mother Théodore's cause was old, historic, and colorful, dangling the possibility of global recognition for the sisters' devotion to Catholic education and their community-minded grit. It held the promise of massive media exposure, of luring big crowds of tourists and pilgrims to the little enclave. If Marie Kevin succeeded in her rare venture, Mother Théodore would become only the eighth American to be designated a Roman Catholic saint. She would be the first American saint named since 2000, when Pope John Paul II had canonized Katharine Mary Drexel, a Philadelphia-born nun who, during the early twentieth century, spent her energies and much of the $20-million family fortune to build more than sixty schools and missions to serve Native Americans and African Americans. But achieving saintly status for Mother Théodore was not wholly supported by the nuns at the Woods. And Marie Kevin heard—and often took personally, according to a friend—the swipes and criticisms hurled by a minority of sisters who disliked the cause.

That sort of rancor had, in fact, been brewing for decades at the Woods. To pinpoint just how many detractors the cause had among the sisters—as well as why they stood against it—congregation leaders had surveyed their nearly five hundred members in 1993. According to convent records, 290 sisters answered the query and, of those respondents, 10 percent said they believed the cause should not be pursued. One sister said she felt a "sense of repulsion" for the sanctification effort. Another 7 percent of the nuns labeled themselves as ambivalent—torn between a desire to magnify Mother Théodore's fame and a reluctance to spend time and money on a process that might not benefit the order. If those two percentages accurately reflected the feelings of the full congregation, about seventy-five of Marie Kevin's fellow sisters either thought her work was foolish or didn't care if the entire enterprise flopped.

The opposition to the cause had two primary arguments: first, that it was an unwise and irresponsible use of the community's funds. Sister Nancy Reynolds, the congregation's general treasurer from 2004 through 2009, refused in an interview to reveal the costs incurred by the order during the nearly century-long beatification and canonization push, saying, "I've never told our sisters what that number is, so I wouldn't tell anybody else." She added that none of the other sisters, including the other convent leaders, had asked her for an accounting of expenses: "They know how much we spent in the last year [of the cause] for all the stuff, but nope, that has not been a question. We were working on the canonization for many, many years. So you can imagine how much it cost us. And no, I won't give that number out to the public." In 2005 the Archdiocese of Indianapolis (which simultaneously oversaw the campaign to sanctify Mother Théodore) opened a cause to canonize Simon Bruté, the first bishop of the then-diocese of Vincennes—and the man who first requested that French nuns come to the Indiana frontier. When the Bruté cause was launched, archdiocese vicar judicial Monsignor Fred Easton estimated its cost would eventually reach about $250,000 but could run as high as $1 million. The nuns who stood against Marie Kevin's work winced at such numbers.

Yet something deeper than money annoyed the strident opposition and was the source of their second argument: that in seeking the canonization, the sisters would be forced to kowtow to the men at the Vatican. The cause's opponents were, according to the survey summary, "unwilling to have us involved in the process which they saw as an extension of hierarchical control of women religious."

This raw distrust—even outright dislike—of the Roman Catholic Church's ancient male-dominated culture and command structure had been interlaced with the sisters' reality since the community's earliest days, when Mother Théodore faced browbeating and banishment from Bishop La Hailandière. But the place and value of women within the Catholic Church was a knotty narrative that coiled backward nearly two millennia, to the first centuries after Christ. During that era, the Church found "three ways to neutralize" the women in religious orders, according to the French philosopher and theologian Jacques Ellul. "One, it imposes on women silence, passivity, obedience, and self-effacement, as though such things were valid for all women. Two, it makes the status of virginity superior to all others, thereby excluding women from their social role and from the true nature as those who bear and transmit life. Thirdly, the church engages in idealizing the Virgin Mary, who becomes a model of submission. ("Be it done unto me.") By exalting women in the ideological sense, men find it possible to maintain a clear conscience while virulently abasing women in the real sense."

Women were, of course, still barred by the Vatican from reaching the priesthood. Still, as Marie Kevin confronted frosty resistance from fellow sisters who loathed the Vatican's entrenched sexism, Pope John Paul II was, in fact, elevating the duties many women held within the Catholic hierarchy. In the 1990s women assumed control of pastoral and administrative tasks in some parishes without priests, and others were named as diocese chancellors—the staff members responsible for handling all formal documents, writings, and records used in diocesan business. The pope also wrote a 1995 letter apologizing for the Church's long-standing lack of appreciation for female achievements, and he denounced the "long and degrading history" of sexual violence against women. At the same time, however, John Paul refused to lift the ban on female priests, arguing that the male-only league of priests was nondiscriminatory because it stayed true to Christ's vision for Church rule. Jesus, he wrote, had only picked men as his Apostles—a cue the Church had followed ever since.

The bitterness some Woods sisters held toward Catholic sexism was deeply personal, not merely a vague disappointment over past oppression, male-oriented theology, or hiring decisions. From time to time, modern Catholic power brokers still reminded the nuns who was in charge. Cardinal John O'Connor of New York ignited public and media outcries when, during a 1991 Father's Day homily that chastised feminists, he borrowed a quote from then-Cardinal

Joseph Ratzinger, who would become Pope Benedict XVI: "We are not authorized to change the 'Our Father' into 'Our Mother.'"

For the Sisters of Providence, that anti-authority discord had also been cultivated in the parish schools and churches across Indiana, the Midwest, and the eastern United States where they had worked as teachers and principals. Sister Diane Ris, the convent's general superior in early 2001, had held some casual conversations with nuns at the Woods to try to tap deeper into those feelings, especially since some of the sisters cited that explicit anger as their prime reason for opposing the cause. "Many—I don't know how many—but numbers of our sisters had been treated badly by priests . . . just lording [their authority] over them with actions that were disrespectful," Sister Diane said. "These were good people [who stood against the cause] but they had experienced something that had soured them. They felt if this is the way the Church was, then something is wrong. And, they asked, why would we contribute to something [governed by the Church]? They were having a hard time getting past that."

Marie Kevin was, in her self-view, a feminist, although she was quick to add, "Not a rabid feminist. Maybe if I was younger, I would be more rabid." She liked to refer to biblical passages in which the prophet Anna preached to crowds about Jesus, yet added that modern religious women were "not allowed to preach in the Church. God is pushing that issue through the need we have for priests today." Despite espousing those opinions, however, Marie Kevin remained a target for snippy comments from sisters who felt she was being something of a sellout to the men in Rome.

"It wasn't easy for her to do that job. A lot of nuns didn't want this canonization to take place," said Kathy Fleming, a former Sister of Providence and a retired Indiana school principal who had befriended Marie Kevin when Fleming was a teenager. "The Rome-dominated male Church makes a lot of women angry, makes me angry. . . . [The fury over the cause] all centered around Rome and some people just plain didn't think it was a necessary process. They also had other big problems [at the Woods] that they needed to deal with, and so the cause, some thought, was sidelining them. . . . Marie Kevin was hearing from ten percent of the community but that ten percent was very vocal. It upset her a lot. . . . It was horrible.

"She's not the type of person who would sit down and complain about it," Fleming added. "But I knew."

Many years later, Marie Kevin would be asked if jibes from the anti-canonization faction hurt her personally. After all, not only had she shaped her world by emulating and embodying Mother Théodore's path and her teachings, but she had risen from her deathbed in 1994 to lead the canonization cause. Marie Kevin saw the cause as her reason for living and, perhaps, her legacy.

"There has always been a small percentage in the community who didn't think we should go along with this cause. I think that was a mistake on their part," Marie Kevin said. "Others were saying, 'We know she was a saint. Why do we have to go through all this [to prove her sainthood]?' I told them, 'We know it. The world doesn't know it. And the world needs models of holiness.'"

Moreover, Marie Kevin claimed, the digs and discontent she faced never ruffled her feelings.

Some of her friends contended, however, that Marie Kevin indeed felt the sting of the disharmony. And, they said, it didn't just slice through her cheery façade; it rattled her will. In fact, she expressed doubts about her daunting duties to at least one friend. Marie Kevin even privately suggested that perhaps another nun might be better suited to please all the constituencies at the Woods and see the cause through to a conclusion. She temporarily considered abandoning the job.

At the same time, the pressure to deliver sainthood for Mother

Théodore was mounting. Marie Kevin, of course, felt a fundamental need to please the convent leaders who had placed their faith in her. And she felt a responsibility to the majority of sisters who fervently yearned to see the founder sanctified before they died. But there was one other burden that weighed on Marie Kevin—and it was something the promoter of the cause did not often discuss with outsiders.

Marie Kevin had done the math. She had sifted through the numbers of nuns coming and going. Older sisters at the Woods were dying at a much faster rate than that at which young novices were entering the convent. At that pace, she figured, the community would be decimated by natural attrition in about twenty-five years. But Marie Kevin believed that Mother Théodore's potential sainthood—a global celebration and endorsement of her living aura, her charism—could revive and perhaps bolster the future of her community in the Indiana hinterlands. In many ways, Marie Kevin was laboring for the very survival of Saint Mary-of-the-Woods.

CHAPTER FIVE

The Prayer

He didn't know where to start, and he wasn't sure he could even find the proper words. Above all, Phil McCord simply hoped God was listening.

Entranced by the lush organ music flowing from the balcony, and coveting a slice of solitude, McCord had drifted into the basilica like one of the dead leaves swirling in the breezes outside — no clear purpose, no plan, certainly no script. Just a mind brimming with dread and terror. The organist suddenly stopped tapping the keys, stood, and left her perch. From a sixth-row pew, with the Church of the Immaculate Conception momentarily his private temple, McCord breathed in the blissful hush and absorbed the scene: the high galleries to his right and left, the red marble walls, the powdery fresco of angels greeting the Virgin Mary. On both sides of the massive room, stained-glass windows blazed with the images of strong women and famed biblical miracles. On a window behind him, an Old Testament heroine named Judith clutched the severed head of a defeated enemy general, while on a pane to his right, Saint Peter walked on water.

How odd that McCord would find himself here on the third day of 2001 — at this seminal, horrible moment in his life — inside such a sublime shrine to Catholic dogma and devotion, deep in the cradle of hundreds of Catholic nuns. He had been raised otherwise. His mother, Marjorie McCord, a Christian Scientist, had cited her faith when refusing to take her only child to the doctor to be treated for tonsillitis. Phil had nearly died from the infection at age five. His

paternal grandmother, also a Christian Scientist, had told young
Phil not to play with his neighborhood pal, a Catholic boy, because,
she said, all Catholics stored guns in their basements in preparation for an armed global conquest. His deeply devout father, Paul
McCord, a Baptist lay minister and head of the board of deacons
at his church in Anderson, Indiana, had lugged his little boy to a
weekly blur of prayer meetings, potluck dinners, and Sunday services. And many years later, after Phil attained his prized job as the
convent's maintenance chief, Paul McCord had urged his son to "go
to a real church."

While not formally loyal to any religion, and certainly not a
praying man, Phil McCord nonetheless held a fondness for many of
the sisters and their earthly missions. He basked in the community's
zesty history and thoroughly adored the bucolic outpost he had been
hired to preserve and repair. Sometimes he even attended Mass,
although that was rare. On January 3, as his decaying right eye
sagged and ached, he sat alone in the Woods' most precious place,
yearning to find the will to endure a looming corneal transplant —
and all the macabre risks and the lengthy recovery that would come
with it. When he had entered the church, he never intended to pray.
Suddenly, however, he felt the urge to talk, maybe even to talk to
heaven.

"God, you've probably heard about my eye problems. Of course
you have, you're God. Well anyway . . . " he began. His awkward,
one-way communication sounded more like a backyard chat with a
neighbor over beers.

McCord's own theory of prayer was beautifully practical and
seemed to have been plucked from an engineer's playbook: God
gives each of us the intelligence and skills to solve our own problems. So we shouldn't seek God's aid, he believed, for such mundane matters as, *Can you put my favorite team in the playoffs?* Or, *Can
you boost my credit score?* According to McCord's personal doctrine

of self-sufficiency, God was too busy to cast his attention on life's little, selfish stresses. But when the issue was truly and profoundly harrowing—and when you had exhausted all available options, when you saw no earthly answers to your woes—then, and only then, should you look above, McCord felt. He had reached that moment. He looked above. And he did something he had not planned when his day started. He pleaded with God.

"I try to take care of things by myself, try not to bother you with a lot of things. But I can't do this myself," McCord prayed. "I've tried fifty ways to resolve this situation. I can't seem to do it. Can you give me the courage and strength to get through this surgery?"

Never once did he ask for a cure. He merely needed, he told God, a friendly push. He simply wanted some peace with this decision.

His head fell quiet again. He focused once more on the plush sanctuary that enveloped him. Just beneath the church floorboards, Mother Théodore's remains lay within a coffin attached to the ceiling of the dark, chilly crypt. On an October night in 1908, Sister Mary Theodosia Mug had ventured into that chamber and asked the founder to rescue an ailing sister. In the tomb, Mary Theodosia had wondered aloud if Mother Théodore had any influence with God. McCord began to ponder that same question.

He had read and heard much about Mother Théodore's rough-country history and about Mary Theodosia's storied cure. And he was keenly aware of the sisters' hunt for a modern miracle. Given his Baptist background, McCord had only a vague grasp of the Catholic concept of intercession. Still, he figured, it couldn't hurt to try. Just as Mary Theodosia had done one floor below almost one century earlier, he prayerfully asked the Woods founder if maybe she could have a word with God—a word about McCord's blind right eye and the operation he faced.

"Well, Mother Théodore, this is your house. And I am your

servant," McCord prayed, first feeling the need to introduce himself as one of the modern-day Woods workers. "If you have God's ear, if you could exercise that on my behalf, this would be a good time. If you can help me get through this, I would appreciate anything that you could do for me."

A small cluster of nuns shuffled into the church and took their customary seats near the altar. Dozens more soon would follow, nestling into pews for the 11:30 a.m. daily Mass. McCord saw that as his signal to return to work. He had been inside the basilica for about fifteen minutes. Had he even said his prayer correctly? He wasn't completely sure. Had he requested intercession in the appropriate manner? Again, he did not know. He had rambled through the prayer, he realized, hadn't even offered a proper conclusion. Yet he noticed something—a subtle yet unmistakable change. While his right eye remained a blurry, tender fright, he somehow now felt lighter, more relaxed.

As he stood and strolled toward a side exit, he exhaled deeply—a powerful, cleansing sigh. His head, packed with panic minutes earlier, swelled with fresh conviction about his surgery and his future. As he reached the door, he truly felt his prayer had been answered.

OK, I can do this now, he thought. *I'm a big boy, I can handle this. Thank you, God. That's just what I needed.*

As he reached his office a few buildings away from the Church of the Immaculate Conception, he smiled and thought, *Maybe there is something to this prayer thing.*

With a slow shake of his head, the bearded man recalled one of the biggest crises from his childhood. Behind a wry smile, he admitted how outlandish the story sounded more than fifty years later.

An emergency family meeting had been called at the McCord

home in Anderson, a company town flush with money and pious folks. Soon, a small but fiery group of people squeezed close to the kitchen table. They had come for an intervention.

One by one, taking their turns at the circular table, they confronted Phil McCord's aunt as she listened. She had known they would be upset. They spoke their minds with urgency and with passion, and they tried to convince the woman of her monumental error and her potentially damnable sin.

She was thinking of converting to Catholicism.

"It was almost like she was joining a cult, the way they were trying to talk her out of it," McCord recalled with a smirk, reclining in a cozy chair in the lobby of the Providence Center, the welcoming hub for Woods visitors. It was a gorgeous, bright day in May 2008. In two more days he would turn sixty-two years old. On the carpeted lobby floor, his long legs stretched straight in front of him, feet crossed at the ankles of his blue jeans. Sunglasses dangled from his shirt collar. He was relaxed and jovial as he threaded together, anecdote by anecdote, the moments that shaped his pragmatic faith—the Christian Science denials of modern medicine he had heard from one side of the family, the seemingly unending string of church events he attended with his Baptist dad, his grandmother's distrust of all Catholics, and the McCord elders' general fear of what they deemed to be Catholicism's dangerous persuasions.

Phil McCord, himself, had long been grounded by the accepted maxims of evolution, physics, chemistry, biology, and modern medicine. Yet he was equally convinced of a higher power. His mind and imagination were open to all possibilities. He firmly acknowledged that even the smartest humans had not cracked many of their world's mysteries. He was a believer. He was not a churchgoer. When it came to formal religion, probably to his father's dismay, he identified himself as "more Catholic than anything."

"I am not really observant," he acknowledged, as rays of

Indiana sunshine splashed the side of his face. Nuns walked near
his plush chair. Some offered grins and waves. He waved back with
an equally broad smile.

To the sisters, the non-Catholic caretaker represented the pre-
carious balance between faith and science, between the notion of an
imperceptible higher authority and a palpable reality that could be
measured.

"There is a real conflict for me between those. Always has been,"
McCord said in a voice that was gravelly, yet hypnotically soft. An
engineer like McCord always looked at an unknown and studied it
to determine its cause and effect.

He fell silent for a few seconds, trying to mentally navigate and
then give voice to his dissonant thoughts on theology. "I guess,
where 'I don't know' ends, 'I believe' begins. That's why they call it
faith. Otherwise they'd call it proof."

McCord existed at the narrow nexus of belief versus reason,
and his life story exuded that perpetual tension.

Born on May 23, 1946—following several miscarriages by his
mother—he had registered only four pounds on the hospital scale,
putting him on the fringe of unhealthy baby weights. But he grew
into a precocious, bright, and sometimes mischievous boy in the
union town of Anderson, the seat of Madison County, and, then,
a thriving, middle-class city in central Indiana on its way to a
peak population of seventy thousand. In Anderson, the primary
employer and social focal point was General Motors. Roughly one
in three Anderson residents drew paychecks from the company in
those years, and the automaker operated so many plants in the city,
company bosses made sure to stagger shift schedules to prevent
Anderson's streets from becoming clogged each afternoon as plant
employees drove home for supper. McCord's mother, Marjorie, had
two brothers who worked for GM. Phil McCord's father, Paul, had
four brothers on the company rolls, and Paul himself worked for

GM as a tool-and-die maker, helping assemble starting motors and cranking motors. Paul McCord's father had been a GM plant super-intendent, and Marjorie's father also had been a company man. The townspeople had dubbed GM "generous motors." If both spouses worked there, a family's household income likely rose into the nation's ninety-fifth percentile. Nestled an hour's drive northeast of Indianapolis, Anderson boasted clean, cozy neighborhoods and a suburban feel. At Phil's high school, about nine of every ten stu-dents went on to college. Anderson also served as the headquarters of the Church of God, which was formed to promote a primary alle-giance to Jesus Christ in a way that would transcend all denomina-tional loyalties. For a time, Church of God followers did not allow women in the congregation to wear lipstick or pants, did not allow musical instruments at Sunday services, and espoused a belief that Catholicism was a false Christianity. But there were many Catho-lics in Anderson, along with Presbyterians, Jews, Methodists—and the Baptists to whom Paul McCord preached. Anderson was, in short, all about job, family, and faith.

Voraciously inquisitive, eager to question, interrogate, and ana-lyze, yet chronically prone to flit from interest to interest, young Phil feasted on the written word, devouring hundreds of books and magazines on a wide mix of topics, including his favorite, history. As an only child, he also absorbed his parents' attention. The McCord family often traveled the American roads together, especially south and east of Indiana. By the time Phil was ten years old, he had toured every Civil War battlefield. He learned the piano, pleasing his mother by mastering pieces by Romantic-era composers like Mozart and Beethoven, while also sneaking in some Elvis Presley rockabilly tunes when his mom wasn't listening. When he was in the first grade, teachers told Paul and Marjorie that their son was intellectually advanced and that he perhaps should be enrolled at a private school for more challenging study. The McCords couldn't afford that, and they preferred their son to be raised at home in a normal social setting. In the fourth grade, Phil's public school principal took him to Ball State College, about twenty miles away, where experts tested his intelligence and found his acumen to be years beyond other children of his age. Consequently, his teachers set up a special independent study course, and in time, Phil read his way through the entire school library. Not surprisingly, other kids became envious and often taunted him. Making matters worse, his eyes began growing weak when he was just six years old, forcing the little boy into his first pair of eyeglasses. As time passed, he required thicker and thicker lenses.

"When the report cards came out, kids would knock at my front door and ask to see what I got. I got ganged up on. It was a lot of competition, a lot of jealousy. I was the one who was considered weird, and I guess I was. So I turned into a pretty good fighter," McCord later recalled.

But he won new friends by funneling his smarts into underhanded pranks and explosive schemes. He and other boys set up a Van de Graff generator (an electrostatic machine) just outside the school physics lab, causing the hairs on the heads of passing girls to stand vertically as they walked by, which in turn led the girls to scream and the boys to laugh. He made mortars out of soup cans and fireworks. Using his dad's compressor and a metal tube, he launched potato bombs 150 feet through the sky. As a college boy, he and other students stole a security guard's Cushman cart, stripped it down, and reassembled it on the roof of an eight-story dormitory.

During childhood Sunday-school classes, Phil became known for his playful curiosity and his attempts to disassemble accepted precepts. He tried holding philosophical debates with his instructors and the other kids. They were not, he recalled, equally comfortable testing what they perceived to be the Bible's ultimate certainty.

"No, Phil," he once was corrected, "this is the immutable word of God."

"Well, actually, no," Phil had responded, "I looked into the history of it, and that doesn't fly. Actually, this is the word of man interpreting or presenting these things. It is not the immutable word of God."

"I tried to apply the scientific method to theology," he explained. "That's what always got me into trouble. It creates some discord.

"But on the other side of my mind—the theoretical, philosophical side—I always was intrigued by faith. I'm kind of a believer in spite of myself."

The competing concepts were evidenced in one of his favorite childhood toys, a telescope. He enjoyed peering at the unreachable specks of light in the night sky. He let his head rummage through the hazy conundrums and vast wonders of space, the incomprehensibility of its size, history, and meaning. At the same time, though, he puzzled over the stars' positions, applying his knowledge of astrophysics to that task. He truly admired precision and measurement. He realized he could deduce almost any brainteaser he encountered if he simply took it apart and cut it down to manageable, understandable pieces. He was forever breaking down everything from garage gadgets to complex philosophies and viewpoints. As a young boy, he nourished that affection for destruction at construction sites and at bridge-repair jobs throughout Anderson. His mother—a secretary to the Anderson city engineer and, later, to the Madison County engineer—often took Phil to municipal building projects, where he watched surveyors gaze into scopes to triangulate, calculate, demarcate, and map. They were immersed, he noticed, in the principles of trigonometry, geometry, and mathematics. In a sense, they were reconfirming bits and pieces of place and time, of Phil's town, of his existence. From that point on, he was drawn to a career in engineering—a perfect match for his twin, simultaneous yens

for exactitude and enigma. Engineering used definitive and understood schools of science, like chemistry and physics, to decipher
many of the most complex natural mysteries, to reveal unexplained,
unexplored slices of our world, and to invent new truths. "Engineering is quite different from science," author Walter Vincenti
wrote in *What Engineers Know and How They Know It.* "Scientists try
to understand nature. Engineers try to make things that do not exist
in nature."

Of course, one mystery that defied measurement was love. And
at age seventeen, Phil was purposely introduced to a sixteen-year-old
farm girl who attended Highland High School, located just northeast of town in a rural swath of cornfields and cattle pastures.
Debbie Vermillion, a nurse's daughter, was plain-spoken and sometimes sarcastic. She helped her parents raise a flock of sheep on
their four-acre spread. In her spare time, she dispensed grain to
the chickens and cows at her grandmother's farm—a large nearby
property that also contained a sprawling soybean field. After school,
she honed her entrepreneurial skills in Junior Achievement—her
club met at a local radio station and completed various broadcasting
and advertising projects with station employees. Phil, meanwhile,
attended Madison Heights High School in a suburban Anderson
township where most adolescents felt heavy academic pressure as
they worked toward college acceptance. Phil also participated in
Junior Achievement—his group teamed with General Motors to
sterilize safety glasses for plant visitors. The daughter of the area
Junior Achievement director knew both Phil and Debbie separately and secretly decided to have them meet at her house under
the pretense of a club get-together. Immediately, a mutual crush
was kindled. Phil teasingly called Debbie his "country bumpkin,"
and she dubbed him her "city slicker." Their courtship was swift.

"He made me laugh. He was also very intelligent," Debbie
recalled. "He would comment on various things—politics, science,

everything—and then I had to go home and look them up to see if he was right."

He always was.

She fell in love with his ingenuity and his spoken desire to do whatever was possible to make his world—and her world—a better place, to make it cleaner and greener. He was an avowed environmentalist and recycler in the early 1960s. They married on January 25, 1964, when Phil was still seventeen and Debbie was still sixteen. In time they would have three children: Philip Todd, Michaela, and Aaron.

By age eighteen, Phil already was leading a surveying crew in Anderson after two summers on the job, and he had received his professional registration in that field, reducing his immediate need for a college degree. The couple moved to Indianapolis to chase higher incomes, Phil in the surveying field, Debbie in nursing, initially working with pre- and postsurgical patients. In the early 1980s they moved back to Anderson, where Phil took an engineering job at the community hospital and decided—for advancement purposes—to seek an undergraduate degree in economics and then to obtain his master's degree in business administration. He completed all those studies in five years at Ball State College, just up the road in Muncie, Indiana.

Their careers next took the McCord family near the shores of Lake Michigan in northwestern Indiana, to the city of Valparaiso, where Debbie secured a nursing job at Porter Memorial Hospital and Phil became that medical center's head of engineering. After seven years at Porter, however, Phil failed to land a big promotion he had been expecting. Disappointed, he launched another job search. The Sisters of Providence had been searching as well—for a new head of facilities management. After the nuns' six-month candidate hunt had come up dry, they bought a one-time classified ad in the *Chicago Tribune*. On the same day the ad appeared, Phil

McCord—for the first and only time as a reader of that newspaper—
thumbed through the want ads. He spotted the opening at Saint
Mary-of-the-Woods. His subsequent phone conversation with the
Woods' human resources chief went smoothly, and he was invited
to the campus on the outskirts of Terre Haute for a personal chat.
The interview also went well. And the next morning Phil awoke at
a quaint campus guesthouse and opened his eyes to the almost cin-
ematic scene of bright new snow and horses galloping atop a shim-
mering blanket of clean, white flakes in the pastures. Pure serenity.
He felt at home. By the spring of 1997, he and Debbie were fully
settled in their two-story, green-shuttered, cul-de-sac house in an
upscale residential development just outside Terre Haute.

McCord showed up for his new job with energetic, novel ideas,
including plans to help mesh his earth-friendly ways with the campus heating and power grids by using the discarded stalks and husks
from the sisters' crops of corn, legumes, and alfalfa. He also came to
work wearing thick eyeglass lenses. His vision was worsening. He
had been diagnosed as a child with both myopia and astigmatism,
common defects that cause distant objects to appear fuzzy. But
as McCord's age climbed into his fifties, his doctor in Valparaiso
began to suspect that McCord's waning sight was probably due to
bilateral cataracts—a clouding of the eye's own lenses.

In healthy eyes, light streams in through the *corneas*—the clear
domes that shield the front of the eyes. Light then flows through the
apertures in the centers of the eyes—the pupils—and then through
the lenses, just behind the colored section of the eyeball, also called
the *iris*. The job of each lens is to focus that light beam onto the retina—a membrane on the back wall of the eyeball that works something like camera film, capturing light and re-transforming it into
the crisp, colorful objects in the field of view. When a lens becomes
clouded, doctors call it a cataract. They are more common in elderly people and usually develop in both eyes. In McCord's case,

prescription steroids he had taken to treat adult asthma may have prompted his early onset of cataracts. If lenses fog over, they scatter incoming light as opposed to sharply directing the beam back to the retinas. Cataracts don't hurt. But for someone with cataracts, looking at the world is a little like peering through a frosted window. Cataracts can turn reading, face recognition, and night driving into frustrating chores.

The day McCord first stepped into his new Woods office, his uncorrected visual acuity was measured at 20/800 in his right eye and 20/1,000 in the left. People with normal acuity have 20/20 vision. Someone with 20/1,000 vision has to stand twenty feet away to see an object that visually healthy people can see from one thousand feet—nearly three and a half football fields. When McCord donned his clunky glasses, his vision improved to 20/50. Legal blindness is considered to be 20/200.

"I was basically blind. I could barely drive at night, and I didn't unless I knew the road really well," he said. "My vision was very dim and blurry, and everything had a yellowish cast to it."

In fact, only partial sunshine was able to seep into his eyes, and that began to disturb McCord. He described it as being "like living in a world without light."

In 1998 his new eye doctor in Terre Haute diagnosed the cataracts. But he also noted that the cataract in McCord's left eye was six months more advanced than the one in the right. The doctor recommended postponing any removal surgery until the right eye could catch up or—in ophthalmological lingo—"ripen." Cataract surgeries are rarely done simultaneously on both eyes, so as to give patients a chance to let one eye heal fully before the second is repaired and temporarily covered. Ophthalmologists prefer to perform the surgeries several weeks apart; waiting for McCord's right eye to ripen would allow for that schedule. By September 2000, both his cataracts were equally severe, and McCord's doctor referred him to an ophthalmologist, Dr. Jeffrey Jungers, at the Associated Physicians and Surgeons (AP&S) Clinic in downtown Terre Haute.

Jungers was tall, athletic, and friendly, with square brown eyeglasses and gray hair that he kept short on the sides and stylishly mussed on top. He was a 1978 graduate of the Southern Illinois University School of Medicine and had joined the AP&S practice in 1983. Behind his office desk, a bank of windows offered a view of the redbrick St. Joseph University Parish Catholic church across the street, three blocks from the Wabash River. In front of his desk, a small television was sometimes silently tuned to CNBC, showing a steady crawl of stock prices. To the right of that TV, Jungers kept a pair of well-used running shoes tucked under the wooden visitor's chair. He once participated in a five-kilometer breast-cancer-benefit race beneath the lush green canopy that cloaked the Saint Mary-of-the-Woods roads. During the previous few decades he also had looked into the eyes of many nuns, removing cataracts from some sisters. During his first examination of McCord, on September 1, 2000, Jungers used drops to expand his pupils. Then, as McCord reclined in a padded chair, the doctor leaned near his face, squinted through an optical microscope, and assessed each lens and each retina. He confirmed that the cataracts had reached the same maturity and he decided to remove the left cataract first.

On September 21, a Thursday, Phil and Debbie McCord drove about fifteen minutes from their home to the Wabash Valley Surgery Center on Terre Haute's north side. The routine procedure—called phacoemulsification or simply "phaco"—would last about fifteen minutes, would require Phil to swallow one Valium pill to steady his nerves, would be painless, and would involve just one temporary suture.

Phaco is the most common and most advanced cataract-removal

procedure, according to the Eye Surgery Education Council. After the treatment, patients have to don a protective shield for one day, and by the time they remove that covering, their vision has almost always cleared. What's more, some patients discover that they can see distances without the aid of their old eyeglasses. More than two million cataract surgeries are performed each year in the United States, about 95 percent of which are successful. By the morning that McCord sat for his first cataract surgery, Jungers had performed more than 3,500 phaco procedures. He put McCord further at ease by telling him, "I'm pretty good at it."

The twenty-seven-step operation begins with the application of two local anesthetics—one in the form of drops, the other injected into the eye via a hair-sized tube. A lid speculum is installed to keep the eye open, and one temporary suture is tied to fix eye muscles in place. Then, using a small tray of tiny blades, the surgeon makes six micro-incisions, starting at the edge of the cornea. The openings allow the ophthalmologist to burrow into and navigate through several eye layers to reach the damaged lens—an oval, peachlike structure that contains a hard pit (called the *nucleus*), a circular layer of surrounding softer material (called the *cortex*), and a cellophane-bag-like outer skin (called the *capsule*). At step sixteen, the surgeon slices a minuscule hole in the capsule. Then he brings out the primary anti-cataract weapon: a penlike ultrasonic wand that is inserted through the small capsule incision. The probe is armed with a vibrating titanium tip that, when activated, emulsifies the diseased lens into about four fragments, each roughly the size of a pinhead.

During his work on McCord's left eye, Jungers turned on the buzzing phaco tip for thirty-four seconds—a relatively short burst for that procedure. The shattered cortex and nucleus were flushed and vacuumed out of the lens capsule through a suction attachment on the probe. The eye chamber, which just a second before had held the lens, was reinflated with a lubricant to protect the surrounding cells. The phaco handpiece was slowly removed from the eye. Finally, using all the same incisions and a tool called an injector, Jungers implanted, inside the empty capsule, a folded and artificial intraocular lens made from silicone. The new lens—measured to match the size and power of McCord's old lens—quickly unfolded and anchored itself behind the pupil where the cloudy lens used to reside. The artificial lubricating fluid that Jungers had pumped in minutes earlier was aspirated out and McCord's left eye was splashed with a final dose of drops—steroids to prevent inflammation plus a drug to maintain normal eye pressure. The speculum and suture were removed and McCord was wheeled to a recovery room.

McCord's medical records showed the procedure was completed without a hitch, and Jungers later described it as "uneventful . . . a normal case." After removing the clear shield and gauze the next day, the fresh vibrancy of the world's colors caused McCord to take a few excited deep breaths. After fifty years of seeing the world through something resembling a blurry tunnel, he instantly enjoyed peripheral vision—he could see things in the angles to his far left and right, out of the corners of his eyes. He needed Debbie to drive him around town for the next week as the healing progressed. But from the passenger seat, he noticed he could read distant street signs that before—even with his glasses—he couldn't see unless his car was idling next to them. His vision was measured at 20/20. McCord prodded Jungers to perform the second surgery as soon as possible. He couldn't wait for full, resplendent sight—a sensory delicacy he had not relished for forty-eight years. The next cataract removal was scheduled for October 12, 2000, at the same medical center with the same doctor.

The cataract removal on McCord's right eye seemed to go just as well. After the eye was deadened by two anesthetics and pried wide with a speculum, Jungers followed the same intricate steps, painstakingly tunneling toward the graying lens through precise, petite incisions. According to medical records, the doctor switched on the phaco probe's vibrating tip for an even shorter period than he did in the left eye—22.8 seconds—and he purposely operated the unit at 45 percent of its full power, enough to chop and remove the hard nucleus. The cortex was next irrigated and aspirated out, and the lens fragments were "vacuumed" from the lens chamber. A Bausch & Lomb LI61U foldable intraocular lens was inserted into the capsular bag "without difficulty," Jungers later noted in his records. Finally, McCord's right eye was moistened with a few drops of Celestone (an anti-inflammatory steroid) and a touch of Lopidine to maintain eye pressure and promote healing. Again, a shield was placed over the eye. The surgery lasted fifteen minutes. "It went fine," Jungers told McCord afterward. "I think you will be happy with this."

But when he awoke the next morning—Friday the thirteenth—everything felt different to McCord in contrast to the happy aftermath of the first operation. The right eye ached and seemed heavy. When he shed the gauze and shield that had guarded the eye overnight, he was quickly disappointed: the vision in that eye was blurry, while light and color appeared dark and dim. The eyelid drooped like a half-drawn shade, and the right side of his face felt as if it was sagging. He was mildly concerned, hardly reveling in the post-op bliss he had experienced twenty-two days earlier. Tapping her nursing skills, Debbie noticed some puffiness and redness in and around the right eye. Phil popped a Tylenol pill for the pain and climbed into the car as Debbie drove him for a scheduled follow-up visit with Jungers.

From the ophthalmologist's reclining chair, Phil described his vague pain and distorted vision. "That happens sometimes," Jungers told him. The doctor used his optical scope to survey his work and the artificial lens in an attempt to pinpoint the cause. Immediately, Jungers's instruments detected elevated pressure inside the right eye—a tension caused by a nonstop buildup of fluids, also seen in glaucoma patients. Normal intraocular pressure was measured at about 10 to 12 millimeters of mercury. In McCord's eye, the pressure approached 40 millimeters. The second obvious problem: McCord's cornea—the eye's transparent, protective dome used to help focus vision—was strained by edema or swelling. In other words, the extra fluid and pressure inside seemed to be pressing up and against the bottom of that clear dome, irritating and stretching it. Such a complication was not infrequent following cataract surgeries, Jungers later explained. He prescribed two glaucoma drugs— Trusopt and Alphagan—which McCord would use along with the anti-inflammatory steroid drops and antibiotics he was already taking. McCord was instructed to come back in a couple of weeks for a recheck. But within five days of the second procedure, McCord already knew his post-op recovery had stalled. His right-eye vision was stuck in a murky haze. The dull throb remained. He confided to his son that it felt like someone had jammed a thumb into his eye. It was watery and it blinked rapidly, and he often dabbed the weeping wreck with a tissue. Back at the Woods, his coworkers noticed it and some described the eye as "angry."

On October 30 and again on November 6, McCord returned to Jungers's office where the puzzled—and increasingly worried— doctor continued to see the corneal edema and measure a high intraocular pressure. At the November 6 appointment, Jungers revealed to McCord that he might require a corneal transplant if the medications failed. But there were still other drugs to be tried. Jungers tinkered with the mix, adding an anti-inflammatory steroid called Pred Forte and a non-steroid called Acular, which was sometimes used to treat watery eyes in people with seasonal allergies. He also prescribed new drops called Muro 128, a sodium chloride solution designed to work like a sponge, drawing moisture out of the irritated cornea. Several weeks later the eye pressure began to ease back to normal, but the cornea was growing more inflamed. The root of the eye's tenderness remained a mystery. Jungers was certain, however, that trauma from the cataract removal was not the genesis because the phacoemulsification time had been so brief and only a small amount of energy had been directed into the eye. Still, something had happened, a complication beyond anyone's anticipation that had caused McCord's eye chemistry to cascade out of control and that now threatened to destroy his cornea.

McCord, meanwhile, was tumbling deeper into discouragement, exhausted by the eye's raw sting. He was living life half blind, and his world was shrinking. Reading and driving became tiresome. He bumped into furniture when he walked in his own house. Between November 6 and mid-December, McCord was evaluated six more times by Jungers. On December 14, the doctor gave his patient some sobering news: The cornea was dying.

"There is nothing more I can do," Jungers said.

In order for McCord to fully see again, an eye surgeon would have to slice out the ravaged section of McCord's cornea, then stitch in a used cornea—a piece of healthy human tissue cut from a dead body. That, Jungers informed him, was the final option. Time had expired. The ugly, sore mess inside his eye was known in medical books as bullous keratopathy, a blister-like swelling that occurs rarely after cataract removal. Deep within the cornea's endothelium—a delicate layer of cells that line the inside of the blood vessels—death and destruction had irreversibly changed the landscape. As the eye's uncontrolled swelling caused scores of endothelium cells to perish, the few remaining cells had desperately rearranged themselves to cover the cornea's surface. But in doing so, those surviving cells had become weirdly shaped and enlarged. The endothelium had, consequently, increasingly lost its blood-pumping ability, and the corneal nerves had been stretched and ripped. After two months of constant irritation and abnormal fluid levels in the eye, the cornea had reached a stage, Jungers decided, where it could not heal or be healed. Too many cells had been permanently lost.

For McCord, the news pierced emotionally deeper than his day-and-night eye pain. His frustration and despair instantly lapsed into a cold-sweat panic. He was told there was a 20 percent chance that his body's immune system would reject a transplant. He was told the new cornea might carry a hidden infection. He was told his eye might hemorrhage during the surgery, and that he could suffer serious breathing problems under anesthesia. He was told that his vision might not return for several months, if at all, and that he faced years of other potential complications.

"It took me a long time to get past the idea of having my eye operated on in the first place; that had been kind of a major step for me. So now, having to do it again, with a procedure that is riskier, looking at up to two years of recovery time, I was not happy," McCord recalled. "So much so, I was considering not having it done. I was thinking, 'Can I ever do this?' and 'Can I let this happen?' and 'Do I want to go through that?' The first cataract surgery had been perfect, and now this. I was depressed."

Some forty thousand corneal replacements are performed annually in the United States, making it the most common form of transplant surgery. Thousands of ready grafts are temporarily stored in eye banks—there are about one hundred such facilities in the United States, including one in Indianapolis. And the transplant process is indeed grisly if not meticulous. After a willing donor dies, his or her two corneas (and often their organs) are harvested during a sterile surgical procedure. The donor's blood is typed and tested for disease. Often the eyes are removed entirely, placed in a preservation fluid, and driven or flown to the nearest eye bank. There the eyes are processed, the corneas snipped out and graded from zero to four—zero meaning the cornea is perfectly clear, one meaning it contains a trace of haze, two meaning it has a slight haze, three meaning it shows enough haze that the iris is not visible, and four meaning that only the pupil is visible in the eye. The retrieved corneas are placed in a special liquid medium that, with refrigeration, can keep the tissue healthy for fourteen days. The donor's identity is kept secret. In 2008 American eye banks received more than 92,000 corneas.

The first successful corneal transplant was completed in 1905 by an Austrian doctor, Eduard Konrad Zim. In that case, the donor—an eleven-year-old boy—was still alive. An accident had hurled tiny metal bits into the boy's eyes. His vision was forever erased, but his corneas remained viable. His corneas were removed by Zim and then stitched into the eyes of a Czech man whose corneas had been burned one year earlier during a mishap involving chemical lime. One of the two corneal transplants was successful and the Czech man regained partial sight. As of 2009, corneal replacements successfully restored vision 90 percent of the time, although in some of those cases, tissue rejection later forced surgeons to perform new transplants. If several grafts fail, doctors can also try synthetic corneas, but those are pricey (about $10,000 apiece), and they work only 60 percent of the time.

The operation itself sounded like a fairly simple sequence but carried an ominous technical name: penetrating keratoplasty. A surgeon, using a cookie-cutter-like tool called a trephine, would carve a circle through and around the diseased swath of McCord's cornea, then remove a button-sized disc of tissue. The donor cornea, selected from an eye bank by its grade and its blood type, would be cut to fit that fresh hole. The doctor would place the healthy corneal flap over the opening and sew it in place using a fine surgical thread. Like cataract removal, corneal transplants were an outpatient procedure. Jungers already had someone in mind for the job, Dr. Stephen Johnson, a transplant specialist who worked just eighty minutes east of Terre Haute at the Midwest Eye Institute in Indianapolis.

Johnson's office was on the second floor of an elegantly decorated medical building in a corporate center on the north side of the Indiana capital, just past the Interstate 465 interchange. To meet with Johnson, his patients climbed a wide, wood-railing staircase and entered the eye clinic's spacious, carpeted waiting area, which included sofa chairs and an eyeglass fitting room. Johnson was nearly bald, with a salt-and-pepper beard and eyes that became narrow when he smiled. According to his website, he graduated from the Indiana University School of Medicine in Indianapolis and was one of the first surgeons in the United States to study radial keratotomy. He had been in private practice since 1983, and billed himself as one of the state's top LASIK physicians. Two days after Christmas in 2000, McCord took a familiar position in Johnson's office—in another eye doctor's chair—and he allowed Johnson to appraise his broken cornea.

Johnson confirmed Jungers's diagnosis of bullous keratopathy and judged McCord to be a good candidate for transplant. Without such surgery, McCord was told he would not recover the vision in his right eye. Johnson scheduled a follow-up exam for January 26, 2001, when he would measure the cornea in final preparation for the surgical graft. As McCord left Johnson's office that day, he knew that his donor was still alive, that he or she was maybe even living somewhere close and perhaps was still quite healthy.

Would he go through with it? He wasn't sure.

"I had pretty well exceeded my quota for letting people stick needles in my eye," he said later. "And then there was the 'ick' factor of a cadaver. I have worked in hospitals much of my life. My wife is a nurse. Not too much gets to me.

"This did."

So, as he drove back to Terre Haute, the intrinsic fixer and gifted mender thought about canceling the most important repair of his life, thought about living out his days with a perpetually wounded eye. He thought about *not* fixing it. Traveling the wintry highway at sixty miles per hour, he was mired in dread.

Five nights later he would quietly mark another New Year's Eve with Debbie, scared that his next few months — or perhaps his remaining years — would be dominated by partial blindness. After the brief holiday, he would return on January 2 to his job at the Woods and try to occupy his mind with new carpets and old furnaces. And the day after that, walking head-down toward his office on a nippy Wednesday, he would momentarily allow himself to follow that luscious stream of organ music.

He would grant himself permission to make that unplanned, uncharacteristic detour into a Catholic house of worship. He would ask Mother Théodore Guérin for a moment of her attention and for a dose of her famed backwoods strength. And in that instant he would be able to smile again.

† † †

The supper table had always served as the social centerpiece in the homes of Phil and Debbie McCord, where most of the small conversations, big decisions, and evening laughs transpired. The circular, natural-wood dinette in the couple's breakfast nook indeed functioned as the soul and nerve center of their suburban Terre Haute household. Three nearby bay windows offered a view of the weathered brown fence that hemmed their grassy backyard. On the chilly night of January 3, as Phil slid into one of the wood-backed chairs, he happily inhaled the aroma of Debbie's frying hamburger patties.

Phil looked exactly the same: he had the same dangling right eyelid, as though he had suffered a stroke or paralysis on that side. And yet something about Phil was different, his wife noticed. He also seemed as though he had something to say.

So she waited, and she studied him and tried to pinpoint what had changed since he had left for work that morning.

After dark, his right eye always blazed its most ferocious shade of red. That was a sign, Debbie McCord knew, that Phil was tired. Sometimes his forehead carried a more pinched expression. That was a sign, Debbie understood, that Phil was upset and nervous— the kinds of things a wife and a nurse noticed. That night, Phil was exhausted. But he was not stressed, she thought.

As he munched his first bite of burger, he seemed more at peace than he had since the cataract operation had gone awry. Finally he spoke.

"Debbie, you'll never believe what I did."

"What did you do?"

"Well, I went to church."

She stared at him blankly. Church? *That isn't exactly a headline, Phil,* she thought. He wasn't the most religious man, but he worked for a group of nuns, caring for, among other things, their quaint chapels and their big church. With her usual hint of sarcasm, she challenged his claim.

"Phil, you go to Mass all the time with the Sisters—or at least when somebody there dies."

"No, I went by myself."

"Oh?"

"Yeah, I was walking down this hall that connects to the church and I thought I'd go in for a minute. It was kind of a peaceful place to be. I just"—he paused—"I just calmed down a little."

Now she watched him smile. Now it was making sense to her. Always so analytical and grounded, lately he had been petrified about his pending transplant, and about all that could—once again—perhaps go wrong. Now Debbie recognized the change in Phil. His old, easy way was back, as if he had shed the ballast of all his worry.

He told her about the prayer.

"I sat there and I said, 'Mother Théodore, can you help me be brave?'"

He watched Debbie's head tilt slightly, like she was surprised. He was strong-willed and prideful, a man who mended his own troubles. Phil knew his moment of vulnerability would strike her as unusual.

"It was so halting and stumbling. It was such a lousy prayer," he said. "But you know, Debbie, after I left the church, I felt kind of good."

"What do you mean?"

"I felt," he said, "relaxed."

That winter night, for the first time since the trees had dropped their leaves back in October, Phil McCord slept deeply and purely.

CHAPTER SIX

The Cure

The morning after his clumsy prayer, Phil McCord dressed himself in sweats and roamed across his snow-splotched front yard to fetch the newspapers. To his eyes, the world appeared just the same as it had the day before: half dark and half blurry. Still, the deep chill of Wednesday had lifted. Calmness filled the cul-de-sac.

He snatched his plastic-wrapped papers—the *Terre Haute Tribune-Star* and the *Indianapolis Star*—returned to the breakfast nook, and spread the pages across the table. His sipped a cup of coffee and scanned the lead story in the local paper. GROUP RENEWS DAYLIGHT SAVINGS TIME BATTLE, proclaimed the banner headline above an article about a proposed push for Indiana to finally join forty-seven other American states that annually turn their clocks ahead or back one hour in the spring and fall. As he flipped through the other pages, he skimmed by an ad trumpeting the grand opening of a new Eye-Mart store in town, and he spotted a sports column about a basketball showdown later that evening between hometown Indiana State University and the University of Northern Iowa. He swallowed a last splash of coffee, then stood and climbed the stairs to the second floor.

At the top of the steps, just down the hallway from the master bedroom where his wife was stirring, McCord turned right into a small den adorned with a sewing machine and a hanging sign that read DEBBIE'S ROOM. A few steps left through the den brought him to his own bathroom. On one wall, a glass-framed poster offered a catchy medley of baseball quotes from former stars describing the elegance and pure simplicity of the game—the kind of hardball wisdom that Coach McCord preached to players on the Saint Mary-of-the-Woods softball team. He cranked the shower on hot, stepped in, and scrubbed up for the workday. He toweled off, then faced the sink. A tube of Crest toothpaste, a toothbrush holder, and a soft-soap dispenser were scattered atop the vanity. He peered into the reflection—past the speckled splashes of old, dried soap. He raked his fingers through his cheek whiskers, trying to decide whether or not to trim his beard before dressing. Then, with one hand still cupping his face, his eyes met the eyes in the mirror. His breath caught in his throat.

That's odd, he thought.

His right eyelid had retreated to its normal tucked position. Within his now fully opened eye, he could actually see the entire blue iris. The once-red sclera had softened to a much paler shade of pink. His vision remained cloudy on that side. But overnight, the fluid-filled heaviness that had dogged him for months had vanished. So had the ache.

Is this real? he thought.

He walked briskly down the hall and into the master bedroom to get a nurse's opinion.

"You know, I think my eye is better," he announced, sounding like he needed convincing.

"Well," Debbie said, beginning her examination, "it's not bloodshot, and it's not as swollen."

"Yeah, it feels a lot better," he agreed, now with an eager edge. "Is it real?"

"Can you see?" she asked.

"No, but it's not *as* blurry as it has been," he said.

"Well, you should tell your doctor."

"OK, but it's probably just wishful thinking."

After eighty-three days of uncertainty and misery, McCord intended to tamp down any sparks of excitement for a few more weeks, until his scheduled exam with the transplant surgeon. So that Thursday morning, there were no prayers of appreciation, no raucous cheers of celebration. There was just a rising curiosity—along with the fresh peace he had found one day earlier in the basilica.

The engineer in McCord could certainly do the math: less than twenty-four hours after issuing a divine distress signal, his eye had visibly, perhaps even dramatically, improved. Cause and effect? He was not blind to that. So the man would allow himself at least a twinge of hope.

Was it real?

The man of science required more proof.

On the north end of campus, in the shadow of the Italian Renaissance–style bell tower that soared above the sisters' "big church," Facilities Management employees trickled into a redbrick building that resembled an old schoolhouse. From a large desk that overlooked a conference table and two tall windows, the boss checked his morning phone messages and his to-do list—the never-ending upkeep of the antique motherhouse and its scattered network of residence halls, dining halls, student classrooms, and ministry centers. One of the first people to greet McCord that Thursday was his administrative assistant, Sharon Moore. She was twelve years his senior and a Terre Haute resident. As a pair of non-Catholics working closely together in a community of nuns, McCord and Moore had bonded during his few years on the job. He had opened up to her about his anti-Catholic upbringing. She had revealed to him the details of her open-heart arterial-bypass surgery. Often she gently prodded McCord for a medical update on his dimming vision. For months she had heard in return only quiet grumbles and whispered worries. That morning, however, Moore immediately saw that the right eye's crimson glare had been replaced by something closer to a pink gleam.

"How's your eye doing?" she asked.

"Sharon, I think it is better," he said, offering just a shade of a grin. "The pressure is different."

"It looks much better! The angriness, the swelling, it looks much better!" she said.

McCord didn't tell her about his prayer to Mother Théodore. During the brief conversation, there was no talk of supernatural cures or heavenly healings. In her mind, Moore found his physical transformation, she said later, to be "really and truly . . . amazing." But in his head, McCord still wasn't sure what to make of it. He certainly wasn't making a big deal out of it.

After a morning spent on the technicalities of plumbing, grounds maintenance, and the construction of a new health-care wing, McCord chauffeured a few nuns on a thirteen-minute ride from campus to Terre Haute, where they would assemble with other Woods workers for a staff lunch at a local restaurant. In the backseat of McCord's gold-colored Chrysler, Sister Jenny Howard gazed out at the hardscrabble streets of West Terre Haute — a satellite of Terre Haute with about two thousand residents and a median household income of below $26,000. West Terre Haute was home to Providence Place, the affordable-housing complex launched via the $50,000 reciprocal gift the nuns had presented to Pope John Paul II at the 1998 beatification ceremony.

With wavy, graying hair cut short above her ears and an amiable manner softened by years of globe-trotting travel, Sister Jenny was part of a select group of six nuns who had been elected in 1996 to the convent's leadership team. The governing body included the general superior (at that time, Sister Diane Ris) plus five general councilors. The five-year terms of the current team all were about to expire. On the organizational chart, Sister Jenny was McCord's boss's boss. She also was his friend. And she happened to be the niece of Sister Dorothy Eileen Howard, who had nursed Mary Theodosia during her final days.

Sister Jenny and McCord had some things in common. Each adored the American wilderness and spending time aboard boats. She often camped and canoed with other nuns through the boundary waters of northern Minnesota, while McCord spent countless warm afternoons trolling Lake Michigan in his motor craft. An Indianapolis native, Jenny had initially considered becoming a nun at age six—the first year of many she spent at Catholic schools under the tutelage of the Sisters of Providence. As a student, Jenny noticed how convivial and content the nuns appeared, and how sweet they were to each other. Even as a girl, Jenny felt especially close to God, and she felt called to serve anyone trapped at the world's economic margins. Still, she wasn't sure her yearnings meant she should surrender her life to a religious convent. She had wanted someday to have children, and to find love. But after dating throughout her young adult years and failing to connect with the right man, she abandoned her motherly visions and joined the Sisters of Providence in 1982 at age thirty.

When McCord was hired fifteen years later, the engineer and the nun became cordial colleagues and, later, good friends. About three times each week, they shared a large meeting table with other Woods employees in order to dissect and discuss the latest campus repairs and upgrades. He was an exceedingly quiet, unassuming, and careful man, she noticed. Whenever McCord and Jenny had a few minutes alone, though—before or after meetings—he spoke candidly to her about work issues and, sometimes, about his private anxieties. Whether their conversations covered daily business or life's meaning, their exchanges were unflinchingly honest. On that first Thursday of 2001, en route to the staff lunch in Terre Haute, McCord let Jenny do all the talking. From the backseat, she enthusiastically chronicled her recent journey to El Salvador—the people, the land, the flavors. On that day, Jenny hadn't yet spotted anything physically different about McCord. No one else in the car had really noticed. As he drove, McCord said nothing about the overnight recovery to his miracle-hungry friends. But eventually there would come a crucial night in McCord's life when the nun would sit opposite the engineer in a crowded, cacophonous room, would hear his angst and listen to his questions, and, with a few delicate yet precise words, would help escort him out of the darkness.

† † †

Twenty-three days after McCord's prayer, he drove back to Indianapolis for his scheduled pre-transplant appointment with Dr. Johnson. By Friday, January 26, 2001, McCord hoped his calmer eye truly signaled some sort of significant healing. His vision remained murky, however. To him, a transplant still seemed unavoidable.

"So, how are we doing?" Johnson asked after McCord had settled into the exam chair.

"I think," McCord said, "it is better. But I'm at the point where I don't know if I'm hoping it is better and just trying to convince myself it is better, or if it is *really* better."

"Mmm, hmm. OK, yeah," Johnson mumbled with cordial skepticism. He swiveled an optical scope toward McCord's face and trained the lens to scan the patient's cornea and to explore beyond his dilated pupil.

"Hmm," Johnson said.

"Hmm, what?"

Johnson leaned back from the scope's eyepiece, picked up McCord's medical chart, and quickly skimmed the notes and numbers he had jotted the previous month. He returned to the scope and then returned to the chart.

Clearly, something had him bewildered.

"What?" McCord repeated.

"Well, you know, it *is* better."

"Well, good. Better like, 'We're going to wait awhile and reevaluate before we do the surgery'?"

"No, better like, 'You don't need the surgery.'"

McCord's heart thumped a bit harder. His head floated in euphoria.

"What did your cataract surgeon do?" Johnson asked.

"He didn't do anything." In fact, McCord hadn't seen Dr. Jungers since mid-December.

"Well, what did *you* do?"

"What did *I* do?" McCord said, hurling back some attitude. What was *he* supposed to have done?

Then he remembered.

"Well," McCord told the doctor, "I just said a prayer."

Johnson smirked. "Well, it worked."

"Is this unusual?"

"Oh yeah, *very* unusual."

One question remained. Would his full eyesight ever return? Would he ever have 20/20 vision in the right eye as he now did in his left? Since October, McCord's left eye had been transmitting images with a crispness he hadn't known since childhood. Would his right eye finally complete the brilliant picture?

Yes, Johnson said, likely it would. The doctor explained that inside the right eye, a filmy scar tissue had bloomed near his implanted lens. It was a routine complication that developed after about one quarter of cataract removals. It had probably emerged at roughly the same time his cornea had healed, thus extending his shadowy vision. But a quick burst of laser energy would probably disintegrate the buildup without hurting the new lens. Jungers would handle that cleanup procedure, Johnson said.

"There is nothing more," Johnson added, "that I need to do."

The doctor seemed genuinely happy for his patient. But McCord later described the surgeon's reaction to his tale of the prayer and morning-after healing as decidedly "blasé." McCord added, "I have no idea what he thought. But his attitude was kind of, to be candid about it: 'Shit happens. Is that a miracle? I don't know.' It was, in a sense, like he was unwilling to lend his name to some witchcraft.

"I understand that. I worked in hospitals for twenty years. My wife is a nurse. You can't be around the medical profession without seeing [mysterious] things and saying, 'Wow, I can't explain that.' Things will happen to patients [that defy medical science] and doctors will ask, 'Was that a miracle or divine intervention? Well, it wasn't anything I did, so describe it any way you like.' That pretty much was Dr. Johnson's attitude: 'I can't say why this happened, but I'm not going to leap to a spiritual explanation.'"

McCord was anything but blasé, but he wasn't thinking about miracles, either. The confirmation from Johnson left him feeling physically lighter, emotionally recharged. As he stepped out of Johnson's office, bounded down the carpeted staircase, and strutted to his car in the lot outside, he recited again and again in his head the same glorious, seven-word sentence: "I don't have to have a transplant! . . . I don't have to have a transplant!"

Johnson, meanwhile, jotted down the details of his final examination on McCord, including the eye measurements and his overall observations. He included everything but McCord's mention of the prayer. Then he sent the file to Dr. Jungers in Terre Haute. When McCord visited Jungers's office again five weeks later, on February 28, 2001, the patient never disclosed his divine request for healing, Jungers later said. McCord was simply eager to clear out the remaining haze in his vision.

"What about the laser? When can we do that?" McCord asked.

"The room is open. We can do it right now," Jungers said.

"Let's go!" McCord said.

Like the transplant surgeon in Indianapolis, Jungers was confounded: What had caused the spontaneous regeneration? He told McCord that once the cornea had reached such a hideous state — held together by painfully stretched cells — only a transplant, in his opinion, could have mended the eye.

For the last time for a long while, McCord reclined in an eye doctor's chair, allowed Jungers to affix a speculum to hold his lid open, and waited for an invasive procedure to begin. This time he was not nervous at all. Jungers aimed the beam at the protein buildup and, with a series of laser pulses, quickly cleared away the unwanted membrane.

In that instant, McCord could see. Not perfectly yet, as there were intermittent flashes of light and temporary dots from the laser's zaps. But he could see out of both eyes. He could see the eye chart, and he read the black letters to Jungers with glee in his voice.

"Now," McCord told Jungers, "I have sight."

Now it was real.

The vision in his right eye was measured that day at 20/50 — considered a minor impairment. When McCord returned to Jungers's office about a week later for a follow-up check, the eye had further healed and its measured vision was nearly 20/20. It remained so for years.

Miraculous? Not in McCord's mind. Not yet.

To the engineer, he would only go so far as to dub it "a pretty remarkable thing." But the man with something of a split personality on faith did have another conversation with whoever might be listening in heaven.

He said a short prayer of gratitude. It would become something of a ritual.

Many mornings thereafter, after opening his eyes and visually devouring the tiniest details of his bedroom or the rich texture of the Indiana landscape beyond his second-story window, he would offer a simple appreciation.

"Thank you very much."

† † †

When it came to medicine, Dr. Jeffrey Jungers put no stock in the power of prayer.

He was the eye doctor of choice for many of the local nuns in Terre Haute and he had enjoyed jogging through their godly grounds just across the river. But he described himself as "not a religious person at all." Jungers, in fact, later summed up the McCord episode as merely a baffling bit of science, a happy quirk of nature.

Did McCord's divine plea play any role in his swift, strange recovery, he was asked. The ophthalmologist answered by mentioning the largest medical study ever undertaken on the possible healing powers of prayer. Funded by the British-based John Templeton Foundation—which supports projects exploring the nexus of religion and science—the $2.4-million study enlisted more than 1,800 patients who had undergone heart-bypass surgeries. Researchers also enrolled a squad of designated praying people, including devout Protestants and Catholic monks. They were given the patients' first names and the first initial of their last names. They began praying the night before the patients' operations and continued for two weeks, asking God for "a successful surgery and a quick, healthy recovery and no complications." The volunteer patients, meanwhile, were randomly split into three clusters: some received prayers but were not told of that; some received no prayers but also were not informed; and some knew they were getting prayers from the strangers. In groups one and two, there were no differences in their post-surgery troubles—each group averaged a complication rate of 52 percent, researchers found. But in group three, 59 percent of the patients suffered complications. The study was published in an April 2006 issue of the *American Heart Journal*. Researchers theorized that disclosing the prayer chains to some patients perhaps caused "performance anxiety" in group three. The project reached one statistical conclusion: prayers did not matter. That matched Jungers's thinking.

"I can flat-out tell you," Jungers said, "I don't believe in miracles."

Dr. Stephen Johnson's religious leanings, meanwhile, were not clear. He did not respond to several interview requests I made to him via e-mail and telephone. I e-mailed Johnson's office coordinator, Patti Bailey, in October 2008 to solicit an answer from Johnson about a long-pending interview request. Bailey responded with an e-mail: "When I approached Dr. Johnson the other day about the subject, he looked at me and very sternly said, 'I don't want to hear another word about this. Is that clear?' He then turned and went about seeing his patients. I have worked for Dr. Johnson for 10 years and can read him quite well. When he said he doesn't want to hear another word about this, then that is what he means. I don't know the details of why Dr. Johnson is reluctant to speak with you."

Johnson's firm stance against discussing the McCord case would surface again two years later—in that instance, casting a shadow on Mother Théodore's cause for sainthood. Not surprisingly, when it comes to matters in which the medical and the mystical collide, some doctors are, at best, uncomfortable with the commingling of topics and, at worst, offended when God gets the credit for their work.

But the notion that the two worlds are interlaced is as ancient as the Egyptian pyramids. And the dance—or duel—between human faith and human health has been in constant flux ever since. Two

thousand years before the life of Christ, polytheistic Egyptians
believed a disease was a sign of friction between the sick person or
the sick village and the ruling gods. Or, they thought, the sick people were perhaps being punished for displeasing the gods. To enact
a cure, a healer—sometimes a priest—was summoned to remove
invading, angry spirits. Yet even within this mystical approach,
some Egyptian healers were known to try herbs and rudimentary
surgeries to restore health. In Ancient Greece, many citizens held
similar views about the fusion of their physical status and their
devotion to an exhaustive roster of higher powers, including Ascle-
pius (the god of medicine) and Hygeia (the goddess of health).
Some Greeks believed illness arose when people angered the gods
through bad behavior, while other Greeks thought a body's failing
was tied to spirit possession.

Science, however, began to sprout more modern concepts in the
five centuries before Christ, as Greek doctors started to search for
the natural, physical causes of disease. Hippocrates, born in 460
BCE on the Greek island of Cos, forged a medical career on a now
well-worn maxim: Seeing is believing. Observation, Hippocrates
maintained, should be a physician's primary tool. He concluded that
diseases could be explained through a rational study of the human
body, and he espoused the long-term physical values of fresh air, rest,
and a healthy diet. He rebuffed the old thinking that superstitions or
unhappy spirits somehow fueled sickness. Through his analysis of
human anatomy and his inspection of patients, Hippocrates learned
that some disease symptoms hit different people harder than others,
and that some people seemed better armed to withstand an illness.
What's more, he was the first physician to posit that one's beliefs,
thoughts, and feelings emanated from the brain, not the heart. He
taught his concepts at a medical school he founded on Cos as well
as during his excursions throughout Greece. He has been dubbed
"the father of medicine," and his affirmation of medical ethics—the

Hippocratic oath—continues to be recited by modern doctors. Still, four hundred years after the death of Hippocrates, many cultures— including new legions of Christians—put their belief behind a new brand of medical restoration: the divine touch.

During the first centuries after Christ, tales abounded of holy men who suspended nature's laws, often by citing the name of an almighty spirit. Earth's religions and their most sacred books gushed with supernatural claims. In a passage from the Koran, the Muslim prophet Muhammad flew through the night from Mecca to Jerusalem on the back of a winged horse. The Buddha was said, according to believers, to have walked through the air on a golden bridge he created. The Old Testament contains wondrous descriptions of Moses turning his rod into a serpent, drawing water from a rock, instructing Aaron to transform the Nile into a river of blood, and, most famously, parting the waters of the Red Sea to allow the children of Israel to cross it unharmed. Miracles cited in the Old Testament were often steeped in pestilence or death: frogs, lice, locusts, and hail. They appeared to affirm God's authority.

In the New Testament, by contrast, many supernatural events were bathed in mercy and seemed to gently symbolize the divine grace and purity of Jesus and his Apostles. The Bible lists thirty-five miracles performed by Christ, and seventeen of those are medical in nature, including healings of people with leprosy, blindness, palsy, edema, a blood disorder, a shriveled hand, and fever. In the case of Lazarus, a man was even brought back from death.

As Christianity spread throughout Europe, claimed miracles typically followed Christ's health-restoring blueprint. As a result, within the early Christian church and, later, inside the Roman Catholic faith, alleged supernatural acts generally involved spontaneous or unexplained healings. That medically focused trend in claimed miracles remained true into the twenty-first century. Catholics believed there was another reason for this cure-rich tendency in alleged miracles: if death seemed imminent, people were more apt to pray for God's intercession. According to Catholic doctrine, that prayer plea was the theological crux of any miracle equation, the key to Catholic saint-naming.

During the first four centuries after Christ, curative miracles were not linked to or driven by the cults of saints. From roughly 415 CE to 928 CE, Christian clerics and their faithful followers ravenously absorbed, accepted, and repeated numerous tales of supposed supernatural healings without scrutiny or suspicion. According to an essay written several decades ago by Father Paul Molinari, an Italian theologian and Jesuit priest who prepared numerous sainthood causes in Rome, that era "was in no way governed by critical or scientific standards, while the quality of medical research was not only crude, it could scarcely be said to have existed at all." In that age, faith *was* medicine. Over the span of the next millennium, a certain saintly tinge was added to the religious mix.

The fall of the Western Roman Empire in the fifth century gave way to the Middle Ages—a millennium marked by the towering authority of the Christian Church and by brutal pandemics such as the Black Death of the mid-fourteenth century. Many of the clergy dedicated their lives to housing and treating the ill; they became known for their compassion and their healing touch. Some priests even wrote medical dissertations. And when the clerics' rough therapies sometimes saved people, the cures were deemed divine wonders.

As that generation of priests and monks died out, they gained new reverence by being named saints. And their miracle work was believed to live on through their relics—pieces of their bodies, clothes, or the objects they had used. Touching, wearing, or even being near a relic was thought by many faithful to relieve sickness. To medieval Christians, this notion of heavenly magic was backed by the Bible itself: the New Testament portrayed the curative power of items once grasped by Christ or his Apostles. What's more, the faithful saw relics as a tangible bond between man and God, between life and the afterlife. The veneration of relics soon matched the followers' staunch belief in certain Church sacraments like baptism, matrimony, and the Eucharist.

The most holy of all relics were those said to have been removed from the body of Jesus or his mother, Mary—or were reputed to be items they touched while alive: a tatter of Mary's veil, for example, or a chunk of wood from the actual cross on which Jesus was crucified. England's Walsingham Abbey displayed for visitors a liquid that was said to be the breast milk of the Virgin Mary. More common, however, were the relics of local European saints who had performed alleged miracles while alive. Those relics were guarded and treasured, and their purported life-restoring value created a flourishing market in which exorbitant prices were charged, and where fakes and duplicates proliferated. One European church exhibited and flaunted what they believed to be the brain of Saint Peter. One day the cherished memento was accidentally moved and onlookers realized the so-called relic was merely a slab of pumice stone.

Throughout the Middle Ages, Christians routinely embarked on long pilgrimages to see the saints' tombs—and to be close to their relics. When smaller relics were available for sale, some pilgrims purchased the holy trinkets simply as a way to create their own shrine to that saint back at their home church. The new shrines then helped lure flocks of the sick or the devout, boosting the congregation and the number of coins in the collection plate at that local parish. This was business. And the trade got desperate and dirty. Merchants were known to rob random graves, steal bones, and pass them off as saintly relics. Other relics were routinely stolen from one cathedral only to show up at another. Far darker, however, and far more barbarous, were the mass murders carried out, at least in part, to retrieve sacred relics. During the religion-fueled medieval military campaigns called the Crusades, armed Christians—including the Knights Templar, a monastic order—invaded eastward from Europe to recapture Jerusalem and the Holy Land. Amid the massacres of Muslims, Jews, and those of other faiths, the crusaders also plundered and carried home a grisly list of biblical relics, supposedly including wood from the cross on which Jesus was killed; his blood and sandals; the crown of thorns that Jesus wore during his crucifixion; and the shroud he was buried in; a lock of Mary's hair; the skull of Saint John the Baptist; the shinbone of Saint Peter; and an arm from the Apostle Simon. While belief in the healing potency of relics never completely vanished among many people of faith, a new and radical sensibility was poised to transform medicine—and shed the cozy alliance between that still-young branch of science and theocratic Christianity.

With its roots in Florence, Italy, and its first breaths said to have been taken among artists and intellectuals of the late 1300s, the cultural reawakening known as the Renaissance swept in a massive and fresh fascination with and celebration of the human race, siphoning off some of the entrenched social devotion to the saints and the Almighty in heaven. In many circles, humanism gained equal footing with—or surpassed—communion with a higher power. The potential genius of the mind was explored, pushed, and displayed. The scientific method—a quest to paint a reliable, verifiable depiction of this world—found fierce followers. Men of astronomy, mathematics, and engineering gathered empirical evidence, invented new tactics to test their reality, and acquired proof through direct observation. As the secular inevitably clashed with the spiritual— the here-and-now versus the great beyond—Renaissance thinkers challenged the authority of the Catholic Church as the lone source of wisdom. Science and art often were merged to feed the chase to decipher who we were, where we were, and why we were here. Leonardo da Vinci delved into the subtle twists and sinews of the

human body, splashing his notebooks and paintings with painstakingly precise portrayals of the human form. The Renaissance
gave way to the Enlightenment in the 1600s and 1700s—and to an
immortal roster of philosophers and inventors. They included Benedict de Spinoza, who questioned the origin of biblical texts, and
the master scientist Sir Isaac Newton, who invented calculus and
figured out why things dropped down and not up. These men only
intensified the rising, mammoth thirst to discover earthly truths,
cementing a widening belief in human reason, natural law, and universal order. Some historians have viewed this "Age of Reason" as
a moment when science and faith became polarities, if not enemies.
In 1600 the Italian philosopher Giordano Bruno, a known propo-
nent of the notion that the sun sat at the center of the solar system,
was declared a heretic by the Roman Inquisition and burned at the
stake. Thirty-two years later, Galileo Galilei, an Italian physicist,
astronomer, and another heliocentric advocate, was charged by the
Church with heresy for publishing his findings, was forced to publicly recant his belief that the earth revolved around the sun, and
was placed under house arrest for the remainder of his life.

Of course, science, and particularly the study of medicine, roared
ultimately forward through the next three centuries—thrusting our
knowledge of the human condition to unprecedented levels. Nearly
halfway through the twentieth century, the Roman Catholic Church,
still searching for and endorsing medical miracles, proffered a significant nod to the world's more technological ideologies. On October 22, 1948, the pope established the Consulta Medica, its advisory
body of about one hundred Italian doctors. At the behest of the Vatican, the Consulta meets in panels of five doctors to review claims of
divine healing and the members cast votes on whether those cures
can be rationally explained or whether they deviate from natural
laws. In making their decisions, the Vatican's paid team of physicians
reads through patient and witness testimonials and analyzes X-rays,

MRIs, biopsies, and reams of medical files. Their final say never contains the word "miracle." The group merely renders a majority opinion on the case's scientific explicability or inexplicability. They dissect about forty cases per year for the pope. The post–World War II launch of the Consulta marked a rare twentieth-century occasion when scientific method and theological study were fused for the same cause. But there was precedent for this in Rome. About fifty years earlier, the Holy See had stepped gingerly into the scientific realm— specifically (and somewhat ironically) into astronomy. In 1891 Pope Leo XIII opened the Vatican Observatory on a hillside next to the dome of St. Peter's Basilica. The Vatican had dabbled in star study at its smaller college-affiliated observatories during the late 1700s and the 1800s. At one of those facilities the Jesuit priest Angelo Secchi had become the first astronomer to classify stars according to their spectra, and he was one of the earliest scientists to declare the sun to be a star. Pope Leo founded the Vatican Observatory, historians say, to neutralize chronic accusations that the Catholic Church was hostile toward science. By 2009 that papal-run research center was headquartered just outside Rome, at the pope's summer residence in Castel Gandolfo, Italy, and it was still using men of faith to probe the stars. Jesuit Brother Guy Consolmagno, a Detroit-born graduate of the Massachusetts Institute of Technology, worked at the Vatican Observatory and informed journalists he felt that science could indeed coexist with miracles—but only if science was not considered a tool to prove or disprove divine intercessions. "Science ultimately cannot pass infallible judgments on miracles, because science is not perfect," Consolmagno told the *Philadelphia Inquirer* in a 2000 interview. "Still, it can be useful; an event that has an obvious natural cause is clearly not a miracle. . . . Science by its nature comes up with general principles, but it's always trickier—maybe impossible—to have one hundred percent certainty about any specific historical incident."

In something of a mirror image to the classic, secular chapters of the Renaissance and the Enlightenment, spirituality regained a sturdier foothold in medicine during the decades after World War II. At the chilly zenith of the Cold War, following the detonation of two U.S.-made atomic bombs on Japanese cities, with American and Soviet military factories continuing to churn out, test, and hoard nuclear warheads, and amid the runaway ascent of computer intelligence in many Western cultural corners, more people — faith-oriented and otherwise — began casting a wary eye toward science. As Richard P. Sloan held in his book *Blind Faith: The Unholy Alliance of Religion and Medicine,* these technological accelerations became the seeds for a swell of distrust in machines and, ultimately, a broadening dissatisfaction with contemporary health care. The person — the unmeasurable soul of the patient — was becoming lost in the faceless haze of space-age doctoring. New Age paths and ancient Eastern healing won converts, including many people who argued that Western medicine's loud progress came at a dehumanizing cost. The sick, and those trying not to become sick, increasingly sought a whole-body, holistic flavor to their care. To some, that meant God needed to be in the exam room or the surgical suite.

Since 2000, a number of doctors have made sure to inject faith into their bedside manner and into their arsenals of gadgets and pills. These include doctors like Dale Matthews, a long-time internist and medical instructor in Washington, D.C., author of four books, including *The Faith Factor: Proof of the Healing Power of Prayer,* a member of the Christian Medical and Dental Society, and a media-friendly face for the restoration of the Almighty in health settings. Matthews, who often spoke of his prayerful moments with patients, or of his scribbling out New Testament scriptures along with prescriptions, told a newspaper interviewer in 1998, "Faith seems to be good for what ails you." He told another in 2002, "I look for spiritual pain, and spiritual pain cannot be treated with aspirin."

The robust reappearance of religion in traditional health care accompanied an awakening among physicians toward the possibility of the supernatural, according to a 2004 survey of 1,100 physicians conducted by the Louis Finkelstein Institute for Religious and Social Studies, part of the Jewish Theological Seminary in New York. The poll found that 74 percent of U.S. doctors believed miracles had occurred in the past, and 73 percent thought they could still occur. The same research showed that 55 percent of doctors said they had witnessed treatment results in their own patients that they deemed miraculous. Most of the doctors acknowledged to the pollsters that they prayed for their patients.

But the rift between faith and medicine remained—particularly as some conservative Christians promoted "intelligent design" as an alternative to evolutionary theory. Dr. Neil Scheurich, a psychiatrist at the University of Kentucky College of Medicine, contended in 2006 that the time had come for a fresh separation of church and medicine. He asserted that religion was no less important but no more important than any other value that patients held dear.

In the modern era, Catholic miracle investigators—like Sister Marie Kevin Tighe—often collide with uncooperative, unresponsive, or even unkind doctors as they try to gather facts. Marie Kevin encountered just such friction in Boston when she talked to the doctors of throat-cancer survivor Eddie Mulkern. And she would face a similar hesitancy when she eventually approached Dr. Stephen Johnson, the corneal-transplant specialist.

But in time, Marie Kevin also would find a doctor who would happily try to help her sell a miracle to Rome.

† † †

From its lavishly frescoed ceiling to its pink marble floors, the Church of the Immaculate Conception echoed with delicate footsteps and soft organ notes as another morning Mass concluded in the spring of 2001. Most of the nuns were heading to lunch. At the rear of the church, Sister Charles Van Hoy, now in her seventies and long since retired from her grade-school teaching job, strolled toward the exit and prepared to step into the sunshine. Then the back door opened. Phil McCord walked into the sanctuary.

Sister Charles knew Phil well and was familiar with his severe eye condition. Almost all the nuns were aware of it. On campus, nuggets of gossip and stray personal news were quickly dispersed via a chatty telegraph that McCord once dubbed "the Sisters' Grapevine." At the Woods, there were no secrets. If one sister knew, all knew.

Sister Charles had not seen McCord for a while, since sometime before the holidays. He looked good, she thought. She asked about his eye.

"It's better!" he said. He began telling her his story about the unexpected healing.

As he spoke to the nun, McCord spied the church pew where he had offered his prayer. He described to Sister Charles his plea for inner peace on January 3, and he told her of his visual reawakening the next morning. The tale took about two minutes to tell. The nun listened in silence, as if she was not the least bit surprised.

"Well," she said, "that is a miracle."

"It is to me," McCord agreed.

Sister Charles watched him walk into the basilica, a calm and happy man who had apparently returned that morning to pray. Their brief exchange stuck with her. Every nun at the Woods knew that Sister Marie Kevin had been chasing a second proven miracle to secure Mother Théodore's sainthood. Shortly after Sister Charles departed the church that morning, she crossed paths with Marie Kevin in a corridor at Providence Hall, the motherhouse atop the old crypt, the very building where Sister Mary Theodosia had heard the voice and experienced her own cure.

"Did Phil McCord tell you about his eye?" Sister Charles asked.

"No," Marie Kevin replied.

"He was having so many problems with it. He prayed to Mother Théodore, and now it is better."

For both women, the conversation was calm and casual. But as promoter of the cause, Marie Kevin knew it was her duty to follow up on every alleged healing performed in the founder's name. When she returned to her office just down the hall, she dialed up McCord at the Facilities Management building. She asked him to repeat his story to her. He reviewed for Marie Kevin his eye's medical history and told her of his deep stress about the planned transplant, his unpolished prayer, and what he had seen in the mirror the next day.

This has merit, Marie Kevin thought.

"Can we get together and talk?" she asked.

"Come on over," McCord invited.

At his office that day, the nun bombarded the engineer with a spray of additional questions: Was a cornea transplant the only way to fix the eye? Why had he asked Mother Théodore for intercession? What had he said to her exactly? As a non-Catholic, how did he even know about intercession?

He patiently answered all her queries.

This is worthy of investigation, Marie Kevin thought. Outwardly she remained stoic. She still wasn't convinced that McCord's healing met the theological qualifications of a potential miracle.

She thanked McCord for his time and walked across campus to her office. With the conversation fresh in her mind, she typed up an account of the chat and e-mailed the narrative from Indiana to Italy. It was addressed to the latest in a century-long line of postulators, advocates assigned by the sisters to handle and manage Mother Théodore's cause in Rome. But Dr. Andrea Ambrosi was altogether different from any of the past postulators on the case. To begin with, he was not a priest.

With more than three hundred causes on his résumé—the dozens of men and women he had helped reach beatification or canonization—Ambrosi was a highly educated canon lawyer, once dubbed a "saint maker" by the media. He was one of only three laymen in the world who earned a living by guiding or pushing miracle claims through the tortuous and political Vatican bureaucracy. His mystical work had taken him to more than thirty countries. He was tall, vivacious, and dapper. And unlike so many of the Vatican-affiliated men with whom the nuns had dealt over the previous decades, Ambrosi was utterly captivating. He beamed with human warmth. He hugged and smiled freely. And in his tiny, book-crammed office, he employed three bright young women as his assistants—a sort of *Charlie's Angels* of the angel business. Marie Kevin adored him. She described him as "congenial and jovial, with amazing listening skills" and a man "who is always on task, who approaches everything very intently." Quite simply, she admired his savvy.

Ambrosi was known to grind through the theological minutiae and the medical grit of each cause he took on, yet he also was a master at building miracle cases that would satisfy the scrupulous Vatican experts. Named by the sisters as Mother Théodore's postulator in 1994, he had needed only four years to complete what his predecessors had not accomplished in ninety years—shepherding the alleged miracle of Mary Theodosia to Vatican acceptance and thus securing Mother Théodore's beatification. His reputation also would land Ambrosi two of the most famous modern American canonization causes: Cardinal Terence Cooke, who had served as archbishop of New York from 1968 to 1983, and Archbishop Fulton Sheen, who for twenty years sold Catholicism to the masses through his popular radio and television programs. In the field of saint-making, Ambrosi was a star.

Not long after Marie Kevin revealed the McCord saga to Ambrosi,

he e-mailed her back. His response was to the point. He told her
to contact the Metropolitan Tribunal at the Archdiocese of Indianapolis with a clear message: the postulator and the nun were
about to launch a joint inquiry into the possible miracle of Phil
McCord.

Marie Kevin already had booked a pleasure trip for herself and
a friend to Rome for late September 2001. Ambrosi requested that
sometime during her vacation, Marie Kevin visit his office so they
could hash out—and perhaps pare down—all the potential miracles on her docket, including the improbable cancer cure of Eddie
Mulkern. Privately, Marie Kevin still thought the disappearance
of Mulkern's throat tumor would be their ultimate selection for the
potential second miracle to present to the Vatican. The McCord
healing, she worried, might seem just a bit too convenient to the
cardinals in Rome. It involved one of the sisters' own employees
and had occurred right on their own campus. She had her doubts
about the case.

But then so did McCord.

After Sister Charles suggested that his visual rescue had been
a supernatural event, McCord struggled to make the intellectual
connection between his healthy right eye and a church-defined,
biblically tinged, straight-from-God miracle. *A miracle?* he thought.
In that context, the word carried an otherworldly depth, a
once-in-a-generation significance, and a momentous weight.

If it was a miracle, McCord couldn't fathom why *he* had been
the recipient. Among the six billion people on the planet, why him?
Why now? And what was next? If God had indeed touched and
healed him, did that mean he was destined to do something more
vital, perhaps something historic, something to pay back that ultimate favor? Did he owe a heavenly debt? He began to mull all
those unknowns. For years he would mentally trip over those questions again and again. Of course, McCord was never the kind of

man to stop his examination of anything at the surface. He was compelled to dig deeper toward the core of an issue, down to where the answers hid. So once more he peeled back the skin of the situation—the simple, warm notion that his prayer for peace had been answered—and he began to rummage through the mysterious reasons and theological questions that made up the essence of his wondrous recovery.

That quest for meaning initially would puzzle him. Later, it would haunt him.

CHAPTER SEVEN

The Saint-Maker

J ust across the Tiber River from Vatican City, a shady cob-blestoned street stirred with a fresh burst of morning life: the gentle clinking of coffee cups, the staccato chatter of men in ties gabbing on cell phones, and the shuffle of green-aproned clerks hauling crates of fresh fish, plump tomatoes, and fat lemons into sidewalk cafés. A grocer inspected his outdoor trays of potatoes and artichokes. A newsstand vendor looked over his oddly diverse display of computer magazines, Barbie coloring books, and postcards featuring a grinning pope.

Via di Tor Millina was fully awake, already drenched in the vapors of cigar smoke, engine exhaust, and freshly baked pizza dough—although it would be a couple of hours before the daily cavalcade of tourists wandered over from the artists' square, Piazza Navona, in search of a lazy, alfresco lunch.

In the middle of the narrow avenue, a three-story building with brown shutters stood in silence against the rising bustle. A bulging plastic trash bag awaited pickup on the front stoop. On a wall next to the glossy brown front door, a panel of buzzers displayed eight names, one for each of the flats inside. A motorcycle rested on its kickstand inside the tiled lobby. To passersby, Via di Tor Millina 19 looked like a humdrum stack of sleepy apartments, just another century-old edifice on another achingly quaint Roman street. But upstairs on the second floor, behind a faintly lit window, a man sat at a wide desk and briskly scratched his pen across a legal pad. He was engrossed, arranging his proof for one more earthly miracle, helping pave the eternal way for one more future saint. When it came to defending claims of divine healings and promoting canonization causes, the natty lawyer had built a happily hectic caseload. Coffee breaks were rare. Brown-bag lunches were gobbled at his desk. For Dr. Andrea Ambrosi, business was good.

On October 1, 2001, a balmy, seventy-degree morning, Via di Tor Millina was the primary destination for Sister Marie Kevin and her friend, Kathy Fleming, a longtime school principal and former Woods nun. The two had recently landed in Rome for a ten-day vacation that included one work meeting—a critical briefing with Ambrosi. The agenda: five possible miracles to consider.

Fleming had promised to pay for their overseas junket if Marie Kevin—who had visited Rome twice before—agreed to guide their tours. In truth, Fleming had not been too eager to jet to the ancient hub of Catholicism. The Italian capital was, she said, "too churchy for me." But a young man and former co-worker at Fleming's suburban Indianapolis school, Our Lady of the Greenwood, was about to be ordained as a deacon in Rome, and Fleming wanted to attend that ceremony. In addition, she delighted in Marie Kevin's gentle company. Fleming had in some ways patterned her life after Marie Kevin, who was fourteen years older than she. Fleming had joined the Sisters of Providence at eighteen, essentially on a whim: "I just felt it was the right thing for women to do, and I really didn't give it a whole lot of thought." After graduating from the Woods novitiate, she initially taught eighth grade at a school in Bloomington, Indiana, eventually rising to become the school's principal. At age thirty-six, however, Fleming decided to break her sisterly vows and depart the community: "A friend of mine once said, 'A lot of people ask why Kathy left. Well, she never figured out why she went in.' There was," Fleming said, "a lot of truth in that."

Fleming had nonetheless maintained a lifelong friendship with a sprightly campus nun, Marie Kevin. In fact, their personal ties stretched back to the 1950s when they had met on one of Fleming's saddest days — back when she was grappling to find emotional footing following a sudden family move to Indiana. Fleming was then fifteen. Her younger brother had enrolled at St. Philip Neri Elementary School in Indianapolis and immediately began raving about his smart and sweet eighth-grade teacher, Sister Marie Kevin, who put her students before the books and who really listened to the kids. Fleming had never known her brother to like any nun. She decided she had to meet this woman. One afternoon she knocked on the back door of the convent at her brother's school. "What can I do for you?" Marie Kevin asked. Fleming burst into tears. "I just hate the school I'm going to, and my brother loves you. He's doing so well. I made all A's back in Virginia but at this school I feel dumber than all get-out. I just can't do it." The nun responded with a kind smile: "You are a smart young woman and you can do it. You will turn it around and keep with it! Just study your head off!" For thirty minutes, Marie Kevin quietly convinced Fleming that she was indeed smart enough. More than fifty years later, Fleming hailed that exchange as a "life-changing moment." In time, Fleming would be the one to give Marie Kevin a dramatic pep talk.

As their ten thirty meeting with Ambrosi ticked closer, a taxi whisked the nun and the ex-nun on a brief ride west from their lodgings at the Pontifical North American College, an American seminary near the Trevi Fountain downtown. As they neared the sprawling Piazza Navona — thick with completed and unfinished scenic watercolors resting on a sea of easels — Marie Kevin pointed out a flurry of antique landmarks, like the gray-domed Sant'Agnese in Agone. The basilica, named for Saint Agnes, was constructed on the spot where Agnes was said to have been killed in the year 304. Marie Kevin stared at the cold stone façade of the church. The legend of Saint Agnes was laced with some familiar saintly themes. At age thirteen, Agnes, a member of Roman nobility raised in a Christian family, had been ordered to marry the son of the Roman prefect Sempronius. When she refused and invoked her faith, the prefect first ordered that the girl be dragged naked through the streets and raped — Roman law did not permit the execution of virgins. According to church lore, the men who tried to rape Agnes were instantly blinded and "her honor was miraculously preserved." Sempronius then demanded that Agnes be burned at the stake. But the pile of wood would not ignite. Finally a Roman officer drew his sword and sliced off the girl's head. Agnes was eventually canonized as a martyr. Almost two thousand years later, on the arched ceilings of the basilica's interior dome, frescoes depicted Agnes's violent end and her heavenly form. She was the patron saint of young girls. Some folk customs held that girls should practice love rituals on Saint Agnes Eve (January 20) to find their future mates. John Keats wrote of that superstition in his poem "The Eve of Saint Agnes." Fleming had once attended St. Agnes Academy in Indianapolis.

Like no other city, Rome teemed with saintly names — from St. Peter's Square to Porta San Paolo. It was the place where hundreds of saints had lived and died (or were martyred). It remained the place where the newest saints were made for a modern world through an ancient means. The two women in the cab's backseat had long yearned for Mother Théodore to join that select club. In Rome, their wish could become a reality.

Marie Kevin seemed excited. She looked forward to Ambrosi's magnetic grin and his booming hospitality. She had spent time with him twice before in Rome, including at Mother Théodore's 1998 beatification. In her hands that morning, Marie Kevin clasped a few typed sheets of paper — bullet points for the five potential cases she would discuss with the postulator. The top spot on page one was occupied by the alleged miracle involving Eddie Mulkern. Marie Kevin had admitted to Fleming that she felt Mulkern was the best choice — medically more dramatic, and a case that didn't involve a

paid worker at the Woods. Fleming had agreed. "Mulkern had cancer of the larynx, and you don't get cured from that," Fleming said
later. "No question, I wanted the Boston case to go through, too.
I thought it would look better publicly not to choose an employee
of the Sisters of Providence." Fleming also had shown the medical
records of the two leading candidates — Mulkern and McCord — to
her father, a physician who believed not in miracles but in "good
doctoring." She had spread all the documents in front of her dad on
her family room table in Indianapolis. Using a handheld lens to read
the small type — and jokingly wearing a Sherlock Holmes cap to help
him "look for a miracle" — Fleming's father had skimmed silently
through the two folders and then announced his verdict. He sat up
a bit taller in his chair, put his magnifying glass down, and pointed
to the Mulkern case. "This," the doctor had said, "is phenomenal."

After Marie Kevin and Kathy reached Ambrosi's building, they
climbed a dim flight of stairs and entered a narrow, bright foyer
lined with many shelves of red-bound books — some of the 450
positios Ambrosi had overseen for blesseds and saints, would-be
blesseds and prospective saints, and those who had ultimately been
denied that title by the Vatican. The postulator greeted the nun with
a smile and a kiss on the cheek. Ambrosi understood English but he
almost always spoke in Italian, allowing his hired English translators to paraphrase his words. For this occasion, however, he raised
his eyebrows, held out his hands, and carefully posed an opening
question in Marie Kevin's native language:

"Did you bring me a miracle?"

For a steadfast Catholic who plied his godly trade at the Vatican,
and who drew inspiration by sifting through saintly lives, Dr.
Andrea Ambrosi was surprisingly abrupt when asked a seemingly
logical question.

Did you ever consider becoming a priest?

"No!" he said.

In fact, as a city boy in the 1950s and 1960s, his career fantasy matched the cheer-filled dreams of countless kids on the opposite side of the Atlantic: knocking down buzzer-beaters as a basketball player. Lanky, athletic, and eventually reaching a height of six feet two inches—taller than most Italian men—Ambrosi played high-school hoops and yearned to join A.S. Stella Azzurra (Blue Star), his favorite team in Italy's professional basketball league. He never possessed those kinds of physical gifts, however. What he had was a deep love of God, a passion for family, a tight pack of friends, and an analytic mind well suited to practicing law. Those were his priorities—"probably," he added, "in that order."

He was born in Rome on August 13, 1947, to Alvaro and Giovanna Ambrosi. In fact, the Ambrosi family had been in Rome for "a few" centuries, he said. He was baptized at the Basilica of Saint Vitale, which had been built in the year 400 and consecrated by Pope Innocent I. All the Ambrosi women were homemakers, including his mother, Giovanna, who held, he said, "very close reins" on Andrea and his older sister, Alessandra. Alvaro Ambrosi worked in public administration but detached himself for a few hours each day to relax with his favorite games—tennis and bridge. The parents raised their kids in the strict Catholic faith, and he described his childhood as "stable and serene." As a boy, Andrea Ambrosi attended Catholic boarding schools in Rome, including a Marianist elementary school and the Brothers of La Salle High School. At home, he listened to family members (including his uncle, a Catholic monsignor) tell tales of the laymen who toiled behind the scenes at the Vatican on various sanctification causes. The stories stayed with him.

As he neared adulthood, that type of work—to him, sacred work—seemed an ideal way to put his rigorous religious beliefs into a law practice. He eventually enrolled at the Pontifical Lateran University in Rome, a Catholic college run under direct papal authority. He earned a doctorate degree in civil law as well as canon law, the legal code of the Roman Catholic Church that covered everything from marriage to confession. In 1971, the same year he was married, Ambrosi began an unpaid internship at the Congregation for the Causes of Saints—the special wing of the Roman Curia (the central governing body of the Roman Catholic Church) that oversaw beatifications and canonizations. He was twenty-four years old. The Congregation for the Causes of Saints was then in only its second year of operation. But its roots—and its primary duties—predated the births of Peter the Great, Johann Sebastian Bach, and Isaac Newton, the publication of the King James Bible, and the invention of the flintlock musket.

On January 22, 1588, Pope Sixtus V revolutionized Catholic saint-naming procedures by creating the Sacred Congregation of Rites. He assigned the new department two tasks: regulating the exercise of divine worship among Catholics and handling the causes of prospective saints. Prior to 1588, the vox populi, or "spontaneous local attribution," had remained a primary engine for naming saints. Consequently, that largely scattered, disorganized, and indiscriminate method had churned out thousands of Catholic saints, including some whose lives were merely myths. The Catholic Church had taken its first strides in 1234 to try to centralize saint-naming rituals. It took still another papal decree—issued four centuries later—to finally place full Roman control over the process. In 1634 Pope Urban VIII required that the Vatican be involved in all sainthood causes, through its Congregation of Rites.

That configuration remained virtually the same until May 8, 1969, when Pope Paul VI divided the Congregation of Rites into two new bodies. One—the Congregation for Divine Worship—dealt with liturgical practices within the Church. The other—the

Congregation for the Causes of Saints—became the investigatory arm for alleged miracles. And the new saint-naming wing was further split into three divisions: a judiciary to enforce canon laws, a historical section, and the skeptically minded priests who manned the office of Promoter of the Faith. The Congregation for the Causes of Saints was led by a prefect (a cardinal), a secretary (often an archbishop), and an undersecretary (usually a monsignor). In all, it contained thirty-four voting cardinals, archbishops, and bishops, plus a working staff of twenty-three people. In 1984 the Congregation would add still another section called the Study, which formed future postulators.

In 1971, when Ambrosi began his Vatican internship, canon law stipulated that anyone seeking employment in the canonization field required training at the Congregation. For his tutelage, Ambrosi was assigned to the office of Promoter of the Faith. There, priests toiled to uncover any selfish or secret motives behind a saintly candidate's apparently virtuous or heroic deeds. Equally important, they attempted to expose and suggest natural explanations for all alleged miracles brought to the Vatican as part of sainthood causes. The Promoter, in short, aimed to sniff out fakes, frauds, and those unworthy of eternal celebration. Established in 1708 by Pope Clement XI, the office provided a checks-and-balances system meant to add credibility and caution to what might otherwise be runaway sainthood causes—for example, heavily financed campaigns waged by large congregations, or emotional crusades for deceased nuns or priests who remained feverishly popular in death. Ultimately the Promoter of the Faith was responsible for raising doubts and asking adversarial questions about each cause—questions that had to be answered and addressed by the pope's jury of cardinals and bishops, if the causes were to proceed. As with many archaic Vatican practices, Ambrosi's new workplace carried an official Latin title: *advocatus diaboli.* Devil's Advocate.

When Ambrosi began his internship, the Promoter of the Faith was Father Rafael Perez, a stocky and engaging Spanish monk then pushing seventy. He and four assistants, all canon lawyers, were headquartered in a starkly furnished, unmarked third-floor office above St. Peter's Square. Their workspace also was jammed with hundreds of fat scarlet binders, each containing the arguments, defenses, and alleged proof backing all active sainthood causes. Though his professional label sounded sinister, Perez laughingly admitted in a 1974 interview that his Vatican colleagues teased him about his title, occasionally asking the other priests with whom he lived, "How can you sleep under the same roof as the Devil's Advocate?" But Perez did not consider himself to be "an enemy of saintly people," nor, he added, was he "working day and night to destroy their candidacies." Perez and his staff felt they merely carried a centuries-old duty to "make sure that everything done in the saintly cause is done according to canon law . . . We look into the candidate's whole life," he said. "He may have done great things when he was fifty or sixty, but what about earlier? We attempt to illuminate obscure phases of his career."

That's where the newest man on the team would focus his attention. "I had to present myself there three days a week and was given causes to work on, to pick apart," Ambrosi recalled. He helped prepare and write what essentially amounted to background investigations on would-be blesseds and saints, rooting out any potential weak points in their otherwise sterling lives. Meanwhile, on his Congregation off days, Ambrosi led something of a Vatican double life. He also worked for a pair of canon lawyers in Rome who pushed canonization causes. At that firm, Ambrosi earned enough money to support himself and his wife. He aided the lawyers as they authored *positios*, wrote up backing information for alleged miracles, and answered any questions posed by the Devil's Advocate. This meant, of course, that a portion of Ambrosi's workweek was

devoted to selling certain canonization hopefuls while the remainder was spent arguing against other prospective saints—like a lawyer spending time as both a prosecutor and a defense attorney.

Between the two jobs, Ambrosi said he learned and collected
far more tricks of the trade while he searched for cause flaws. "This
was something very important to my career because I was one of
the very few—there were only three [laymen]—who had this type
of training," he said. "I enjoyed finding the defects." Years later,
his knack for pinpointing possible glitches in sanctification causes
would help Ambrosi as a postulator. He gained a quick eye for
discriminating between the strong causes and the flimsy ones. He
also developed the ability to anticipate and resolve questions about
alleged supernatural cures long before they reached the pope's
medical and theological experts. "To be a good defender, you have
to know how to be a good accuser," he said. His Vatican internship spanned three years. On December 20, 1974, Perez awarded
Ambrosi with a decree stating that he was formally qualified to join
the saint-making profession.

Amid all his on-the-job education, Ambrosi further kindled his
already vibrant faith. Studying the virtues and often harrowing
lives of martyrs and would-be saints inspired him to live up to a
higher standard. Later, during his careful audit of Mother Théodore's years in Indiana, he would be enticed by her emotional resil-
ience, and by how she induced people under stress to trust God
fully, to elevate their own grace despite bitter living conditions.
He reveled in the glow of helping a congregation see its founder,
or a cherished former priest or nun, reach saintly status. Serving
the Church gave him an unmatched thrill. But in 1983 Pope John
Paul II unveiled a series of sweeping and still-controversial reforms
that helped Ambrosi turn his spiritual fire into a far more lucrative
living.

As a young Polish priest, Karol Wojtyla had made a special

pilgrimage to post–World War II Italy, trekking southward to the tiny town of San Giovanni Rotondo, near the shores of the Adriatic Sea. There, in 1947, he confessed his sins to a charismatic monk, Pio of Pietrelcina—known as "Padre Pio"—who claimed to possess the marks called stigmata, or Christlike wounds on his palms. Fifteen years later, Padre Pio prayed for one of Wojtyla's friends who recently had been diagnosed with cancer. The cancer soon went into remission, and Wojtyla believed Pio's prayer had spawned a medical miracle. In 1978 Wojtyla, a firm believer in supernatural moments, was elected to lead the Roman Catholic Church as Pope John Paul II. During his lengthy reign, he transformed the Vatican into what some critics later dubbed a "saint factory." On January 25, 1983, John Paul II unleashed that saintly assembly line by issuing the apostolic constitution *Divinus Perfectionis Magister*, which dramatically reshaped the rules for beatifications and canonizations. Boiled down, the pope eliminated the powers of the Promoter of the Faith and his Devil's Advocate's function, and he halved the number of miracles required for sainthood from four to two. The reforms, John Paul maintained, were meant to make the saint-making process faster, more collegial, less costly, and more productive. He sought to sell the Catholic faith by naming more saints from all corners of the globe.

As part of his overhaul, John Paul made one more significant move. For centuries, canon law had mandated that only priests could serve as postulators—the specially schooled clerics whose role was to examine, collect, and research historical and theological material about prospective saints and then present their cases for canonization to the Holy See. But after January 25, 1983, laypersons were eligible to work as postulators if they possessed the proper canon law degrees and training. Ambrosi was perfectly positioned to become one of the first postulators to pitch miracles to the Vatican while wearing a tie instead of a priest's collar.

During his first three years as a postulator, Ambrosi slowly fashioned a one-man canon-law firm. At first his income was too low to rent an office, so his Rome apartment doubled as a workspace. By 1986, however, he was caring for enough sainthood causes to afford the three-room flat on Via di Tor Millina, a prime location within walking distance of Vatican City. With each cause taking years if not decades to complete—and with Ambrosi reaping legal fees (or "honoraria," as he called them) from the rabid backers of those would-be saints—his business was solidified. Eventually he would hire a series of young women to transcribe and translate reams of witness interviews, medical records, and saintly historical accounts that spanned eight languages. One was Italian (later replaced by an American woman), one Swiss, and the third Ukrainian. He preferred working with women because they followed his directions without question, as one of those assistants later explained. For a time, Ambrosi also employed one of his three children—his daughter, Angelica, who also had earned a doctorate degree in canon law. While at the firm, Angelica wrote *positios* for her father.

To locate and land causes, Ambrosi sometimes relied on his Vatican contacts. Later he created a slick website to globally market his Ambrosi Legal Firm in nine languages (including Latin), with a description of his services, an explanation of saint-related canon laws, a long list of his successes, and three photos of a smiling Ambrosi greeting or listening to Pope Benedict XVI.

As a young postulator, he picked up a number of German causes, including an ongoing canonization push for a World War II nun with a nursing degree who had earned the nickname "the Angel of Love." In 1936 Sister Maria Euthymia Üffing was assigned by her order to work at a hospital near Düsseldorf. Her duties there intensified when Nazi forces began invading nations throughout Europe, Asia, and North Africa. As Allied fighters later regained that ground and enclosed Germany, Sister Maria Euthymia was given a new task. In 1943 she was placed in charge of a special isolation ward at the hospital—a wooden shack that housed British, French, Russian, and Polish prisoners of war who were ill with infectious diseases. According to the testimonies of some of those prisoners, the nun risked her own health to treat the POWs, spending hours at their bedsides in an effort to make them feel safe and at home. She died from cancer on September 9, 1955. The day after her death, several nuns gathered to pray at her open casket. One of the sisters had recently suffered severe burns when her hand became entangled in the rollers of an ironing machine. Standing at the coffin, the nun prayed to Sister Maria Euthymia to mend her wounds. According to Vatican records, the skin on the nun's hand was inexplicably healed soon after her plea. Forty-five years later—with Ambrosi heading her cause as postulator—Pope John Paul II deemed that skin restoration a miracle. On October 7, 2001, Maria Euthymia was beatified. In the annals of Catholic lore, Maria Euthymia's story had been largely obscure beyond her small band of advocates. But Ambrosi had spotted deep potential after reviewing her contributions—and he had delivered the goods. In fact, Pope John Paul's speech during her beatification ceremony hinted at the tall odds her cause had faced: "Her life shows us that seemingly small things can be very important in God's eyes. From the human viewpoint this sister was not a star in the limelight, but her silent work was a ray of light to many people that is still shining today."

Ambrosi's reputation as a razor-sharp defender of causes spread quickly through the American Catholic community via word of mouth. In addition to the highest-profile U.S. causes still under his watch—those for Archbishop Fulton Sheen and Cardinal Terence Cooke—Ambrosi simultaneously served as postulator for a bevy of other active and weighty American canonization campaigns. There was Father Patrick Peyton, an Irish-born priest and early multimedia evangelist who used radio, television, films, and a stable of Hollywood stars to sell his "Family Rosary Crusade," and who coined the motto "The family that prays together stays together." There was Father Nelson Baker, the Buffalo, New York, native; Civil War veteran; and prosperous grain entrepreneur who later joined the priesthood, applying his business acumen to a slew of charity ventures, including homes for orphaned boys, unwed mothers, and infants. There was Henriette DeLille, born to a white father and a mixed-race mother in slavery-era New Orleans, who had taught school classes to nonwhites (defying the laws of the time), and who, along with two other free women of color, had launched an order of nuns, Sisters of the Holy Family. And there was Bishop Simon Bruté, the first bishop of the then-Diocese of Vincennes, who in the late 1830s had asked a community of French sisters to send six of their best nuns to a farm clearing in the Indiana forest where they later built a Catholic outpost, educated thousands of American children, and molded six generations of religious women.

The often-stalled canonization hopes for the Woods' magnetic leader became Ambrosi's responsibility on July 26, 1994. He got the job through one of his old Vatican allies—a priest from Brooklyn and a key player at the Congregation for the Causes of Saints since 1981. Monsignor Robert Sarno had long been the only American in the Vatican's saint-naming wing. Sarno was a theological stickler who soon would become involved in the exceptionally swift and perhaps boosterish drive to beatify and canonize the world's most famous nun, Mother Teresa of Calcutta. Sarno often served as a go-to source for U.S. media members reporting on sanctification work, appearing on CNN and the CBS program *60 Minutes*. He could be prickly with the media if they asked uninformed questions, yet he could sermonize poetically about the modern need for saints and the meaning of miracles. Moreover, the well-respected Sarno was a staunch fan of Ambrosi—and of Mother Théodore.

By 1992 the Sisters of Providence had grown frustrated with

their latest (and eighth) postulator in Rome, Father Antonio Ricciardi. That same year Vatican appraisers had finally declared Mother Théodore "Venerable," meaning her life was deemed "heroic in virtue"—the critical gateway to possible beatification. At the Woods, however, celebration over the announcement was tempered by some grumbles. The sisters were incensed that they were never told of the pivotal decision by Ricciardi, their Rome-based advocate and a man to whom they were paying money to propel the cause. They were alerted well after the event by fellow Sisters of Providence in Belgium who had read about the development in their local newspaper. Ricciardi had been Mother Théodore's postulator since 1980, and the aging Franciscan priest was apparently "not well, and obviously not in the condition to handle this case anymore," recalled Sister Nancy Nolan, the convent's general superior at the time. "We hardly ever heard from him except that we'd get a bill every once in a while. So after that, we decided, 'this is too much.'"

Not long after the founder's veneration, Sister Nancy dialed up an old friend from Brooklyn who had attained a lofty position at the Vatican, Monsignor Sarno.

"We don't feel Father Ricciardi is in any kind of health to continue with this," she complained.

Sarno was quite familiar with the allegedly miraculous healing of Sister Mary Theodosia Mug in 1908, and he was similarly unhappy that the probe into her cure had been shelved and shunned in Rome for almost one hundred years. He offered a solution.

"You need Dr. Ambrosi," Sarno had said. "He can look at cases that come in and immediately see whether or not they're worthy of being sent on. He knows how to prepare and present the [miracle] cases. You really need to get Dr. Ambrosi on this."

Sister Nancy asked Sarno if he would be willing to ask Ambrosi to consider taking control of Mother Théodore's cause. Sarno readily agreed to make the call.

After getting the proposal from Sarno, Ambrosi ambled through the daily pack of tourists milling in St. Peter's Square, made a right-hand turn between two newsstands laced with papal postcards and key chains, and entered a four-story blond-brick building — headquarters of the Congregation for the Causes of Saints. Directly across the street stood an identical four-story blond-brick building — also filled with Vatican officials with various duties. And at the far end of the solemn piazza, the opulent dome of St. Peter's Basilica shimmered. He took an elevator to the third floor and stepped into a cold corridor of spartan offices. In one of those unadorned rooms, he sat at a table. He opened the thick file of witness testimonies and medical records describing the eighty-six-year-old cancer rejuvenation experienced by Mary Theodosia on a cold autumn night at the Woods. He read a curt note clipped to the case file — a message apparently left by the past postulator. Its words stunned Ambrosi.

"Not worthy of consideration," it read.

Ambrosi knew the postulator who had authored that damning message, and he respected him. He also knew Sarno and thought highly of the monsignor's positive opinion of the case. The note perhaps explained why the cause had stalled.

Ambrosi sat frozen for a few minutes, conflicted. "I waited a long time to open that," he later admitted. But soon after he began scanning the material, Ambrosi suspected he was indeed looking at a long-ignored miracle. The past postulator, he believed, had been horribly mistaken. Eventually he also devoured many of the zesty triumphs and dark tribulations that colored Mother Théodore's life story. As always, he took a moment to tumble all the pertinent medical and theological equations through his mind before rendering his own verdict on the supernatural promise of the cure and the potency of the cause. His evaluation didn't take long.

Sarno later phoned Sister Nancy at her campus office and relayed the decision: Ambrosi would indeed become their new postulator.

But he wouldn't come cheap.

How expensive was Ambrosi? When presented a series of basic questions about the firm's commercial aspects, one of Ambrosi's assistants said that he did not discuss his fees, his honoraria, his profits, his office budget, or his own salary. He did not and would never make those figures public, the assistant said. When asked directly about his fees, Ambrosi responded, "I can say that the amount of payment that is applied by me is that of a normal lawyer; however, in our sacred forum there are no legal procedures that can be carried out in just a few hours. My case is rather unique since I am a lawyer who travels all over the world . . . [with] a staff that speaks eight languages." And Ambrosi saw his firm not as a business enterprise, the assistant said, but as his "life's work." Fee payments came to the postulator directly from the congregations backing the causes, as did reimbursement checks to cover the substantial travel expenses incurred by Ambrosi and the assistants who accompanied his trips abroad to vet facts and to interview survivors, witnesses, and doctors. The Congregation for the Causes of Saints stipulated that canonization crusades could not be brought forward unless and until the would-be saints' promoters had set up a fund to pay all the bills, according to one of Ambrosi's assistants. The Vatican also set aside reserve money to help finance those causes launched by poorer churches or congregations, the assistant said.

At the Woods, questions about money—particularly about Ambrosi's costs—were deemed off limits to the public, particularly among some of those footing the bills. In addition to the congregation's treasurer—who refused to release financial figures, and said she never revealed that accounting even to community leaders—the nun who had hired Ambrosi said she could not recall his fee structure. "We had, in the congregation, a separate fund that was set up so people [including local parishioners and alumni of the Catholic schools where the sisters had taught for decades] could donate to

Mother Théodore's cause. That was the fund from which we took money to pay a postulator," Sister Nancy Nolan said. "I hate to say it, but I don't recall how much. I never felt that we paid an exorbitant amount." Sister Marie Kevin also shrugged off a question about Ambrosi's charges: "I can't name the total cost. I believe everything we had to spend was donated by people."

But Marie Kevin's friend and traveling companion—and, later, her vital partner in shaping a case for the alleged second miracle—did remember some of those legal bills. According to Kathy Fleming, Marie Kevin mailed a number of five-figure checks to Ambrosi. She saw at least one check written for $40,000 and another for $11,000. "It's an extremely expensive process. Very expensive," Fleming said. "And I think it is way more expensive than even Sister Marie Kevin understands it to be. She's the type of person who will go in to a store to buy a new suit, and it bloody well had better be cheap or on sale or she wouldn't be buying it. But she could requisition a $40,000 check to send to the postulator like it was nothing. And her attitude was like, 'I have to do it, so I'll do it.'"

As a businessman, Ambrosi was shrewd. He capitalized on his exclusive credentials. One example: his title. Early in his career, Ambrosi realized that American doctors—whom he needed to help build many of his biggest miracle cases—typically were reluctant to speak with lawyers. If they heard that a lawyer from Rome was flying to the United States to interrogate them about a past medical case, "oftentimes they would run in the other direction," Ambrosi said. So he tweaked his professional designation. Equipped with his doctorate degree from the Pontifical Lateran University in Rome, the Italian lawyer began presenting himself as "Doctor Ambrosi" to ease tensions with the American physicians. His business cards, his website, and his employees similarly used that title.

After more than twenty years as a professional postulator, Ambrosi had two homes, along with his Piazza Navona office.

During the week he lived in an apartment in central Rome, just one block from the Tiber River and a short stroll down the hill from the lush, expansive Villa Borghese gardens. Fleming, who visited the flat, described it as "palatial." On the weekends he traveled with his wife to their second home, thirty-eight miles north of Rome—a house located in the historic village of Caprarola. He had adored that small town since childhood, when he first visited there with his family to inhale its Renaissance charms and fresh air. Tucked into rolling, tree-covered, volcanic hills, Caprarola included the five-hundred-year-old, pentagon-shaped Farnese Palace along with the Church of Santa Teresa. Built in 1623, the Church of Santa Teresa was based on a drawing by Carlo Rainaldi, a seventeenth-century architect who designed many famous Roman churches, including Sant'Agnese in Agone, the basilica near Ambrosi's office.

Ambrosi often attended Mass at the Church of Santa Maria. On Sunday mornings he would worship while gazing at the trio of original, imposing masterpieces that adorned the front of the chapel. The paintings were by three leading Baroque artists, including Guido Reni, whose striking creation hung just above the main altar. Its title: *Madonna del Carmine and the Saints*.

† † †

A few minutes before reaching Ambrosi's office to muse about miracles, a momentarily jarring event befell the seventy-seven-year-old nun and scared her traveling companion. Marie Kevin collapsed in Piazza Navona.

She tripped over a curb and tumbled awkwardly, smacking loudly into the concrete surface of the outdoor artists' mall. Years later the two women would offer markedly different versions of the spill. Marie Kevin said, "I barely remember it," adding that Fleming "makes everything sound dramatic." Fleming, however, recalls being quite frightened for her friend. Crouching over the crumpled woman in the piazza, Fleming instantly flashed back to her doctor father's medical advice: don't immediately touch an older person after a fall; if their sudden contact with the ground cracked a hip or a leg bone, trying to help them up could further displace the bones.

"Can you move your legs? Can you move your hip?" Fleming asked with worry.

"I don't feel any pain at all," Marie Kevin said, glancing back up at her.

Fleming became silent. Her mind raced. *Oh Lord*, she thought, *she might have severed her spinal column.*

"I just stood there looking at her," Fleming would say later. And then the ex-nun fleetingly believed they might need a small miracle to complete their mission. She made a private plea to the woman of the hour. *Mother Théodore,* Fleming prayed, *you've got to help us through this!*

Two Italian men raced over to the sprawled, white-haired woman, gently clasped each of her arms, and carefully helped her stand. After brushing the roadway grit from her clothing, Marie Kevin resumed her short walk toward Ambrosi's front door, embarrassed but otherwise fine.

The tale was merely a footnote to an otherwise decisive day. But it raised two questions—one theological, one scientific. Was it proper to ask saints (or prospective saints) for relatively smaller favors, like mending a possibly injured leg—or for the strength to go through with an operation? Put another way: for people of faith, were there—or should there be—limits on the kinds of miracles they sought? And, more broadly, did miracles still possess a legitimate foothold in the modern world, at a time when old mysteries (such as how our genes overpower life-threatening illnesses) were being solved as science and technology surged?

As part of his Vatican career, Monsignor Sarno had long brooded over such eternally slippery questions. The balding priest

with a faint Brooklyn accent was a physical study in human precision. On a warm, late-winter Tuesday morning in 2009, his writing
desk was fastidiously arranged: on the open page of his monthly
calendar, previous days were neatly slashed to note their passing;
incoming white envelopes were sleekly piled, ready for reading;
and a scarlet-covered, bound *positio* sat open, a pen tip marking
the sentence where he had momentarily halted his perusal. A second desk, pushed against his writing table, held a computer and
keyboard. A crucifix was centered above his office window, which
offered a perfect view of St. Peter's Square, three floors below. He
wore a short-sleeved black shirt beneath a black sweater vest, and a
priest's collar. When he spoke, he used lyrical tones that sounded as
rhythmic as a well-practiced sermon, and he punctuated his points
by slowly jabbing a clenched left hand, inside which he clutched
his eyeglasses. The framework of his voiced thoughts was equally
meticulous, and as his voice echoed off vacant Vatican walls, he
began to explain his views on miracles, particularly their role in the
beatification and canonization process.

"What is the miracle? It is God's confirmation that the person is
in heaven, and that they have God's ear," Sarno said.

Under Catholic doctrine, miracles were seen as divine rubber
stamps—supernatural signals that prospective saints were worthy
of beatification and canonization, otherworldly proof that the venerated dead could hear intercessory prayers and could ask God to
intervene in earthly problems.

For whom were miracles meant? Not just for the lone, fortunate
recipient, Sarno said. "We believe the miracle events are given for
the entire Church and for our entire humanity."

Purported miracles—specifically, gauging the competency of
miracle examinations performed by local dioceses—were also part
of Sarno's job. (He had taught procedural law at the Pontifical Gre-
gorian University; his doctoral dissertation was used by Catholic

dioceses around the world as a guide for the inquiries made in canonization causes.) When alleged miracles were presented to the
Congregation for the Causes of Saints—as occurred about twenty
to twenty-five times each year—staff members verified that canon
law was indeed followed by the local tribunals that first tested the
alleged miracles. If mistakes were detected, the cases were denied, or
sent back to their home parishes for supplemental work. The Congregation was much like a judicial review board, double-checking
that the correct medical and theological questions were posed to
the right people during the trials, and that the documentation was
complete.

Ninety-nine percent of all presented miracles, Sarno estimated, were medical in nature—largely because the cures had been
documented by doctors and nurses. On rare occasions, the Vatican weighed nonmedical miraculous claims. One case involved a
1988 flash of superhuman strength allegedly exhibited by a Peruvian sailor who simultaneously managed to save himself and his
crewmates aboard their leaking, sinking submarine. As that sailor
struggled to close a door against a sudden gush of ocean water, he
prayed to a long-dead nun famous in his homeland. In that moment
he somehow sealed the hatch and saved the boat. A naval investigation later found that no human possessed the physical strength to
overcome thousands of pounds of water pressure. On June 6, 2003,
Pope John Paul II beatified the nun to whom the sailor had prayed,
Sister Marija Petrovic.

"Crying statues? Apparitions? That's not our concern here,"
Sarno said. "We never ask doctors if this was 'a miracle.' We ask
them for the flow of events. We try to find a direct link between
prayer and cure. The goal is to get to the truth."

After more than two decades of investigating, Sarno's personal
truth on the topic was globally broadcast in June 2002, aired during a CNN story on Padre Pio's canonization campaign. In an

on-camera interview, CNN reporter Christiane Amanpour asked of Sarno: "Is there such a thing [as miracles]?"

"That's a strange question to ask someone whose life is dedicated to studying the possibility and the reality of miracles," he replied. "I believe in miracles."

But in the realm of miracles, did faith empower or permit the prayerful to ask a saint—or a saintly candidate—for the strength to undergo an operation, or for help in finding a job or a missing wallet? Were there boundaries to what was an acceptable prayer for intercession? Sarno had been asked that question before, because prayers came in all forms and because woes that perhaps seemed crucial and desperate to some people were, of course, all relative to the larger circumstances of their lives. Moreover, there was a theological issue at play: many Catholics believed people should never request favors directly from the saints, that they should only ask the saints to pray for them. So, was it inappropriate to ask Saint Anthony to help us find our lost car keys?

"Well," Sarno said in a 2008 interview, "there is always the problem of personal piety and popular piety, and making sure they are in keeping with the teaching of the Church. It is up to the bishops to see that people understand the Doctrine of Communion of the Saints, and how it teaches that the Church in heaven and the Church here on Earth is one family, united in faith and hope and love. Therefore we pray with each other and for each other. In reality, we should be praying for the saints to join us in praying to God. . . . The saints do help guard us, and I don't suppose there is any harm in asking Saint Anthony to help us find our keys, as long as we understand that doesn't mean Saint Catherine couldn't also help us find them."

Certainly, there's no dearth of saints or blesseds to whom the faithful can pray—more than ten thousand have been named (though no exact head count exists) throughout Catholic history and within the Roman Martyrology, according to Church estimates. During the twenty-six-year pontificate of John Paul II—when beatification and canonization rules were loosened—the pope beatified more than 1,300 people and canonized another 482—more than the combined number named by his predecessors spanning the past four centuries. Though Pope Benedict XVI returned some restrictions to the sanctification process, the Vatican had, as of 2008, a backlog of some 2,200 pending miracle claims still to judge. But under Benedict's papacy, the Vatican's fever to seek and approve miracles seemed to have cooled a degree. Benedict believed God could work miracles, as he told a crowd in St. Peter's Square in January 2008, adding that "where Jesus comes, the Creator Spirit brings life and men are cured of diseases." Yet compared to his forerunner—a crowd-rousing superstar and a faith-driven marketer—the German pontiff was considered by observers to be more professorial and more cerebral than John Paul. Benedict was also a scrupulous theologian. Under his watch, the Vatican demanded more rigor in the saint verification process, emphasizing, for example, the need to show that candidates had "a true reputation for holiness" long before they were ever considered for beatification. Some Vatican observers dubbed Benedict "the pope of reason." Rome-based Raphaela Schmid, a German philosopher who had studied Benedict's writings, contended the pope had reached a circumspect balance between Catholicism's quest for intellectual respect and the religion's showier displays, like relics and miracles, and that he had effectively established, Schmid said, that "both have a place in the Church."

At the Vatican, Sarno readily acknowledged that technological leaps were shifting the ancient work of miracle corroboration, particularly among the doctors at the Consulta Medica. "Our experts," he said, "tend to be more critical and more precise." Medical miracles were simply becoming harder to prove. Physicians had a better grasp of the molecular foundation of diseases such as cancer, and fewer health events—no matter how rare—were left unexplained. Scientists had discovered that in some cases cancer cells were spontaneously eliminated when specific genes switched on or off. Some of last century's overnight disease recoveries—its Vatican-endorsed "miracles"—may not have seemed so medically mysterious to modern doctors. Once more, though, the Roman Catholic Church had ready a countermove to keep its saint-making branch bustling. Father Paul Molinari, who had served as the postulator general for the Jesuit Order, admitted that proving the inexplicability of certain medical cures soon would grow even more laborious as DNA researchers uncloaked additional genetic truths. He and other postulators had suggested that instead of requiring two medical miracles for sainthood, the Vatican could instead judge a candidate's "moral miracles"—how their immaculate ideals, heroic acts, and holy examples inspired other men and women to live differently.

For the skeptics of Church-approved medical miracles, such a fundamental course change would have been welcome. Some of the most famous miracle doubters—including three noted philosophers of the seventeenth and eighteenth centuries—had long collectively stumbled on the same point: nature's laws were hard and fast, permanent and sacrosanct; they didn't bend, they couldn't be momentarily lifted, and they didn't change with time. Miracles, by definition, were events ascribed to God that occurred "above" the laws of nature, according to the *Catholic Encyclopedia*. For more nuance, Pope John Paul II offered this nugget during a January 1988 homily at the Paul VI Auditorium: "Miracles are not in opposition with the forces and laws of nature but constitute only a certain experimental suspension of their ordinary function, not their annulment." But that, said spiritual cynics, was exactly the illogical rub. Nature's laws could not be postponed, could not be even briefly evaded. Gravity pulled, the Earth spun, living things aged and died—infinitely and always. "Nothing, then, comes to pass in nature in contravention to her universal laws . . . she keeps a fixed and immutable order," wrote Benedict Spinoza, a seventeenth-century rationalist. "We may, then, be absolutely certain that every event which is truly described in Scripture necessarily happened like everything else, according to natural laws." In other words, Spinoza felt Jesus and his disciples were subject to nature's principles like all other humans, making it impossible for Christ to stroll atop water. In the 1700s the Scottish economist and philosopher David Hume held that the laws of nature were established by the "firm and unalterable experience" of people and, further, that because miracles "violate" natural principles, "the proof against miracles . . . is as entire as any argument from experience can possibly be imagined." Simply put, our collective truths about living in this world had been reinforced, minute by minute, since humans took their first breaths; those truths constituted our reality, and there was no debating reality, Hume argued. Finally, there was Immanuel Kant, a German philosopher and one of the most celebrated thinkers of the Enlightenment. In his 1793 book *Religion within the Limits of Reason Alone,* Kant also leaned on the universal laws but took a more mathematical approach. Those who believe in miracles, he wrote, "soften the blow" against rationality "by holding that [miracles] happen but seldom . . . How seldom? Once in a hundred years?" Under nature's laws, events happened either routinely or never. Therefore, Kant contended, miracles happened either routinely or never. Accepting miracles as a daily occurrence "is not at all compatible with reason," Kant wrote. "To venture beyond these limits is rashness."

At the heart of science, the repeated surveillance and measurement of natural phenomena had helped form the laws of nature. Scientists made their conclusions after seeing and documenting patterns. In the world of microscopes and empirical data, observation and repetition reigned. Even Christian apologist and author Dr. Norman Geisler conceded this point in a 2002 article titled *Miracles and Modern Scientific Thought*: "Unless there is a direct correlation between the presence and absence of the cause and the presence and absence of the effect, then there is no scientific basis for believing it is the cause." Were miracles, Geisler then asked, strictly a matter of faith? "Simply because miracles are not subject to repetition does not mean they do not occur. After all, a hole-in-one [in golf] has happened; desperation shots have gone through the hoop, and some have won at the lottery on their first ticket," Geisler wrote. Science—specifically astronomy—also had put its faith in a broadly accepted model based on a singular event: the "Big Bang." According to that theory, twelve to fourteen billion years ago, our universe began as a hot, dense state, called a *singularity,* only a few millimeters across, from which it expanded into our vast cosmos. Scientists believed the event occurred even though they were not there to see, hear, or analyze it. "So all the theist needs to admit is that singular events [such as miracles] are not subject to scientific analysis. That is, there may be no way to have a scientific understanding of them; they may be understood only by 'faith,'" Geisler wrote. "In this sense, what the non-supernaturalist would call a 'fluke' the supernaturalist may choose (by faith) to see as 'the hand of God.'"

Sarno, the bespectacled priest who studied alleged miracles at his orderly Vatican desk, echoed Geisler's pro-faith hypothesis with the verve of a preacher in the pulpit. If the Holy See's hired medical experts affirmed that a medical cure was not scientifically explicable, Sarno explained, the Vatican's theologians asked the next vital question: was there a cause-and-effect relationship between the requesting of intercession and the unexplainable recovery? "And that is where the essence of the miracle lies," Sarno said. "That requires faith. That is where faith takes over and where science ends. We have to be courageous enough to admit that science is not the only truth in human existence."

                                    † † †

In the tight confines of Ambrosi's book-lined office foyer, Fleming immediately witnessed the friendly spark between the postulator and the nun. "A lot of electricity between them," she later recalled. "He's charming as all get-out, and he always hugged and kissed her when he saw her." To Ambrosi, meetings with Marie Kevin were more like family gatherings.

But the postulator also saw something beyond the nun's gentle affection. A torrid determination radiated from her eyes and in her words. After posing his icebreaking question about whether she had brought him a miracle, Marie Kevin ruffled her papers and offered something of a declaration: "We are going to get her canonized. And this is what we have to get it done."

The group moved into Ambrosi's softly lit office. Marie Kevin and her friend were nestled side by side on a red divan that faced the window. Ambrosi sat at his desk. Near Ambrosi sat his English interpreter, Francesca Lorenzetti, a woman in her late twenties with an American mother and an Italian father, who had graduated from the American University of Rome.

Finally, Marie Kevin began reciting her short list of wonders. She spoke with exactitude, pausing often to allow Lorenzetti time to repeat in Italian. Ambrosi leaned in. He could understand English adequately, but for a judgment so delicate—and, to him, so utterly solemn—he wanted to ensure that he grasped every pathological morsel, each human subtlety embedded within the individual medical mysteries. So while he heard the nun's English words, he watched and listened to Lorenzetti's translations.

Marie Kevin mentioned three promising cases involving children, including two who had been deemed healthy several years after contracting forms of cancer, and a four-year-old boy who was still living—beyond doctors' predictions—with a rare genetic disorder that left him unable to stand, lift his head, or even wiggle his fingers. In all three instances the parents had prayed to Mother Théodore to save their babies. Ambrosi listened patiently, nodding along with each description, though his typically emotive face didn't reveal his private opinions on that trio of prospects. Going into the meeting, Marie Kevin knew the two young cancer patients had probably not been in remission long enough to be considered medically cured, and the sick little boy would never be physically healthy. She moved on.

Marie Kevin revealed the two biggest guns on her miracle agenda. Each tale was rich in prayerful drama and white-coat intrigue. In one story, she told of a Baptist caretaker who, while trying to choose between blindness and a risky cornea transplant, had offered a bumbling, winter-morning prayer at the Woods basilica. That man had awakened a day later with an eye that felt better and ultimately regained full vision. And she chronicled how a Boston telephone technician in the first stages of treatment for a lime-sized, cancerous throat tumor had been informed—as he clutched a Mother Théodore relic—that the growth had somehow vanished.

Fleming studied Ambrosi as he soaked up the peculiar details spilling from Marie Kevin's mouth. She watched him and read him, and the school principal knew right away that their case list had been trimmed to two. "He is so animated. When you talk to him, his face just lights up," Fleming recalled. "And he was very expressive about the larynx and about the eye."

Ambrosi now had to whittle those two strong candidates down to a single robust, airtight case. He instructed Marie Kevin to continue communicating with the archdiocese tribunals in both Indianapolis and Boston. And, according to Marie Kevin's own notes from the meeting, Ambrosi directed her to ask the doctors involved in the McCord and Mulkern cases if either cure was "scientifically explainable," and if it was, to ask how it could be explained. In her notes, she underlined those last five words. At the close of the one-hour meeting, Ambrosi didn't disclose whether he favored McCord or Mulkern, but Marie Kevin's notes from their session reflected that the postulator perhaps tipped his hand. Ambrosi told the women that he and Lorenzetti would travel to the United States the following March, where he would speak personally to the two men at the center of the alleged miracles, as well as to their doctors. And to accomplish these interviews, Ambrosi said he would come to Indiana, the notes indicated. Mulkern would have to fly in from Boston.

"I think he was leaning toward McCord," Fleming said later.

Marie Kevin also sensed the same.

"I still don't feel comfortable with Phil McCord's case," she later would confide to Kathy. "And I know that's the one he [Ambrosi] wants to process."

After exchanging good-bye hugs, Fleming suggested the two women walk back to Piazza Navona to celebrate Ambrosi's urgency and fervor—and to salute the fresh energy that seemed to have nudged Mother Théodore's cause closer to the saintly threshold. Because Marie Kevin did not drink wine, the women went in search of Italian ice cream cones to toast their success. One week later the two women boarded a return flight to Indiana.

Back at the Woods, however, where the cause had long divided the sisters, the nun who rose from her deathbed to seek a clinching miracle would soon be forced to conquer some of those old sanctification foes—and defeat her own rising doubts.

CHAPTER EIGHT

The Choice

When the crisis of faith came, Kathy Fleming was ready to repay an old debt. The former wide-eyed nun—now a worldly wise school principal approaching retirement—possessed the perfect words to save and spark her wounded friend.

Just as that friend had done for Fleming some fifty years earlier, when they met at the back door of a convent house on the east side of Indianapolis.

"I am going to stop doing this," Sister Marie Kevin suddenly divulged to a stunned Fleming one day at the Woods in 2001. As Fleming recalled, Marie Kevin said, "I can't take it anymore."

"This" was her beloved work as promoter. "It" was the opposition, the 17 percent of the Sisters of Providence (roughly seventy-five members of the congregation) who were offended by, hostile to, or just ambivalent about the pursuit of the cause for two primary reasons: men and money. They were unwilling to have their order embroiled in a process they considered an extension of the male-hierarchical control of religious women, and they felt the chase was a colossal waste of money. The anti-cause faction was an old legion at the Woods. The volume of their displeasure seemed to ratchet higher each time the crusade neared a critical stage, such as the 1998 beatification. After the Vatican approved the first miracle, the Sisters of Providence leadership council convened the nuns to discuss and deliberate how they would honor their founder's impending beatification in Rome. But that gathering soon shifted into a referendum on the cause itself as both sides aired their convictions, recalled Sister Denise Wilkinson, who was in attendance. (In 2006 Sister Denise was elected as the Woods' eighteenth general superior; her five-year term would run until 2011.) "We had a meeting, as we always do. We hashed it out. Once the decision was made to go ahead, the decision was made, and then we supported it [publicly, as a group]," Sister Denise said. "That's what our call of obedience asks us to do. And we talked directly about that: if we were going to go ahead with this decision, if that was the decision of the group, then all of us would support it in our own ways. We would celebrate it as a congregation."

Three specific vows, taken by the women when they commit to the sisterhood, were meant to define their calling and help them emulate the life of Jesus Christ: poverty, chastity, and obedience. In joining a community where they were supplied clothing, food, and a bed, they had promised to surrender any hunger to acquire personal riches or expensive comforts, freeing them to serve other people. They had promised not to marry or engage in romantic entanglements or sex so that all their love could be given to God. And just as Christ had obeyed God, the nuns all had promised to follow the laws and commands of their superiors.

But even at a tranquil convent in the Indiana forest, sometimes promises were broken, and some grudges never died. The breach between the pro-cause and anti-cause sisters even drew a grinning mention during a special 1998 beatification Mass held at the Church of the Immaculate Conception for those sisters who couldn't travel to Rome for the ceremony—and for those who purposely decided to skip it. When previous general superior Nancy Nolan, then president of Guerin College Preparatory High School in River Grove, Illinois, was asked to offer a homily at the service, she felt the dicey topic had to be broached because, she said later, "there were a substantial number of sisters who were not up for pursuing the canonization." During her homily, she said, "We couldn't have unanimous consent [on issues at the Woods] even in the sixties, so why should the nineties be any different?" Laughter rose from the pews. "I don't think we ever agree on anything," Nolan later reflected. "That is the way with educated women. We have educated women — as Mother Théodore did — to stand up for themselves, to fend for themselves. But I always knew that every Sister of Providence had great love for the congregation. They would put down their lives for the congregation. The Woods was a very strong glue that held us together." Near the end of her leadership term in 1996, Sister Nancy said she realized the cause had achieved unstoppable momentum. Besides, she added years later, "Who was I to say we wouldn't want the universal Church to declare her a saint?" Still, Sister Nancy admitted she "could understand all the reservations" that lingered. The former superior, who had selected both Dr. Andrea Ambrosi and Sister Marie Kevin to their key positions, tried to rally her fellow sisters at the 1998 beatification Mass by pointing out that "the canonization really isn't for Mother Théodore, it is really for us and it should give us a renewed spirit and renewed energy to follow her example and carry out the mission. Canonization really doesn't put her one step higher in heaven. All it does is call attention to the kind of woman she was — which is the kind of woman we're all striving to be. If this canonization doesn't transform us, if it can't enable us to transform others, then it is in vain."

Her stirring words didn't quell all the doubters. By 2001 some of the most resistant sisters were on the convent's six-woman leadership team. "That was a real struggle," recalled Sister Ann Margaret O'Hara, who was elected general superior in 2001. "Because we knew that the people who wanted us to go forward had absolutely valid reasons, and the people who wanted us not to go forward had absolutely valid reasons. And there were people who felt that way among the council members." Although the congregation had agreed to collectively support the pursuit, the individual feelings of the anti-cause nuns could never be completely hushed. Those conflicting attitudes ultimately shoved Marie Kevin to a breaking point, Fleming recalled.

"Some of the major superiors were for it, but some of them weren't. I think Marie Kevin had to grovel [to the anti-cause superiors], and to what they had to say," Fleming later said. "I don't think she ever lost faith, but it was very difficult for her, and she questioned whether she was the right person to do it, and she thought maybe somebody else would be able to please everybody. Well, we all know that's totally impossible. Ninety percent of the sisters have great respect for Marie Kevin. But there's always that small group, and she is the type of person who would be sensitive to that small group. . . . I think the Devil throws up a lot of obstacles in people's lives. She had a lot of obstacles.

"She let me know a little [about] what was bothering her," Fleming recalled. "But she would find it very difficult to state her feelings [to anyone else] because she's so loyal to the Sisters of Providence. She would not freely acknowledge their weaknesses."

Indeed, when asked, nine years later, about her moment of crisis, Marie Kevin denied that she had ever contemplated leaving her post as promoter, saying only, "I knew there was resistance, but it never bothered me."

Marie Kevin likewise never revealed her frustrations to Sister Denise Wilkinson. But the future general superior was aware that Marie Kevin found any form of sisterly dissension troubling, later saying, "She's a real woman of the Church. I don't mean that the people who felt differently, or saw [the cause] differently, are not. But she really believes that we can solve all our differences and work together, and other people don't believe that."

After hearing her friend give voice to her discouragement — knowing how deeply that agitation had to run for Marie Kevin to consider quitting—Fleming tried to buoy her with tough love and a kind offer.

"Oh, come on, you've brought it too far," Fleming began. "There's no way you can walk out now. I'll tell you what—when I retire, I will help you."

The overture worked. To have Fleming and her potent administrative skills on board would be an instant boon, Marie Kevin understood. Short in stature and long on energy, Fleming was sweet, gracious, and affectionate, yet sharp enough to see through hypocrisy or arrogance, and bold enough to call out those faults in other people. She reveled in preparing big, festive meals for her friends and engaging in spirited conversations about books, religion, and politics. She hosted parties at her ranch-style home in an Indianapolis cul-de-sac, where she sometimes entertained with bottles of red wine on her pool patio or served up after-dinner sips of limoncello in her living room—which was decorated with a human-sized angel statue in one corner. With graying hair and lively eyes, the former Sister of Providence—who took the name "Sister Melanie" while at the Woods—always offered a prayer of grace before eating. She proudly proclaimed her affection for the liberal-minded coverage provided by the MSNBC network and the feminist moxie of Mother Théodore, whom she described as "Indiana's first women's libber." Fleming was a spitfire, a realist, a take-charge woman, and the perfect counterbalance to the good soldier, Marie Kevin.

Initially, Fleming helped Marie Kevin on her two days off each week and on her summer vacations. (That assistance would increase after Fleming retired as a school principal in June 2003.) To study and decipher the intricate medical charts that tracked the decline—and later the unexplained healing—of a blind eye and a cancerous throat, Fleming enlisted her father, the former doctor, along with an old friend, Dr. Robert L. Gregory, who had been an internist and a diabetes specialist in Indianapolis before retiring in 1999.

As Ambrosi had instructed the women while in Rome, each nota-
tion and observation made by the surgeons, physicians, and nurses
for McCord and Mulkern had to be clearly explained for eventual
evaluation by the Vatican's doctors and theologians. With her vol-
unteer experts translating the technicalities, Fleming typed expansive reports on her home computer and printed out reams of copies.
Marie Kevin once walked into Fleming's normally tidy house and
was startled to see numerous stacks of white papers teetering on
coffee tables, end tables, chairs, and sofas—the chaotic products of
dual miracle probes. During 2001, most of the cause-related conversations in Fleming's home remained fixed on the medical minutiae of two curious cures, of cell counts and vision strength, of laser
and radiation beams, of corneal cores and tumor fringes. But some
nights, after all the record-crunching came to a halt, Dr. Gregory
reversed the roles and engaged the former Sister of Providence
with tricky religious questions like, "We have so many saints, why
do you think it is so important to have Mother Théodore canonized?" Fleming loved that type of repartée, and she used Gregory's
query to expound on one of her pet topics. "I think it's very important due to the period in which she lived in Indiana," she told the
retired doctor. "In Indiana back then, the public schools were only
for men and boys. So the only way a girl could go to school was to
attend a private school, like the Woods academy. When you think
about the inequity, it's really awful."

But Gregory's question resonated far beyond the shady campus
of pious women, liberal-arts students, and nuns-in-training on the
outskirts of Terre Haute. More than ten thousand Roman Catholic saints already had been named by the Church, so why did the
Church need to declare more? Why Mother Théodore? Did the
modern world need extra saints?

For generations of Indiana Catholics and for the alumnae who
had been schooled by the Sisters of Providence—the people whose

donations had largely fueled the cause — their pro-canonization reasons ranged from an appetite for Mother Théodore's global glorification to the essential Catholic notion that the saints offered all people a human blueprint for how to lead a heroic life. Millions of Catholics had threaded pieces of saintly devotion into their worlds, naming their churches, schools, and even their children after favorite saints. They were role models, according to many Catholic faithful, and because the circumstances surrounding their individual triumphs and tragedies were so varied, any person from any society could find meaning, lessons, and something to imitate in their lives — as Kathy Fleming had found in Mother Théodore's feminist gumption.

That thinking, in fact, had become the engine for Pope John Paul II's historically frantic canonization pace: Catholics like Sister Marie Kevin believed the 482 saints named during his papacy were central to a "new evangelism." "We need saints because we all need inspiration . . . someone to follow, someone to look up to," Marie Kevin once explained. "It doesn't mean we have to do exactly what every single saint did. One reason we are alive is to become holy, and that means simply to be like God. It doesn't mean we're all trying to be little gods. God showed us [through Jesus] an example of what it's like to be human. The saints are simply living examples of who caught the message that Jesus was trying to give."

While that pastoral philosophy — simply put, "do the right thing" — still reverberated in a modern, cynical world, the veneration of saints has, for centuries, been shredded by many Catholic critics, and it continued to draw fire from hardcore atheists and those who trumpeted other organized religions. In the sixteenth century, Protestant reformer Martin Luther rebuked any belief in saintly intercession as "pagan and idolatrous." The Protestant Reformation, some historians said, led millions of Christians to abandon the concept of sainthood and churchly hierarchies and to embrace the theory that all children of God had equal access to God, and no saint was needed to intercede on our behalf. Conservative Protestants, for example, didn't look to saints for help; they prayed to God and Jesus, not canonized humans. Some Protestants even quoted the New Testament and asked Catholics, "Why do you need saints if Jesus is 'the one mediator between God and man?'" At the Vatican, Monsignor Robert Sarno smiled whenever that biblical verse was mentioned as an argument against praying to saints. "A good question," Sarno said. "Saints are the signposts. Jesus is the road. How can we stay on that road until we get to heaven? God gives us road signs. Just like on our [earthly] roads, the signs help you arrive at your destination safely. God's road signs help to keep us safely along the way. A canonized saint is someone God chooses, to whom God gave special grace—for all humanity to follow, to keep us on that road."

Still, among the thick crowd of named saints, the vast majority once lived as priests or nuns. If saints were meant to serve as role models, how could a Wall Street financier or a Chinese pig farmer find common inspirational ground between their life and the virtuous existence led by a venerated monk, pope, or Sister of Providence? Many progressive Catholic leaders in Rome have long urged the Vatican to beatify and canonize more regular folks, to name more "lay saints" so the faithful could have more everyday examples of holiness. Between the years 1000 and 1987, there were 303 Catholic canonizations, which included several group causes. But those sainthood ceremonies added only 56 laymen and 20 laywomen, and most of those were martyrs. Pope John Paul II hammered away at that imbalance through his blizzard of beatifications and canonizations. Before his death in 2005, John Paul beatified more than 210 laypeople, and he named more than 240 laypeople as saints. Those included Dr. Joseph Moscati, an early-twentieth-century physician in Naples, Italy, who was known for saving scores of patients during both the 1906 eruption of Mount Vesuvius and the 1911 cholera epidemic, giving free medical care to the poor and to those who had lost their homes. Moscati was canonized by John Paul in 1987.

Nearly a decade after Dr. Gregory posed his theological teaser to Fleming, the larger question remained newsworthy. On July 27, 2009, the British daily newspaper *The Guardian* asked bluntly, "Do we need saints?" The rhetorical query was posed in relation to an update from the Vatican that the beatification of nineteenth-century John Henry Cardinal Newman — credited with helping bring the Church of England back to its Catholic roots — had been scheduled to occur in 2010.

"Many find the [saint-naming] practice outdated, and the verification of miracles absurd," the newspaper opined. "Does the Catholic Church really need to add to its [roster] of saints? Moving beyond Catholicism, beyond even religion, is there any value to looking to model individuals as we strive to improve ourselves? Do saints and heroes serve to inspire us or make us feel inadequate?"

† † †

Dr. Nick Rader came to medicine, Catholicism — and, later, to a miracle — through a series of side doors in his life.

Born August 30, 1950, in East Chicago, Indiana, and raised in the Lutheran faith in a home just outside the Windy City, Rader had no lineage of doctors in his family tree or even any plans to become a physician until his first year of college. In fact, he discovered his eventual career path largely because his college fraternity forced its members to leave their house each night to go study. Consequently, Rader earned all A's in his first semester, which included a biology course that he took with several medical students. *Maybe I should look at medicine,* he thought. In time, Rader enrolled at the Indiana University School of Medicine, where he "found ophthalmology to be interesting," he said, ultimately earning a medical degree and completing his residency at that college. In private practice, he specialized in refractive procedures as well as in cataract removal. In 1983, Rader became one of the first surgeons in Indiana to perform radial keratotomy. His eye clinic in Greenwood, Indiana—a southern suburb of Indianapolis—was located less than two miles from Our Lady of the Greenwood School, where Kathy Fleming was the principal and where Rader's daughter was enrolled. Fleming also happened to be one of Rader's eye patients. "We were friends," Rader said.

His wife was raised in the Catholic faith, and after their daughter was born, Rader chose to convert to Catholicism so that the family could attend the same church, Our Lady of the Greenwood, next door to the school. The pastor at that church was, for many years, Father Joseph Reedman. The priest also happened to be one of the patients at Rader's bustling practice. Rader had a young-looking face and thick, graying hair that he wore short on the sides and brushed straight back. He also happened to be on the minds of two women who were on the prowl for a miracle.

As Marie Kevin and Kathy Fleming rigorously prepared for Dr. Ambrosi's March 2002 visit to Terre Haute—where he planned to interview both Phil McCord and Eddie Mulkern—the nun knew she had to quickly bolster her research into the spontaneous mending of McCord's eye; she had to synthesize all the scientific strangeness for the postulator. Ambrosi seemed to prefer the McCord cure, and Marie Kevin still required some convincing herself that McCord's recovery would truly be the smartest choice to submit as their alleged second miracle. Complicating matters was the fact that McCord's corneal specialist, Dr. Stephen Johnson, had refused to aid the miracle investigators. That meant Marie Kevin still needed an ophthalmology expert to interpret the arcane symbols, numbers, and designations that constituted the language of ophthalmologists.

"Would you call your friend?" she asked Fleming, referring to Rader. "Would you talk to him? [Maybe] he can give you further explanation of why this [eye recovery] is important. Then immediately go to your computer, type up what he says, and send it to me."

Fleming phoned her eye doctor. Without hesitation, Rader consented to read and help unravel McCord's medical records. He later flipped through the piles of pages containing descriptions of McCord's exams, written up months earlier by Dr. Johnson and by McCord's cataract surgeon, Dr. Jeffrey Jungers. Those records showed the power and duration of the two phacoemulsification procedures performed by Jungers in the autumn of 2000, the various measurements of McCord's ocular pressure, and his visual acuity before, during, and after his cornea problems. The reports listed the various amounts of drugs and drops with which McCord was treated. And there was a letter from Johnson to Jungers, written after McCord had inexplicably healed. After immersing himself in the hill of facts, Rader called Fleming with his conclusion: McCord's now-perfect eyesight and swiftly restored eye health defied his medical knowledge.

Exactly how and why, Fleming asked, did the eye evade scientific explanation? She needed to relay to Marie Kevin a concise summary of the cure's significance, a simple picture of the case's inherent oddness. Dr. Rader, a Catholic who believed in miracles, wrote up just such an account for Fleming—on a microscopic level.

"You're in essence born with a certain number of cells that line the undersurface of the cornea, and those are called endothelial cells," Rader said. "It's the job of those little endothelial cells to pump water out of the cornea to keep it clear. These cells don't divide or replicate like other cells in your body. They're akin to brain cells: you're born with one set, and as you get older, you slowly [and naturally] lose some of those.

"So what we're really talking about here," Rader continued, "is the density of cells per millimeter. A normal child may have over four thousand cells per millimeter. A normal adult may have a range of 2,000 to 2,600 of those cells. Surgery and other conditions can damage those cells, and when you damage them, the cell count goes down. And when you get down to around six hundred cells per millimeter, there just aren't enough cells there to pump the cornea clear. The cornea becomes cloudy."

When too many endothelial cells die, the cornea dies—and that old cornea must be replaced if the eye's vision is to return, Rader said. Such massive cellular decimation, he added, is typically irreversible.

"Now, you can have some cells that are damaged but not dead and that can slowly recover . . . where the cornea becomes damaged from surgery and slowly recovers over many months," Rader said. "As a scientist, I can come up with ways that this could happen, that someone could [eventually] get better. But not in the way it occurred. What struck me as not possible, in my realm of experience, was for Mr. McCord to have this problem and then pray for intercession and then immediately improve."

To Fleming, the doctor's math was unmistakably clear: even if the injured cells in McCord's right eye did somehow rejuvenate, two thousand damaged endothelial cells wouldn't—couldn't—spontaneously recuperate in one night of sleep. Besides, she reasoned, at the height of McCord's eye woes, two other doctors had personally looked at that same cornea and had deemed it beyond repair.

Case closed, Fleming thought.

She delivered Rader's findings to Marie Kevin. Not long after the promoter heard the eye doctor's colorful synopsis and his belief that the events eluded medical reasoning, the two women quickly realized that Rader could also become a star tribunal witness—if Ambrosi indeed picked the McCord case as the one to pursue for the possible second miracle. The tribunal—the two Archdiocese of Indianapolis priests who would serve as the judge and prosecutor of the alleged McCord miracle—should hear Rader's blow-by-blow views, both Marie Kevin and Fleming decided. Even more, he could fill the testimonial void that would be created if Dr. Johnson held his ground and rebuffed all future invitations to participate.

Fleming arranged for a dinner party at her house, she said, to sell Rader "on the process." In addition to Rader and his wife, she invited Marie Kevin and Father Reedman from Our Lady of the Greenwood Church—Rader and Fleming's pastor, and also Rader's patient. "Father Reedman is such a good friend of Nick Rader," Fleming explained to Marie Kevin, "if Nick knows Father Reedman will be there, he'll for sure come." Rader recalled the get-together as "a social evening, but clearly they brought some [McCord case] information, and I think it was an opportunity for Sister Marie Kevin and me to get acquainted."

Did the dinner party help persuade Rader to become a potential witness? "I actually did not think much of it—it was no decision," Rader said later. "I would have done that anyway," although he acknowledged that the thought of repeating his observations to a Church tribunal was "a bit more intimidating" than simply analyzing medical records for his friend.

Did his Catholic faith enter into his decision to potentially testify? "I think it did," Rader said. "As a Catholic, I felt an obligation."

Ambrosi already had given Marie Kevin the names of several people with whom he wanted to meet informally during his upcoming fact-finding trip to Indiana: Phil and Debbie McCord, Eddie Mulkern and his wife Mary, and McCord's doctors, Jungers and Johnson, neither of whom had seemed receptive to the idea of speaking to the Roman postulator.

Once again, Marie Kevin and Fleming relied on Rader for a favor. Decades earlier, at the Indiana University School of Medicine,

Johnson completed his residency just behind Rader's class. Echoing Marie Kevin's earlier bid, Rader spoke to Johnson about testifying before a possible miracle tribunal. Once again, the answer was no. "Dr. Rader told me that Dr. Johnson is basically kind of shy," Fleming later recalled. "When he heard that we had this trial, he would have envisioned being on the witness stand, having to defend his medical practices with [McCord]. And doctors hate that with a passion."

If both of McCord's primary eye doctors spurned the miracle investigators, the Vatican might consider their absences a fatal weakness in the case. For Marie Kevin, pressure was mounting to persuade Jungers to at least speak privately with Ambrosi and later, hopefully, to appear before a Church tribunal. Marie Kevin already had written Jungers a letter fully explaining the miracle-analysis process and disclosing that the postulator was about to fly in from Italy. In that letter she invited Jungers to meet with Ambrosi in Terre Haute so he could "simply describe the condition of the eye, what you did, and what your expectations [of recovery] were. You don't have to make any statement about what you think, other than the fact that Mr. McCord is now better." Two weeks after sending the letter, however, she still hadn't received a reply from Jungers. She wrote a second letter and, in that note, tried to sell the doctor with some history, saying "nothing like this has happened in Indiana since 1908," mentioning, too, the approved miraculous cure of Sister Mary Theodosia Mug. After reading the second letter, Jungers asked his receptionist to call Marie Kevin at the Woods and schedule a meeting with the nun at his office for the following Wednesday morning, March 6, 2002—a half hour before Jungers's first patient was set to arrive, and three days before Ambrosi hit town. Marie Kevin would have thirty minutes to make her case.

For their chat, Marie Kevin carried a copy of the *Positio Super Miraculo* that had been used to secure Mother Théodore's beatification. The binder was about four times as thick as the Terre Haute phone book. She wanted Jungers to get a flavor for the precision and intellectual severity that embodied her mission and, she said later, "to show him what we're about. He would see all the doctors' names at the top of the pages." When the nun took a seat in his first-floor office, Jungers was initially "very solemn," Marie Kevin recalled. "I was skeptical," Jungers later admitted.

After introducing herself, she handed him the *positio*. At his desk, Jungers began ruffling through the pages. "His whole demeanor changed," Marie Kevin said later. "He told me he would love to read the whole thing." Before leaving, the nun made her final sales pitch.

"Doctor, I'd like to ask one thing of you, and I want you to feel perfectly free to say no. This gentleman from Rome will be here on Saturday and Sunday. And I would like for you to come and meet with him if you could," the sister said.

"I would be happy to do that," Jungers replied.

Marie Kevin later described her reaction: "I nearly fell off my chair."

† † †

On a late-winter afternoon, almost seven years to the day that he agreed to Marie Kevin's invitation, Jungers sat at the same desk and recounted that extraordinary meeting.

As a nonreligious man who did not believe in miracles, why had he said yes?

"I felt I had to go participate or it would not have been good for me in the community," Jungers said, referring to the sisters' steadfast and lasting presence in Terre Haute—and the fact that a number of his patients came from the Woods.

The eye doctor then spun his office chair 180 degrees and faced the window behind his desk. He gazed out at the chilly courtyard of St. Joseph's University Catholic Church, just across the street from his clinic. In October 1840, Mother Théodore had stopped at that same church and had attended Mass before traveling across the swollen Wabash River in a horse-drawn carriage and arriving at her rustic new home, Saint Mary-of-the-Woods. Her name—and her ancient community of nuns—still carried clout in Terre Haute. Jungers felt he had little choice but to help Mother Théodore, perhaps, reach sainthood.

"In fact," Jungers said, aiming his index finger out the window, "there she is."

He pointed to a small stone figurine standing in the church courtyard. The white statue, topped with a light brushing of snow, was a three-foot-high replica of a habit-wearing Mother Théodore. The statue's eyes were fixed directly and constantly on the window of Dr. Jungers.

†   †   †

The agenda for Ambrosi's three-day visit would mix some witness questioning with some tastes of Indiana lifestyle. He and his English translator, Francesca Lorenzetti, landed at Indianapolis International Airport—via United Airlines flight 500 from Chicago—at twelve thirty on Saturday afternoon, March 9, 2002. They drove seventy-six miles west to the Woods and to their accommodations, a campus guesthouse lined with watercolor paintings of Russian churches. They unpacked their bags and prepared for their opening meeting later that day, a get-acquainted session with Phil and Debbie McCord.

The informal hearings were a staple of Ambrosi's practice, arranged and held for each potential miracle case that he considered. "This is my method. First, *I* have to be convinced [of the miracle]," Ambrosi later explained. "With all the experience I have now, I have a nose for these things," he added with a smile, touching a finger to his nose. "In fact, it is quite big. As soon as I am convinced, I will go forward. If I am not convinced, I'll throw the case out myself."

At four thirty that Saturday afternoon, Phil and Debbie McCord arrived at the Woods. They greeted Ambrosi and Lorenzetti and then settled into chairs in a guesthouse parlor. The questions began. One of the first sentences out of Phil McCord's mouth was "I am not Catholic." To Ambrosi, that unsolicited statement added credibility to the man's larger story. One of McCord's next sentences: "Whatever you need, just ask." Ambrosi liked him.

For now, the postulator only needed to hear his tale. McCord complied, walking the postulator through each ghastly detail of his right eye's rapid deterioration and his own emotional disintegration, the desperate prayer he'd said in the basilica just steps away from the guesthouse, the instant feeling of peace that had swelled inside him that wintry morning, and his baffling day-after improvement.

"Something incredible," McCord said, "has happened to me."

Ambrosi was dazzled not just by McCord's account, but by the passion of his retelling. McCord, obviously a man of deep thought and intelligence, had been moved by the wonder of his experience, the postulator recognized.

The McCords said their good-byes. On Sunday, Eddie Mulkern and his wife would take the same seats. That Saturday evening, still electrified by McCord's version of the events, Ambrosi dined with the convent's presiding general superior, Sister Ann Margaret O'Hara, at Pino's Il Sonetto, an Italian restaurant on the fringe of a residential neighborhood on Terre Haute's south side. As he munched on the flavors of his own country, Ambrosi instantly felt at home, bonded by several strong connections he held with people in Indiana. First, he had known Monsignor Fred Easton, the vicar judicial — or judge — of the Indianapolis Archdiocese tribunal, since the 1960s, when they had studied canon law together at the

Pontifical Lateran University in Rome. Should a local Church trial be held to examine the potential McCord miracle, Easton would preside over the inquiry. Second, Ambrosi shared a deep affection for the first love of most Indianans, basketball. In time, he would attend two University of Indiana basketball games, acquiring a Hoosiers banner to hang proudly in his flat near the Tiber River. Finally, Ambrosi enjoyed the easy, cordial atmosphere of Terre Haute, a city of 59,600 people known for its square doughnuts and its French history — translated from French, the town's name means "high ground."

The second case Ambrosi would consider was rooted in one of America's true Catholic hubs, a place with an even richer history, and a city that boasted a professional basketball team. But in Boston, the Catholic Church was simultaneously embroiled in a dark, deeply damaging scandal involving claims of child sexual abuse against dozens of its priests — and evidence that the local Church hierarchy had for years tried to keep the allegations secret by paying off victims and shuffling accused priests to new parishes, where more sex assaults had occurred. One month prior to Ambrosi's Indiana visit, Boston Cardinal Bernard Law had defiantly told worshippers at a Sunday Mass that he would not resign despite the raging controversy. By the end of 2002, however, Law would indeed step down from his Boston post and be reassigned to Rome, and the Boston Archdiocese would be given permission by its financial council to file for Chapter 11 bankruptcy protection.

Clearly, the leaders of the Archdiocese of Boston had matters other than miracles on their minds, Ambrosi realized. On Sunday morning, the midpoint in his weekend visit, Ambrosi toured the burial tomb beneath the Church of the Immaculate Conception. He stood near the body of Mother Théodore as Sister Mary Theodosia had on that October night in 1908. Later, up in the basilica, he attended Mass followed by brunch in the college dining room. And at 12:45 p.m., the postulator sat across from Dr. Jeffrey Jungers in the guesthouse and heard the ophthalmologist detail McCord's two cataract removals and the subsequent complications that had rendered the caretaker half blind.

The questions from Ambrosi "were thorough," Jungers recalled. He could also feel the urgency and excitement exuded that morning by Sister Marie Kevin. "Even though I can flat-out tell you I don't believe in miracles, I didn't want to be the one to [ruin their miracle case]. I didn't feel like that was my decision to make. But I definitely felt . . . a little bit of pressure not to let down the Catholic community," Jungers said later. "They made it clear to me, though, that I wasn't there to make that decision. It was more, was there some clear medical reason for what had happened?"

That day, Jungers told Ambrosi he could not explain McCord's spontaneous cure.

One of Ambrosi's final meetings at the Woods took place at 2:00 p.m. on Sunday—a sixty-minute casual conversation with Eddie Mulkern and his wife. Finally the postulator would hear firsthand about the enigmatic throat-cancer cure. He then would weigh the Mulkern case against the McCord case—point by point, medically and theologically. Only one case would be selected for a Church trial. Only one would be tested as a miracle.

As McCord had done with his eye problems, Mulkern chronicled for Ambrosi his increasing hoarseness, his diagnosis of a lime-sized laryngeal mass, how he had placed a Mother Théodore relic against his throat while praying for intercession, and how he had been clutching that same card when his Chinese oncologist announced he could no longer see the tumor. The medical tale was packed with life-and-death tension, Ambrosi confirmed. Before departing the Woods, the postulator asked Sister Marie Kevin to try once again to solicit cooperation from the troubled Archdiocese of Boston. She would dutifully follow his instructions, sending two letters in 2002 to Monsignor Michael Foster, the vicar judicial in Boston—Easton's counterpart—beseeching Foster to meet with Ambrosi to discuss a potential miracle trial in Massachusetts. Foster, however, had more pressing issues. In August 2002 he became the twenty-second priest in the Boston Archdiocese to be placed on administrative leave after a former parishioner claimed Foster had molested him twice in a rectory bedroom between 1980 and 1985, when the parishioner was a child. The validity of the accuser's claims later was called into question by a report in the *Boston Globe*. In October 2002 Foster was reinstated as the presiding judge of the archdiocesan tribunal. But by then, Ambrosi already had decided which case to pursue. Marie Kevin's letters to Foster amounted to a mere formality.

Ambrosi had, in fact, been permanently swayed on that Sunday afternoon in March, profoundly influenced by something he had heard from Mulkern during their cozy visit in the guesthouse parlor. It was something that had bothered the postulator. Not Mulkern's words or facts, though. Rather, what convinced Ambrosi was Mulkern's voice—still deep, rough, and raspy. Where McCord's right eye had returned to normal, 20/20 vision, Mulkern's throat was cancer-free yet damaged by the disease.

"He spoke," Ambrosi recalled later, imitating Mulkern's gravely tones, "like a person who has had cancer and who might suffer a recurrence."

In October 2002, Ambrosi sent a letter to Daniel M. Buechlein, the archbishop of Indianapolis, requesting that his archdiocese launch a formal trial to examine the alleged miracle of Phil McCord. That same month, Ambrosi also mailed a letter to Marie Kevin, appointing her the vice-postulator "so that you can act in front of the diocesan curia of Indianapolis. For this purpose," Ambrosi wrote, "I give you all the power relative of this duty, including the power of taking care of the expenses and the necessary opportune documents so that the trial may be carried out perfectly." Marie Kevin accepted, and Buechlein wrote Ambrosi back on December 12, 2002, to inform him he "welcomed the process." The trial would begin on January 23, 2003, in a windowless basement room at the Archdiocese of Indiana headquarters. From that moment forward, Ambrosi and the Indiana sisters began praying that the mysteriously healed right eye of a non-Catholic convent engineer would carry Mother Théodore all the way to a canonization ceremony in St. Peter's Square, completing a century-long quest and elevating her as the eighth American saint.

Ambrosi never second-guessed his judgment to bypass Mulkern's recovery—even though Mulkern was still healthy as of 2009, eleven years after his malignant tumor vanished. "It wasn't a definitive healing," Ambrosi maintained in 2009. "A healing has to be definitive, instantaneous, and perfect. I was not convinced." In contrast, Ambrosi continued, "Mr. McCord's illness was extremely serious and it had all the things you want, all the things I look for, [including] the speed [of healing] that is needed when you take the case and present it to the theologians. That gave me the want and the ability to trust the miracle."

But Ambrosi's final choice, Kathy Fleming later suggested, also was influenced by his fondness for Easton. "I think he really wanted to run it through Indianapolis because Monsignor Easton was in charge of the tribunal and he's a brilliant guy and has a doctorate in canon law. . . . I think it was mostly because he wanted to work with Easton." Indeed, Ambrosi later described Easton as "an exceptional person . . . my best friend in the States," and he added that Easton ran "one of the best ecclesiastical tribunals in the U.S.A." Easton, in return, summed up Ambrosi as "very affable, very bright, but [also] firm when he has to be. He sees the big picture, and I find him easy to work with."

As new alliances and new hopes brewed in Indiana, Eddie and

Mary Mulkern returned to their quiet lives and beloved parish in Chelsea, Massachusetts. Since his schoolboy days in classes taught by Sisters of Providence, Mulkern had been rooting for Mother Théodore's canonization cause. For a few precious months in 2002, it appeared that Mulkern and his own brush with death might serve as the final bridge to transport Mother Théodore to sainthood. But in a surreal competition that had pitted his cancer against another man's partial blindness, he had finished second.

"I was hoping" to be picked, he acknowledged. "To be as sick as I was and then to have the situation reversed, I really felt I was part of God's plan. [But] I was very honored, privileged, and blessed to have been included in the project. I felt that God put me there for a reason. I really think He worked through me in His own way."

When facing his demise, Mulkern had placed his full faith in the heavenly power of Mother Théodore. Aching to stay alive for his four children, wanting to live simply to see the births of his own grandchildren, Mulkern had asked a long-dead French nun to salvage his diseased body. In time, Mulkern indeed became a grandfather, twice over.

He would always believe that Mother Théodore had answered his prayers. But nobody would be calling his cure a miracle.

CHAPTER NINE

The Saint Factory

Four miles southwest of the camera-clicking tourist tumult in St. Peter's Square, the mother church for all Catholics stood next to a remarkably hushed urban lawn strewn with wild daises. On the gently sloping front steps, packs of pilgrims often sunned themselves, squinting skyward in godly silence. Even with marble sculptures of Jesus and fourteen saints soaring twenty-three feet above its roofline, the Basilica of St. John Lateran managed to blend into its staid Roman neighborhood. But inside, just beyond its bronze entry doors, the faithful and curious alike could take lush strolls through two millennia of Christian lore.

The cathedral complex, consecrated in the year 324 and once the primary papal residence, housed six papal tombs and gushed with holy history from its gilded ceilings to its wooden altar — upon which Saint Peter once celebrated Mass — to its Holy Stairs, said to be the same twenty-eight marble steps Jesus had climbed on his way to trial. The trove of religious treasures seemed to befit the church's status as the oldest and highest ranked of Rome's four great "patriarchal" basilicas. St. John Lateran also served as the official ecclesiastical seat of the bishop of Rome, the pope.

On the top story of an adjoining administrative building — connected to the basilica through a pigeon-packed courtyard — a small cadre of workers tapped computer keyboards, aiming to author fresh history. After arriving at the basilica, they took an elevator up three floors, exited past a uniformed attendant, walked down a marble hallway, and opened an opaque door: the nerve center of the cause for the beatification and canonization of Pope John Paul II. This was a place built for speed, where in 2009 claims of purported miracles were stacked chest-high—the potential fuel to rocket John Paul to sainthood. The man who had named more saints than all the past popes combined was—just four years following his 2005 demise—sprinting toward that same eternal distinction, at what seemed to be a record pace. John Paul had changed the rules. Now, in death, he appeared to be reaping the rewards of his own streamlining reforms. At its heart, the office for John Paul's cause epitomized the late pope's deep hunger for canonization work. It was a tiny saint factory.

In the hub of the work space, three paper-cluttered desks had been shoved together into an L. Here, a three-woman staff answered phones, opened letters, counted cash, and created content for bimonthly issues of *Totus Tuus* (Latin for "Totally Yours"), a colorful magazine laced with stories and pictures of the late pope's humanitarian deeds and philosophies, appreciations of his virtues, and readers' claims of his cures from heaven. Just behind the writers' desks, a wide closet contained one bottle of Chianti and twenty-seven red binders, each filled with about one hundred pages of letters and photographs from people supporting the sainthood cause.

A few steps outside the room and down the hallway, in a long, narrow room once used for meetings, a conference table was laden with more than a dozen cardboard boxes, all taped, labeled, and ready for a short transport to the Vatican—selected proof meant to bolster John Paul's potential sanctification. Each package had recently been processed in the same room at a makeshift sorting station—one desk where a series of boxes sat with their flaps open. Within each box, heaps of handwritten and typed accounts of alleged miracles and desperate requests for John Paul's intercession grew fatter by the day. "My husband was hospitalized with serious chest pains, a heart attack. I prayed," read one note from an American woman, who claimed her ailing husband later received "a cure in the father's name." Inside another open carton, the eyes of dozens of seriously sick people peered from a round clump of snapshots, including a strawberry-blond woman in wire-rimmed glasses, a Mexican boy with dark, tired eyes, and an unborn fetus. A third box was crammed with mementos of appreciation for John Paul—rosaries, crosses, dried flowers, and scarves.

"Letters, postcards, and in here, so many photographs," said *Totus Tuus* writer Michele Smits as she stood amid the clutter of testimonials and prayers. "People are sick. They want help from the pope, from Pope John Paul, no? These are all for the cause. This is what we are doing to assist. But in here, it is small. You should see what we have upstairs [in the attic]. Up there, even more. Now, we must go to the Vatican, to take these cartons full of gifts."

The Vatican's Congregation for the Causes of Saints is known as "the saint factory"—though used by several eminent cardinals, the nickname was coined by critics of John Paul's prodigious canonization numbers. During John Paul's pontificate, the "saint factory" rolled out an annual average of eighteen canonizations. The previous six popes of the twentieth century (excluding the brief pontificate of Pope John Paul I) had averaged about one canonization per year. John Paul had tapped his saint-making gusto to promote Catholicism in new, politically vital lands, such as China and the Darfur region of Sudan. He had considered the creation of saints a holy spark to rekindle the fire of Catholic devotion—a passion he believed was lacking in the modern Church. Before John Paul was elected by the cardinals in 1978, the Vatican had canonized 302 people since 1592—the start of Pope Clement VIII's reign. During John Paul's tenure, he named 482 saints. Aboard one of the many international flights he took on the papal plane, John Paul was asked by journalists to explain why he had canonized so many.

"Sometimes," he replied, "it is necessary to do something that is too much." In November 2003 the Vatican became so clogged with active causes that the Holy See began recruiting women and lay-people to train as "saint detectives" to help assess the lives of beati-fication and canonization candidates.

Mother Théodore's cause, frozen in papal bureaucracy for decades, gained new heat under the watch of Catholicism's most prolific and passionate saint-namer—ascending just as the "saint factory" operated at full throttle.

When Pope Benedict XVI gained the papacy, some Vati-can observers predicted he would match his predecessor's fertile saint-making pace. Before becoming pope, Benedict—then Car-dinal Joseph Ratzinger—had been a precious cog in John Paul's saintly assembly line. During his twenty-three-year tenure as the head of the Congregation for the Doctrine of the Faith, Ratzinger was described as John Paul's ideological "enforcer" and "confi-dant." When complaints grew louder over John Paul's canonization numbers, Ratzinger declared defiantly, "There cannot be too many saints." Ratzinger had even presented John Paul with a formula to abolish "the miracle clause," *The Times* of London reported in December 2004. The stunning proposal would have eliminated any need for medically inexplicable cures in order to beatify blesseds and canonize saints. In theory, the move would have further accel-erated John Paul's breakneck saint-making tempo. After the for-mula was leaked to the media, one Italian newspaper, *Il Secolo XIX*, predicted such a "revolution in saint making" would meet resist-ance from Vatican traditionalists who viewed miracles as "one of the cornerstones of the Catholic faith." John Paul died, however, five months later. And the miracle-abolishment proposal apparently died with him.

One year and eleven days into Benedict's papacy, he issued a stern message to the Vatican's saint-making division, reemphasizing the need to "safeguard the seriousness of investigations" of alleged miracles, and affirming that "unbroken Church practice establishes the need for a physical miracle; a moral miracle is not enough." In February 2008 Benedict tapped the brakes again, releasing new orders to bring "greater caution and more accuracy" to the earliest segments of the canonization pipeline—the miracle investigations performed in the home dioceses of would-be saints. At that time, Vatican officials acknowledged they had flagged several unspecified "errors" made by local tribunals. More to the point, Benedict's edict seemed to be a calculated retort "to a public perception that under John Paul an excessive number of people were canonized," the Reverend James Martin, author of *My Life with the Saints,* suggested to the Religion News Service in 2008. "Maybe this is serving as a reminder to the faithful that these rules are still in effect." Under Benedict, the "saint factory" was clearly gearing down.

But it was not being mothballed. The comprehensive streamlining changes John Paul had installed in 1983 remained. Meanwhile, some four hundred causes for beatification and canonization continued to rumble through the Vatican pipeline—including the quick-moving cause for John Paul himself. The orchestrated push to beatify and sanctify the late pope—and to do it in record time—began promptly at his April 8, 2005, funeral in St. Peter's Square. On that day a throng of Catholics raised printed banners that screamed the same two words: *"Santo Subito!"* or "Sainthood at Once!" According to John Paul's controversial *Divinus Perfectionis Magister,* any petition to launch a beatification bid had to be presented "no sooner than five years after the death" of the candidate. (For centuries the Vatican had required a fifty-year waiting period.) Under that five-year rule, the late pope's beatification campaign could formally begin on April 2, 2010, but supporters of John Paul's cause strategically employed one of his own saint-making precedents to propel his campaign years ahead of schedule. On March 1,

1999, less than eighteen months after the death of Mother Teresa of Calcutta, John Paul had bowed to public pressure and waived the five-year waiting period for the Catholic mega-sister, permitting her beatification cause to commence. As a result, Mother Teresa was beatified on October 19, 2003, reaching that threshold just six years after her passing, faster than any non-martyr in the modern era.

To bestow a similar favor for John Paul, Benedict rode across Rome on Friday, May 13, 2005, arriving at the Basilica of St. John Lateran. There the pope stood before members of the Roman clergy and announced he was lifting the five-year waiting period for John Paul—less than six weeks after the pontiff's passing. The assembled priests, bishops, and cardinals promptly stood and clapped inside the historic cathedral. Benedict joined them, rising and applauding. Many in attendance noted the significance of the date: it marked the anniversary of the 1981 assassination attempt in St. Peter's Square that had left John Paul battling for his life with bullet wounds in his abdomen, left hand, and right arm. But on a happier day exactly twenty-four years later, the gathering of Vatican priests looked only forward, toward the possible sainthood of their recently deceased leader. Moments after the meeting, Cardinal José Saraiva Martins, then head of the Congregation for the Causes of Saints, told a journalist he held "no doubts at all" that miraculous claims in John Paul's name would be soon found and approved. After that day, a third-floor office adjoining St. John Lateran would serve as the command post for locating alleged miracles made in John Paul's name—the headquarters for his sainthood campaign.

Totus Tuus began publishing in 2006 with a masthead listing twenty-eight editors, writers, and photography experts, as well as the seven translators needed to publish the magazine in Polish, English, Italian, French, Spanish, and other languages—a glossy global pitch for the beatification crusade. Cover stories featured photos of John Paul wearing the papal miter or sporting a construction hardhat and carried titles like "Defender of Man," and "Pope of Solidarity." Annual subscriptions were priced at seventeen dollars, and the magazine's back page offered instructions on how to donate to the cause via international bank transfers. The young postulator for John Paul's cause, Monsignor Slawomir Oder, edited the magazine from his well-ordered office next to the workroom where Michele Smits and her two editorial colleagues were stationed. Born in Poland in 1960 and ordained as a priest in 1989—eleven years into John Paul's papacy—Oder was tireless and organized, according to his cause coworkers. Balding, bespectacled, and soft-spoken, he called his role as postulator, of proving John Paul's sainthood, the "adventure of a lifetime." Yet he acknowledged "always feeling people breathing down my back, asking, 'When is everything going to be ready?'"

As a man of the Internet era, Oder relied on e-mail to field hundreds of claims of medical cures that had followed intercessory prayers to the late John Paul. Oder also employed a new website — available in seven languages—to peddle the beatification campaign to the bustling online world. Site visitors could type in digital prayer requests for John Paul's help, glimpse a live webcam trained on the late pope's tomb in the Vatican grottoes, and read the *Testament of John Paul II*—his civil will. The website also included a link allowing visitors to donate through their credit cards. Indeed, John Paul's swift-moving cause was an expensive venture. For example, in early 2007, Oder's office spent its entire annual postal budget after the website was deluged with thousands of requests for prayer cards embedded with pieces of a white cassock once worn by the late pontiff.

Franciscan Brother Chris Gaffrey, a *Totus Tuus* translator, told the Catholic News Service in March 2007 that it cost five dollars to mail just one prayer card and one copy of the magazine to America, and that, without an increase in donations, the office could not afford to meet the demand. Gaffrey's comment, in turn, sparked media criticism that the people behind John Paul's cause were selling relics—considered sacrilegious by the Church. The Diocese of Rome was forced to issue statements reassuring all Catholics that the prayer cards were "completely free" and that "relics absolutely cannot be bought or sold because they are sacred objects." The Rome Diocese also pointed out, however, that "it is possible for those with the means to make a free-will offering to support the cost of printing and mailing." In 2007 the cause's webmaster, Stefano Chiodo, told the American Public Media radio program *Marketplace* that the website received about 1,200 daily donations, though he wouldn't reveal the average daily tally in dollars. The incoming money, Chiodo said, covered prayer-card printings, staff payroll, and the travel expenses of cause employees who gathered testimonies from people in many countries. "The process," Chiodo said, "has incurred heavy expenses." Cash contributions also flowed to the cause headquarters by mail, as evidenced by the photocopy of a check taped to the closet door behind Smits's desk in 2009. The twenty-dollar check—saved by the office staff as a souvenir—sent by a supporter in Macon, Georgia, was made out "direct to the Pope," and included a warm "God Bless your work" on the memo line. "This one," said Smits, "it's not so much. But we have much more!"

Energized by its modern business machinery—and by Oder's keenly felt urgency—the cause for John Paul charged forward at an unrivaled clip. From November 2005 through April 2006, a five-member church tribunal in Warsaw, Poland, gathered personal testimonies from about 130 people who had known the pope. Meanwhile, historians collected books about John Paul from libraries around the world, and theologians studied his mountain of private writings—all to check whether he ever did or wrote anything that could be deemed heretical. In the spring of 2007, Oder acknowledged to a journalist that the various probes had been completed with unusual swiftness, emphasizing that "speed doesn't mean a lack of seriousness."

Throughout those early investigations, Rome had buzzed with word that a "mystery nun" from France had contacted Oder, revealing details of her allegedly miraculous cure from Parkinson's disease—the same illness that had afflicted John Paul. *Totus Tuus* became the only publication to carry her anonymous account, which led to Church whispers that her case would be presented as the alleged first miracle in John Paul's beatification cause. On March 30, 2007, Oder escorted that nun, Sister Marie Simon-Pierre, before assembled television cameras and microphones in Aix-en-Provence, a city in southern France. There, with a strong, sure voice, Sister Marie raised her arm for reporters and said, "Look, my hand is no longer shaking. John Paul II has cured me." The nun said she had been diagnosed with Parkinson's disease in 2001, when she was forty-two, and that her condition had deteriorated to a point where she could not control tremors in her left hand or left leg. It had forced her to stop driving and had inhibited her ability to write. After John Paul died, she had started praying to him to heal her, she told reporters. On June 2, 2005, exactly two months after John Paul's passing, she was alone in her quarters at the Little Sisters of Catholic Motherhood convent when an unknown voice had told her, she said, to "take a pen and write." She scrawled John Paul's name. "It was weird," Sister Marie said later, "because my hand-writing was easier to read." She went to sleep, and when she awoke at 4:30 a.m., she climbed from her bed "completely transformed," she said. "It's hard to explain how I felt with words. It's too strong, too big, it's a mystery. . . . I was convinced I was healed." Soon, a local Church tribunal was assembled to examine the nun's recovery. According to the archbishop in charge of that inquiry, the trial could find no explanation for her rejuvenation. Oder had received more than two hundred promising reports of allegedly miraculous cures from people who claimed they, too, had prayed to John Paul for intercession. But the postulator said he saw Sister Marie's restoration as the most compelling case, partly because of the poignant symmetry between her suffering and that of the late pope. At the same news conference in France, Oder told reporters the nun also had passed a battery of psychological examinations, and that an expert's analysis of Sister Marie's handwriting samples from before and after her alleged intervention found script differences that were "amazing."

By April 2008 Oder already had combed and cataloged the full agglomeration of testimonies and medical opinions collected after John Paul's death. The postulator had funneled that torrent of papal facts and wondrous claims into a two-thousand-page *positio* that he, in turn, submitted for review to the thirty-four members of the Congregation for the Causes of Saints. Cardinal Martins, the group's leader, subsequently promised the documents would be studied "without losing a moment." In late 2009 the *positio* was approved by the Vatican, and in December, Pope Benedict proclaimed John Paul "Venerable." By then, his cause had been under way for less than five years. The normal lag time for the congregation to simply scrutinize and judge a *positio*: ten years.

Amid the hustle and hurry that seemed to steamroll the cause, the Polish daily newspaper *Dziennik* reported in 2009 that Pope Benedict sought to conclude the beatification process "as soon as possible" because "that is what the world is asking for." In Rome, papal prognosticators began speculating that John Paul's beatification might take place on October 16, 2010, the anniversary of his 1978 election.

Then in the spring of 2010, the Church's apparent haste to sanctify John Paul produced still another complication, perhaps even a setback in his cause. In early March the Polish newspaper *Rzeczpospolita* reported stunning allegations: Sister Marie's symptoms had returned, and the nun may be suffering from, not Parkinson's, but a different nervous-system disorder from which temporary remissions are possible. Further, *Rzeczpospolita* reported that the Consulta Medica's doctors had been unable to reach a consensus as to whether Sister Marie's recovery was indeed inexplicable.

About one week later, the Church attempted to set the record straight, and keep John Paul's cause rolling at its previous brisk pace. Father Luc-Marie Lalanne, who had led the initial Church investigation of Sister Marie's healing, posted a statement on the official website of the French Bishops Conference: "I categorically deny this rumor . . . Sister Marie Simon-Pierre continues to be at this time in a perfect state of health." The Vatican, meanwhile, issued its own terse rebuttal, calling the Polish newspaper's claim "absolutely without foundation," and adding "there's no question of a delay."

Indeed, on May 1, 2011, Pope Benedict XVI beatified his predecessor before 1.5 million Catholic faithful and tourists who had amassed in St. Peter's Square and in the narrow, cobble-stone streets nearby. As John Paul formally moved one step closer to sainthood, the crowd offered tears and cheers and joined in a choir-led hymn. "He restored to Christianity its true face as a religion of hope," Benedict said in his homily. Although the ceremony reignited a new tide of public criticism from some people who had been sexually abused by Catholic priests during John Paul's papacy, the beatification was completed faster than any other in modern times.

The Saint Factory was still intact.

† † †

The intimate letters between "Dusia" and "Br" spanned fifty-five years and filled a suitcase. For decades the cherished notes had been stored in the home of an elderly Polish psychiatrist, discretely tucked away — just like their relationship.

"Dusia," a devout Catholic who aided the Polish resistance following the 1939 German invasion of her country, was captured by the Nazis at age nineteen, and survived torture and medical experiments on her body during her five years in a Nazi concentration camp. After the war, she married a philosopher, gave birth to four daughters, and developed a psychiatric practice in Krakow, specializing in family issues. Eventually her strict views on love and sex had even influenced the Vatican's official position against birth control.

"Br" was short for *brat*, the Polish word for "brother." In 1956, when "Br" was a freshly ordained priest in Krakow, lecturing students and serving as a chaplain to doctors, "Dusia" had yearned for spiritual guidance. The psychiatrist needed someone to whom she could quietly confide, and someone to listen to her horror stories of having witnessed the murders of babies and children in the concentration camp. "Br" had become her chosen confidant. Soon their therapeutic talks sprouted into a tight friendship. "Br," meanwhile, had discovered he equally needed "Dusia." After his parents and older brother died at early ages, "Br"—still a young man himself—had felt orphaned and alone. The priest sought companionship as a frequent houseguest at the home of "Dusia," her husband, Andrzej, and their four children. "Br" often played with the kids, who began calling him "Uncle." Together with Andrzej, "Dusia" and "Br" would often embark on long hikes in the Beskidy Mountains of southeastern Poland, sometimes camping in the high country. There, they discussed God and the everyday issues faced by married couples.

For the next half century, the psychiatrist and the priest exchanged letters as their individual careers blossomed. Long after "Br" earned the kind of worldwide acclaim that prevented him from peacefully, privately roaming wild places with his friends, "Dusia" sent him rich descriptions of the Beskidy peaks they had once visited. From afar, he continued to cherish his role as her spiritual guide. Addressing her as "My Dear Dusia" and signing his letters "Br," he tried to use the written word to soothe her dark memories of the camp—living nightmares that continued to haunt and disturb her. "I ask God every day in the intention of Andrzej and all your children," he wrote to her in one letter in 1978. "God has entrusted you to me with your deep and uneasy 'I' and with your whole life, with everything that belongs to it. I will report on this task before God."

Years later, when an ailing, elderly "Br" lay dying in Italy, "Dusia" was one of a select few allowed to maintain a vigil at his bedside.

In February 2009, then eighty-seven years old, the woman who had long been nicknamed "Dusia" revealed the lifetime of correspondence she had saved from "Br." She published a book, *The Beskidy Mountains Recollections*, filled with the notes from "Br" as well as with her own religious thoughts. She appeared at a press conference in Warsaw, Poland, to publicize her 570-page tome. "Dusia" was Wanda Poltawska. "Br" was Karol Wojtyla.

The discovery of a previously unread hoard of John Paul's personal letters—missives written to a woman friend—rammed an eleventh-hour wrench into the finely tuned, fully revved engine that had been hurtling his cause forward at a frenetic pace unknown in saint-making history. Did such confidential writings contain any inappropriate comments by the pontiff? In his words—or even between the lines—was there any hint of romance between the married psychiatrist and the late pope? On what may have been the eve of John Paul's beatification, neither Vatican investigators nor Monsignor Oder could answer those potentially derailing questions. Like the rest of the world, they had never seen the letters.

From St. John Lateran, Oder leaped into action. He soon spoke with Poltawska, who agreed to share with him all her notes—including some not published in the book. She then took a sworn oath not to disclose to anyone exactly how many or which letters she had surrendered. In early June 2009, Oder told the Associated Press that Poltawska was "a serious person and what she says warrants respect." In that same month, Cardinal Martins, then the emeritus head of the Vatican's saint-making division, said he would ask Poltawska to send photocopies of the entire correspondence to the Holy See for review and to "avoid future possible problems." Martins also publicly accused the nearly ninety-year-old doctor of withholding the letters from the army of theologians who for several years had been digging into John Paul's life. By then, numerous news organizations, including the Catholic News Service, the *National Catholic Reporter,* and Italy's *La Stampa,* were reporting that the once-secret stash of letters had "bogged down" the cause. From that point, verbal attacks on Poltawska from the Catholic hierarchy only gained venom. Cardinal Stanislaw Dziwisz, who also hailed from Krakow and who for decades had served as John Paul's closest aide, slammed Poltawska for publishing the book and claiming "a special relationship where none existed." Dziwisz, however, also was known to have long been hostile toward Poltawska—a frequent guest at the Vatican during John Paul's reign. In early June 2009, Dziwisz told *La Stampa* that John Paul treated all his old friends from Poland with a special affinity. "The difference," Dziwisz said, "is that Ms. Poltawska exaggerates in her attitude, and the expressions and display of her behavior are inappropriate and out of place."

"What is wrong in a priest's friendship with a woman?" Poltawska responded during an interview with the Associated Press. "Isn't a priest a human being?" Further, her book of memories contained no references to amorous feelings between the psychiatrist and the pope, who in the 1950s and 1960s had crusaded together against abortion in Poland and who had collaborated on his 1960 book *Love and Responsibility,* what some biographers view as his seminal tome. Authored when he was Bishop Karol Wojtyla, *Love and Responsibility* argued that while science could explain some elements of the bonds between men and women, only a study of the whole person revealed a full understanding of gender chemistry. He used his book to preach against artificial birth control, premarital sex, and divorce, insisting that those behaviors and acts conflicted with a person's ability to reach true and full contentment. Finally, *Love and Responsibility* asserted that sex was not only meant for procreation, but that it bolstered intimacy within a marriage. His observations on sex also ventured into the medical when he wrote that "organic disorders" and "outright hostility" could flare in women if "the engorgement of the genital organs at the time of sexual arousal is not terminated by detumescence, which in women is closely connected with orgasm." That was just one of the passages where literary critics believed they saw Poltawska's influence. "We worked together on the same thing," Poltawska said in June 2009, amid the media firestorm over her published letters. "We got to know each other in work, not in anything else."

On a more personal level, it was Poltawska's grim diagnosis of an abdominal tumor in 1962 that had persuaded Wojtyla to reach out frantically to one of his spiritual heroes, Padre Pio.

For many Catholics—Wojtyla included—Pio was a supernatural superstar capable of wielding miracles, a man who claimed to have suffered from unexplained stigmata wounds for much of his life. In November 1962, Bishop Wojtyla was in Rome attending the opening meetings of the Second Vatican Ecumenical Council or "Vatican II"—a monumental, three-year modernization of Roman Catholicism that produced, among other historic shifts, the replacement of Latin as the vernacular of the liturgy. One night during his Italian stay, Wojtyla received an urgent letter revealing that his friend, Dr. Polstawska, was hospitalized with a suspicious tumor.

Doctors had told Polstawska they were 95 percent certain the mass in her intestine was malignant. Only exploratory surgery would verify their concerns, and, if the growth was indeed cancerous, Polstawska would have only about eighteen months to live. Wojtyla immediately remembered his 1947 trek to San Giovanni Rotondo to meet and confess his sins to the mystical monk, Pio. On November 17, 1962, Wojtyla dashed off a letter in Latin to Pio, which said, in part, "Venerable Father, I ask for your prayers for a certain mother of four young girls. . . . Now her health and even her life are in grave danger due to cancer. Pray that God, through the intercession of the Most Blessed Virgin, has mercy on her and her family." To expedite delivery, the letter was given to Angelo Battisti, an employee of the Vatican secretary of state's office who also served as the administrator for Pio's hospital, Casa Sollievo Della Sofferenza, located in the same piazza as Pio's friary at San Giovanni Rotondo. According to an interview Battisti later gave, he immediately drove 236 miles from Rome to Pio's personal quarters near the Adriatic coast in southeastern Italy. After Battisti's arrival, Pio instructed him to "open it and read it." Pio silently listened to the letter's contents, then raised his head and, according to Battisti, said, "Little Angelo, to this one, one cannot say no." For the Italian word "one," Pio had used *questo,* a masculine pronoun, which Battisti took to mean Wojtyla. Pio then bowed his head and prayed.

The operation on Poltawska was scheduled for November 23, 1962. On November 24, a Saturday, Wojtyla phoned Andrzej to learn the outcome. The surgery had been unexpectedly canceled, Poltawska's husband said. "The doctors are confronted with a mystery. . . . They could not find anything," he told Wojtyla. The tumor, he explained, simply had vanished from the woman's body. Relieved and believing that Pio had worked a miracle, Wojtyla wrote a second letter to the monk, dated November 28. "Venerable

Father," it said, "the woman . . . was suddenly cured. Thanks be to God! And also to you, Venerable Father, I offer the greatest possible gratitude."

† † †

Wanda Poltawska's suitcase full of once-secret letters from "Br" became the first public crack in what had once seemed to be an impenetrable wall of support for John Paul II's canonization cause. But other thorny issues emerged. At the epicenter of those fresh concerns was Cardinal Angelo Sodano, John Paul's longtime secretary of state. According to numerous news organizations, including the *National Catholic Reporter,* Sodano had been reluctant to testify before the tribunal investigating John Paul's virtues. What's more, Sodano's top deputy for seven years, Cardinal Leonardo Sandri, also had not appeared before the tribunal.

Vatican theologians who were assigned to examine the two-thousand-page *positio* for John Paul's cause balked at the testimonial absences of Sodano and Sandri. They asked Monsignor Oder to supply them with extra documentation, according to *Il Giornale,* a daily newspaper based in Milan, Italy. More bumps followed. In early June 2009, the *National Catholic Reporter* suggested that John Paul's friendship with the late Father Marcial Maciel Degollado loomed as still another roadblock for the cause. Degollado, the Mexican founder of the conservative and enigmatic religious order the Legionaries of Christ, was in 2006 disciplined by Pope Benedict XVI to live "a reserved life of prayer and penitence." The pope gave no public explanation, but Degollado had previously been accused by more than a dozen former priests and seminarians of sexually abusing them when they were children. John Paul had frequently and openly praised Degollado, describing him on one occasion as "an efficacious guide for youth." Sodano was also known as a good friend and defender of Degollado. In 2006, however, Sodano was one of several cardinals allowed to view the evidence that Vatican investigators had amassed against Degollado after the sexual allegations had surfaced against the priest. "Does what Sodano learned about [Degollado] figure into his reluctance to testify on behalf of John Paul II?" the *National Catholic Reporter*'s Tom Roberts asked in a June 2009 column. "Perhaps it is a simple dose of reality that is slowing down . . . the rush to canonize Pope John Paul II. Certainly a pontificate a quarter century long would produce a great deal to investigate."

Indeed, the Catholic clergy sex scandal—and how John Paul handled those disturbing cases—had long been one of the hottest arguments against his sainthood. Oder's office had received and noted those objections—including a December 2005 letter signed by eleven dissident theologians from Europe and Latin America. The group had written a seven-point critique of John Paul that chastised his conservative position on contraception, the limited role of women in the Church, and some questionable financial maneuvers by the Vatican, including the Holy See's links to Italy's Banco Ambrosiano, which went bankrupt in 1982. But a centerpiece of the dissidents' letter was the child-sex-abuse scandal—especially the discovery that American priests who had molested children were not defrocked or handed over to police, but merely transferred to new parishes.

John Paul's so-called "saint factory" remained still another common target for his most outspoken fault-finders. And the bullish forces driving John Paul's own canonization cause with such historic vigor—waiving the five-year waiting period, and submitting his *positio* to the Vatican seven years sooner than usual—stirred echoes of the late pope's own retooling of the saint-making process and his forceful use of canonization as a Catholic crusading tool. Late in John Paul's life, Brother Michael O'Neill McGrath, an American author and illustrator of books on saints, summed up John

Paul's 482 canonizations this way to the *Chicago Sun-Times*: "While they're good people, I'm sure, they're not terribly inspiring. We're not going to spend a lot of time offering prayers to obscure French founders of orders. . . . What kind of an inspiration is that?" Still another American cleric, Father Richard P. McBrien, joined that chorus by openly suggesting that John Paul had hastily rammed certain fad candidates through the canonization pipeline instead of allowing their merits to be tested by waiting a few extra years. "What's the rush?" McBrien asked an interviewer in 2002. "If someone is really in heaven, we'll find out in our time." McBrien was a liberal University of Notre Dame theologian who believed women should be ordained as priests. He, in particular, had vehemently disagreed with John Paul's June 2002 decision to sanctify Padre Pio, saying, "That makes religion into a kind of act, a show, a kind of theatrical operation." As for Pio, and the Christlike stigmata he allegedly bore that elevated the monk into a mystical Catholic icon, O'Brien added in 2002, "What kind of model is that? If a Catholic or anyone else today . . . woke up in the morning and looked down at their hands and saw them bleeding with wounds that they didn't know how they got, what do you think the first instinct of a healthy person would be? 'Oh, thank God, this is a sign of holiness. I'm gonna be a saint'? I think the first instinct of a healthy, authentically religious person would be to call their wife . . . or husband or get on the phone and say, 'You gotta get me to the emergency room.' "

Pio may have had a lifelong fan in John Paul, but for many years the Vatican treated the friar like a scam artist and a pariah. He was born Francesco Forgione in 1887, and took the name Pio when he joined the Capuchin Order of the Catholic Church at age fifteen. He soon gained a reputation as an earnest monk who prayed so hard he sometimes lapsed into trances. In 1916 the Capuchin Order sent Pio to live in San Giovanni. According to legend, he began receiving the bloody stigmata two years later while praying in front of a crucifix. But he initially was said to have been embarrassed by the sores and had tried to hide them. As word spread to Rome about the monk's strange lesions, Catholic leaders dispatched a series of doctors to examine Pio's hands between May and October of 1919. One doctor wrapped the monk's palms in bandages, but as the story went, the stigmata bled through the wrappings. The second doctor supposedly stuck his finger inside the hand holes. The third doctor suspected Pio had caused the injuries himself, perhaps using the power of suggestion. Those were the last official medical inspections of Pio's stigmata, but many local Catholics believed the wounds were real and began talking about more supernatural powers the bearded monk had allegedly exhibited, including the ability to appear in two places at once. His celebrity raged across Europe. The Vatican, however, remained highly skeptical. Several different popes launched investigations of Pio, and the Vatican once bugged his confessional in San Giovanni in an attempt to prove that Pio was a fraud. In 1931 the Vatican even placed Pio under a two-year house arrest. Again his cult only grew, becoming international and more lucrative. According to historical accounts, some of Pio's followers occasionally sliced off bits of his clothing and sold them as souvenirs, while random bandages dipped in sheep's blood were simultaneously hawked as authentic Pio relics.

After Pio died in 1968, San Giovanni blossomed into a busy shrine with annual visitor numbers rivaling Lourdes — the tiny town in the foothills of the French Pyrenees that had become a tourist mecca following a series of reported Marian apparitions in 1858. In San Giovanni, millions of pilgrims began flocking each year to Pio's final resting place. His beatification cause was launched in 1982 by the diocesan bishop closest to San Giovanni, but Vatican investigators never were asked to consider Pio's alleged stigmata. According to Monsignor Robert Sarno, the longest serving American official at the Congregation for the Causes of Saints, the Vatican only weighed whether Pio had lived a life of heroic virtue. And, ultimately, the Congregation's cardinals, archbishops, and bishops found that Pio had, indeed, been a virtuous man, which led John Paul to declare Pio "Venerable" in 1997.

With that papal decree, the Vatican instantly reversed and paved over its once-public distrust and dislike of Pio. Why, then, had the Vatican been so suspicious of the monk so many decades earlier? CNN's Christiane Amanpour posed that question to Sarno in 2002. "We live in a human world. There are people who will question the best of people, their motives, their reasons for acting," Sarno had responded. "Everything is investigated by the Church." John Paul subsequently approved two alleged miracles attributed to Pio. The first involved a forty-six-year-old woman in southern Italy who in 1995 struggled to breathe when a lymph duct burst in her neck and filled her chest with lymphatic fluid. According to the woman, as she was on the edge of consciousness and waiting for an operation to drain the fluid, she dreamed of Pio, and in the dream he said, "Don't worry, I will be your surgeon." When she awoke, a CT scan showed the swelling had reduced substantially; a third CT scan found that the chest fluid had fully disappeared—all within twenty-four hours and without medical intervention. The second case centered on a nine-year-old Italian boy with meningitis, whose mother had prayed to Pio while her son was in a coma.

When John Paul canonized Pio in 2002, Vatican City was swamped by an estimated 200,000 Pio fans—one of the largest crowds ever assembled in Rome during John Paul's papacy. Standing in the sweltering crush that day was Wanda Poltawska, the pope's "Dusia."

CHAPTER TEN

The Trial

An icy gale sliced into the invited guests as they rushed into a back door at the Indianapolis Archdiocese headquarters on January 23, 2003. The visitors included two courtroom stenographers, a white-haired nun on the mission of her life, a dashing "saint-maker" from Rome, and several witnesses to an alleged miracle. The outside chill clung to their thick coats as they descended a sloping hallway and approached the underground library—a windowless room where the secret trial was set to commence.

In the basement of the brick building—originally constructed as a high school—the guests were instantly warmed with hot coffee and good cheer, supplied by a pair of smiling priests. Monsignor Fred Easton and Father Jim Bonke, both canon-law graduates from different pontifical universities in Rome, ran the archdiocese's Metropolitan Tribunal, which typically heard marriage annulments and, increasingly, sex-abuse allegations against Catholic clerics. Easton was a jovial man who, even in conversation, spoke with the dramatic rhythm and lilt of a Sunday preacher. He was a classical music buff who had played his violin before audiences, a born performer. He was the tribunal's vicar judicial, or head judge. Bonke (pronounced *Bon-key*) was a gentle and instantly likable soul whose proudest possession was a football autographed by Indianapolis Colts quarterback Peyton Manning. Bonke also happened to be a supernatural believer who, in 1991, had waded into the purportedly healing waters of Lourdes, France, to pray for his cancer-stricken mother. She later overcame the disease. He was the tribunal's promoter of justice, or prosecutor.

That frigid Thursday morning, Easton and Bonke once again convened their ecclesiastical court—this time to test the alleged miracle of Phil McCord. Their primary tasks: ask the witnesses the proper questions, solicit the pertinent facts, record and transcribe every word uttered in their courtroom, compile all the vital medical records, and then hand the thick case file over to the jury—the Vatican's doctors, theologians, and consistory of cardinals. The tribunal would meet five times over the next six weeks. And although the external wind chill registered minus 22 degrees on the trial's first day, the courtroom environment was anything but cold and adversarial.

As promoter of justice, Bonke would be the lead questioner of all witnesses. Bonke, however, had no intention of verbally squeezing McCord, his doctors, or family members with difficult queries aimed at exposing testimonial inconsistencies. The priest had no plans to aggressively interrogate the witnesses. In fact, Bonke's questions—precisely fifty-one per witness—had been carefully crafted by the postulator, Dr. Andrea Ambrosi, one of the alleged miracle's biggest boosters. "Basically, I stuck pretty much to the script," Bonke said later. "My role was simply to be the interviewer. . . . We tried to have as comfortable a setting as possible . . . to be cordial, to make the experience as pleasant as possible and to try to couch the questions in such a way that [the witnesses] wouldn't feel intimidated."

Bonke, like many priests in the archdiocese, held a lifelong devotion to Mother Théodore's cause. In 1950, when he was a first-grader at St. Catherine School in Indianapolis, he and his classmates had been urged to pray for Mother Théodore's canonization. One of Bonke's cousins was a member of the Sisters of Providence, and his sister had been named Anne-Therese in honor of the Woods founder. "Yes, I was rooting for a favorable outcome," Bonke acknowledged. "I tried to maintain as objective a posture as I could because I felt that my role was not to be a cheerleader of the case. . . . But I can't deny that I was hopeful that the thing would get [approved as a miracle in Rome]."

Easton, too, had been familiar with Mother Théodore's cause since his childhood, when he was taught by Sisters of Providence at St. Charles Catholic School in Bloomington, Indiana. A stickler for Catholic jurisprudence—and past president of the 1,500-member Canon Law Society of America—Easton's utmost concern was ensuring that his tribunal adhered to the strict Vatican norms for conducting local miracle examinations. Similar to any criminal judge, Easton didn't want the McCord case later tossed out on a technicality that occurred under his watch. And while he acknowledged that part of him wanted to see the alleged miracle someday earn Vatican endorsement, he also applied a cynical eye to the facts. "There are two sides of us when we do this, [but] we are very conscious of our fiduciary obligation to be neutral," Easton said later. "I'm very much appreciative of the reality that miracles do happen, and I say that in an age when we find many instances of hoaxes in this area. There are a lot of people who want miracles to happen. Sometimes [however] these miracles are either imagined or contrived."

Although the final verdict would be rendered in Rome, Easton's tribunal would nonetheless seek to "sort out the real from the unreal," he said. "The job description of anyone working in a tribunal is to look for the truth. In most cases, you can't find absolute truth, so we are coming to a moral certitude." The phrase "moral certitude" had been an essential piece of canon law since 1942. That year, in an address to the highest of all Catholic tribunals, the Roman Rota, Pope Pius XII had defined the core concept this way: "To reach moral certitude, judges must be able to exclude the probability of error but are not held to the impossible and paralyzing standard of excluding all possibility of error." A judge's subjective opinion did not matter, according to the code of canon law, and moral certitude could only be found within the presented evidence. American criminal law had been founded on similar underpinnings—"reasonable doubt" was the sacred dividing line between guilt and innocence. Easton's running orders for the tribunal staff were simple: "Let the chips fall where they may." As he later recalled: "That was a folksy way of saying 'be objective.'"

If nothing else, the miracle trial offered Easton and Bonke a welcome diversion from a rising load of grim cases that had recently been presented to the archdiocese tribunal—allegations of sex abuse against area priests. "We've had to deal with a lot of those situations," Bonke said. "It's a little bit painful. It involves hearing the accuser or the victim, and trying to discern and determine whether there is credibility of evidence. Then we have to hear the priest. It's just not pleasant. And these are guys that I know, or have known." Just one month earlier, Easton had helped the Canon Law Society of America compile a special booklet to assist Catholic dioceses across the country in implementing the "Charter for the Protection of Children and Young People." Approved by the U.S. Conference of Catholic Bishops in June 2002, the charter called on each diocese to meet six goals: creating a safe environment for children; aiding the healing and reconciliation of victims and survivors of abuse; promptly responding to any allegations of sexual assault; cooperating with civil authorities; disciplining offenders; and increasing future accountability to guarantee that "the problem continues to be effectively dealt with" by the Church. In the same basement library in downtown Indianapolis where young men had revealed tales of molestation to Easton and Bonke, a convent caretaker and his doctor were about to testify about a purported supernatural event, an alleged healing by God.

"We were working both ends of the spectrum of canon law," Easton said later. "Holiness and evil."

To put an alleged miracle on trial, Easton needed an independent physician on his panel, a medical professional to help cross-examine the witnesses and sniff out any scientific loose ends not covered by Ambrosi's fifty-one scripted questions. For that chore he recruited Dr. John C. Barker, a steadfast Catholic born at St. Vincent's, a Catholic hospital in Indianapolis, and educated at local Catholic schools. Barker had married a girl who grew up just five doors down from his childhood home on the east side of Indianapolis. His medical clinic was located near that same gritty neighborhood. As a family practitioner, Barker had seen and treated, he said, "just about" every illness and injury common to Indiana children and adults. He was folksy—a physician who did home remodeling on the side. He was good with his hands, loved tools and cars. And as a doctor he maintained that blue-collar ethic in his medical practice, referring to himself as "a trench guy." But he also knew something about eyes. His brother, Felix M. Barker, was an optometrist in Philadelphia who had spent years researching eye disorders. He had testified as an eye expert in legal cases and had once appeared on ABC's *Good Morning America* to talk about eye damage caused by the sun's ultraviolet rays. John and Felix often discussed eye science. And one final factor helped put Barker in the third seat on Easton's tribunal: a family connection. Barker was Easton's first cousin. The doctor's father and the priest's mother had been siblings.

Monsignor Easton and Dr. Barker had shared many meaningful moments. Easton had baptized Barker's three daughters as well as two of his grandchildren, and he had performed the wedding ceremony for one of Barker's daughters. Before enlisting Barker, however, Easton had asked Ambrosi about the propriety of placing his first cousin on the tribunal panel. According to Easton, Ambrosi had replied, "There's no problem with that. [Only] if he was a relative of Phil McCord might it be a problem." Barker readily agreed to serve as the medical expert. "I thought I would just help my cousin out," Barker said later. "I certainly went into the process sort of skeptical of the unexplained miracle. [As doctors] we're kind of more science-oriented—facts, and cause and effect. This was a different realm. My cousin said they wanted someone who understands medicine in general to kind of put things in perspective." The trial's six sessions all would take place on Thursdays to coincide with the scheduled days off Barker took from his medical practice. The blood bond between the trial's judge and its chief medical expert marked just one of the familial connections that laced together many of the tribunal's participants, especially its doctors.

Under Vatican rules, if the recipient of an alleged supernatural healing was still alive, he or she "must be examined separately by two medical experts"—known in Rome as *ab inspectione*. Appointed by the local bishop, the two independent physicians were asked to "ascertain the present state of health of the person healed and the duration of the healing," then testify about their findings, Vatican codes stipulated. The first of those roles was given to Dr. Robert L. Gregory—the retired Indianapolis internist and friend to Kathy Fleming who had helped Fleming understand and translate McCord's medical charts in preparation for presenting the case to Ambrosi in Rome. The second *ab inspectione* physician was Dr. James McCallum—a retired ophthalmologist who had practiced at St. Vincent's Hospital and who once had been the eye doctor for both Easton and Bonke. Finally there was Dr. Nicholas Rader—also Fleming's friend and eye doctor—who had agreed to testify about his recent review of McCord's medical records.

One hour before the trial opened, Bishop Gerald A. Gettelfinger hosted a quiet ceremony at archdiocesan headquarters to swear in the tribunal's three leaders plus Ambrosi and Sister Marie Kevin as postulator and vice-postulator of the cause. The moment was largely designed to underscore and secure the highly confidential nature of the proceedings. Gettelfinger was the first in the room to take a

prescribed oath to observe full and complete secrecy throughout
the hearings. Then Easton, Bonke, Ambrosi, Marie Kevin, and the
trial's two hired notaries—Catherine Fislar and Karen Clement—
each recited the oath. Finally, Barker repeated the vow of secrecy
while placing his hand on the Bible, as all the others had done.
Documents containing written versions of the oath were signed
by all eight participants and stamped by the notaries. During the
trial, every question asked and every word of testimony offered in
the windowless basement room would be recorded on audiotape,
then typed into a transcript by one of the notaries. Finally, each
witness—there would be ten in all—would sign their transcript
(also stamped by a notary), and then they, too, would repeat the
oath to "observe secrecy." Until the alleged miracle was decided by
the pope, whatever happened inside the ecclesiastical courtroom
was supposed to stay there.

Ambrosi and his translator had already spent three days in Indianapolis, seeking last-minute facts from several witnesses. Based
on all his pre-trial interviews, Ambrosi had painstakingly drafted
Bonke's fifty-one-item questionnaire. It was precisely worded and
carefully ordered to try to establish the four criteria the Vatican
would need to see in order to approve the alleged miracle—that
McCord's cure was "sudden, complete and permanent," and that
it carried no scientific explanation. Ambrosi's exhaustive list also
had the goal of anticipating and rebutting any doubts that might
later surface in Rome when the Vatican's experts tore into the facts.
The first two questions were simply meant to identify each witness
(name, address, birthdate, and profession) and exactly how they
knew Phil McCord. Forty-two of the questions were medically ori-
ented, such as number forty: "Is it true that the morning after the
invocation, Philip did not feel the heaviness in his eye, which meant
that the edema was gone?" Six questions were theological, including number thirty-seven: "What kind of prayers or formulas did

he use to ask Mother Théodore's intercession?" Only Gregory and McCallum—the independent examiners of McCord's right eye—would be spared the full, scripted interrogation.

For the other eight witnesses who had been summoned to the tribunal, the final question they would hear cut to the very heart of the case and sought to lure them down the path of the miraculous: "If this recovery can be considered scientifically difficult, can you attribute it to the supernatural intercession of Blessed Théodore Guérin?" On that pivotal point, three of the invited guests grappled with private doubts—including the star witness.

† † †

Having been interviewed twice by Ambrosi and once by Sister Marie Kevin, Phil McCord already anticipated the flavor of questions he would face during the trial. Still, he and Debbie both were anxious about their looming appearances before the panel. What they revealed—and how they conveyed it—could either deliver Mother Théodore to sainthood or perhaps dash her chances for eternal glory. Working side by side with the nuns, Phil could almost smell the rising anticipation at the Woods. "Knowing how important it was to the sisters, that makes you a little nervous," Debbie recalled later. "You wanted to make sure everything was right. Everything you said needed to be right."

The engineer could not explain his new vision, could not dismantle the mystery, could not even find the science in his own cure. Working at a hospital for so many years, he had witnessed or at least heard about, he said, "thousands of things" that defied the best explanations of doctors and nurses. McCord took some comfort in the fact that he merely needed to sit before the ecclesiastical court and tell his story, cite the facts, recount the sequence: cause and effect, prayer and cure.

Still, there was an uneasy truth buried within his fantastic

tale — "a real conflict," as he called it. Indeed, what had happened
to him was strange and scintillating, enigmatic and exhilarating.
But he often quizzed himself: Had it truly been grand enough,
momentous enough, and powerful enough to be called a miracle
of God? McCord viewed the healing of his right eye as "kind of a
small thing" when compared to the sickness and sadness faced by
millions of others, including people who prayed that they or their
children would be spared from a medical death sentence. His life,
he figured, must still contain some unknown purpose, some reason
for his divine bounty.

"I thought, 'Am I supposed to do something?' Because I couldn't
figure out anything I had done to deserve this," McCord said later.
"So I thought, 'There must be something I'm going to do.' It's really
kind of hard to accept when you see so many people that are really
so deserving" of God's healing.

"I wasn't cured of cancer or something that major. There have
been so many other [great] things that have happened that are
attributable to Mother Théodore. This really didn't seem to rise to
that," he said. "Why me? . . . What does this mean?"

He had started to unload some of these mind-twirling thoughts
on one of his closest friends at the Woods, Sister Jenny Howard,
his former boss. She was one of the nuns whom McCord had driven
into Terre Haute for the staff lunch on January 4, 2001 — the morning he had awakened feeling different. The morning after his prayer.

On the day he followed the organ music into the Church of the
Immaculate Conception, he had sought peace, not a miracle. Later
he couldn't fathom why he, of all people, had allegedly received
one. He wasn't Catholic. He wasn't particularly religious. He was a
father and a husband and a softball coach, a handyman, not a holy
man.

"It's a special thing," he had said, "but I'm not special."

Jenny was one of the few sisters with whom McCord felt

completely at ease. He could open up to her, trust her, and honestly lay down his troubles to her.

She understood that McCord was a quiet man, usually reserved. So when he spoke, Jenny listened intently. And she chose her words gingerly.

"I think miracles happen all the time to people, but maybe they're not so obvious or so profound that we always recognize them," Jenny said. "Even in my own life, I think it requires an openness on my part, recognizing that God's presence in my life is that close. I don't know about others, but sometimes I like to be in control. So sometimes I'm thinking I'm controlling the situation and I'm not really stepping back and looking at how God is moving in my life, or in the lives of other people. So what that requires is just a willingness to recognize that little miracles happen every day in people's lives."

That Mother Théodore chose McCord, Jenny thought, "is so beautiful. Here is this ordinary person, one of our staff." During Mother Théodore's Indiana years, she was often warmly expressive and openly appreciative of the hired American workers at the Woods. Without them, the French sisters could never have sustained a remote farm and survived the brutal winters. In her diaries, the founder frequently mentioned her gratitude for the staff. To Jenny, that history might also resonate with McCord. "It's just a perfect situation," Jenny said, "that she could show her care and her healing for someone who was part of our staff." Even more, the fact that McCord wasn't Catholic "obviously didn't matter," Jenny added. "It brings much more hope, I think. You don't have to be some obviously holy Catholic person [to receive a miracle]. It's the ordinary, regular, everyday person. It's just being yourself. That's another thing Mother Théodore said: 'You don't have to do anything extraordinary, just do it every day and do it for the love of God.' That's how she lived her life. That's why she was attracted to those who are just everyday people."

The quiet chats with his nun friend were soothing to McCord. Still, it would take Jenny a few more years to find the right words to finally offer him solace, the right logic to help him solve his spiritual conundrum.

In the meantime, McCord would soon face more than fifty questions from a Church tribunal. And the priests would require him to place his hand on the Bible and vow to be honest. When his day of testimony came, he wondered, would a priest ask him to swear that he believed his own cure had been administered supernaturally, that it had come via God's touch? And if asked that, how would be answer?

For a guy with suddenly perfect eyesight, there was so much still beyond his view. But as the trial of his alleged miracle began, one of the things McCord ached most to see was the end of his long road to acceptance.

† † †

At 10:30 a.m. on January 23, the first witness settled into a padded, straight-backed chair at the midpoint of a ten-foot-long conference table. On the far side of the narrow room, she could see a hanging painting featuring the likeness of Monsignor Francis Gavisk, the archdiocese's vicar general in the 1920s. Above her, fluorescent lights glowed. All around her, floor-to-ceiling shelves were packed with canon-law books and past decisions of the Roman Rota, the highest Catholic court. To her right, at the head of the table, Monsignor Fred Easton sat in the judge's seat. Across the table from her, Father Jim Bonke shuffled through the prepared list of questions. Next to him, Dr. John Barker did the same. At the opposite end of the table, one of the notaries readied a tape recorder. The door was shut.

One floor above, next to the archdiocese reception desk, Sister Marie Kevin Tighe sat alone in silence. As vice-postulator and promoter of the cause, she was prohibited from attending or even eavesdropping on the secret sessions. But she wanted to be nearby. The Church trial was perhaps the most important moment in her life. Days earlier, in fact, she had moved out of the small white campus house she shared with two other sisters and had taken up temporary residence in Owens Hall, a Woods dormitory. She did so, she said, so she could shelve all her housemate responsibilities, such as cooking, cleaning, and grocery shopping. She wanted to be free to escort each witness to Indianapolis Archdiocese headquarters on their scheduled day and hour. Her mind was totally wrapped around an alleged miracle.

Like the nine invited guests who soon would follow her, the trial's first witness—a nun devoted to God—was asked to touch the Bible and swear to tell the truth. Sister Jenny Howard did just that, and then she took the oath of secrecy.

As Phil's friend and former supervisor (by 2003, she was the community's vocation director, essentially the head of recruitment), Jenny appreciated why the tribunal wanted to question her. She had spent time with McCord before and after his recovery. She had observed the swift change in his appearance. Privately, though, she also marveled at her own familial link to Mother Théodore's cause for sainthood. Her aunt, Sister Dorothy Eileen Howard, had nursed Sister Mary Theodosia Mug, the purported recipient of the first miracle, as the elderly nun took her final breaths at the Woods infirmary. And Dorothy had testified before local Church investigators in 1958 as they continued to examine the facts behind the first alleged miracle.

Jenny's memories of the events from late 2000 and early 2001 would help the tribunal begin to chew on some of the theological meat of the case. The tribunal wanted to know, specifically, how desperate McCord had felt before praying, how often he typically prayed, where he prayed on January 3, 2001, why he would think to invoke Mother Théodore's name or request intercession from the founder, what his prayer entailed, and whether he had prayed solely to Mother Théodore or if perhaps he had fired off a scattershot pattern of pleas to a litany of saints or other blesseds. During the trial, Easton and Bonke would rely on Sister Jenny and one other Sister of Providence—plus McCord's office assistant, his wife, and his son—to help them scratch out some answers to those theological queries. Four doctors, meanwhile, had been summoned by the panel to explain the medical intricacies and oddities of his recovery, and Phil McCord himself would cover all that ground when his testimonial turn finally came. According to canon law, the proof of a miracle lay as much in the theological substance as it did in absence of scientific reason. Before McCord's cure ever reached the pope's desk for consideration, the Vatican's experts would have to gauge the caretaker's reverent request just as carefully as they evaluated the speed and permanence of his visual healing.

Jenny, like all the witnesses to follow, warmed up with several rudimentary inquiries about her birthdate, her home address, and her ties to McCord. Then the promoter of justice veered into the nun's grasp of McCord's quiet fears—what had most bothered him about the eye problem, and whether he had lost hope of ever regaining full sight.

"How was Mr. McCord curing himself?" Bonke asked.

"I don't know that," Jenny said. "What I do know about Phil is that he is kind of a quiet person. Unless you might directly ask him how he is, how he is feeling, he would not necessarily come right out and tell you. . . . Personal things would come up [while we were] maybe walking to a meeting."

"But the concern," Bonke asked, "was that he would not improve significantly [from his half-blind state]?"

"Right. As a matter of fact, it might get worse," she said. "He talked about the fact that he could become permanently blind. . . .

He was in a lot of discomfort. But it seemed like the risks [associated with the transplant] were high, so he really didn't know if he wanted to engage in that or not."

"I was going to ask—is it true that Phil isn't Catholic?"

"As far as I know. It wasn't like he wouldn't, at times, attend our services," she said. "But he wouldn't on a regular basis."

Jenny had anticipated the tribunal would ask when she first had spotted McCord after his prayer in the big church, so she had brought her 2001 daybook into the trial room. After that question was raised, she opened the book, scanned the January pages, and testified that McCord had, on Thursday, January 4, 2001, driven her into Terre Haute, where they had attended a staff lunch. "Phil didn't bring up anything about his eye," and from the backseat, she had not noticed his reduced orbital swelling, she said. But during a staff meeting on Friday, January 12, she had sat opposite McCord at a conference table in Providence Hall. There, Jenny testified, she "could recognize that his eye seemed different, and that he seemed to be getting better." Following that meeting, when Jenny and McCord had been alone in the room, she had inquired, "How are you, Phil?" He had then acknowledged, "My eye is better." And as they had talked further, McCord had then revealed to Jenny how he had wandered into the basilica, plunked down in a pew, and begged God and Mother Théodore for mental peace.

"He said he had prayed because he was really worried about his surgery," Jenny told the tribunal.

Bonke reached question number fifty-one on his list.

"If this recovery can be considered scientifically difficult, can you attribute it to the supernatural intercession of the Blessed Théodore Guérin?"

"My sense of Mother Théodore is that she is capable of being a personal advocate for whomever she chooses, and was so in this particular situation," Jenny testified. "And I think it happens all the time. It's just that I don't think it's as easy to see or is as obvious, or that it can be explained in a scientific way. So yes, of course, I think she could."

Sharon Elaine Moore, like her boss, was one of the few non-Catholics on the Woods campus. A Terre Haute native nearing seventy, she had been employed by the Sisters of Providence since 1982 and had known McCord since the day she became his administrative assistant. As mutual spiritual outsiders amid a cluster of nuns, it made sense that Moore and McCord occasionally carved out a few minutes to compare their thoughts on organized religion. The tribunal members understood that too.

"Can you tell us," Bonke asked, "what is Philip's faith?"

"He is not Catholic. He told me at one time it was amazing he turned out OK at all," Moore testified. "I think part of his family is Christian Scientist and maybe part is . . . Baptist."

Dr. Barker, meanwhile, saw Moore's appearance as one of his first opportunities to rummage through the medical narrative. As a physician he needed to be able to visualize how McCord's right eye had changed the day after his prayer—the colors of the sclera and the surrounding skin, the sag of the lid, the plumpness of the facial tissue.

"Did you see him that day?" Barker asked.

"Yes," Moore testified.

"How did his eye then compare to the way it normally looked?"

"His eye looked better. His eye looked much better," Moore said. "The angriness under the eye and the swelling and the redness had diminished."

"Did he say anything about the sight out of that eye at that time?"

"No. I don't believe he mentioned the sight. It's just that he felt the pressure in the eye was different. And the feeling *in* the eye, as far as the edema was concerned, appeared to be gone."

Before leaving the trial room, Sharon Moore listened to question fifty-one. The tribunal members were curious whether a non-Catholic would venture into the supernatural, whether she believed her boss's restored vision could be ascribed to the long-dead nun who had built the religious compound in the trees outside Terre Haute.

Was your boss's cure, Moore was asked, due to the supernatural intercession of Mother Théodore?

"In my heart," she answered, "I feel that is precisely what happened."

Minutes after the administrative assistant exited, one of the convent's ranking leaders replaced Moore in the witness chair. Sister Mary Dempsey was McCord's supervisor, and she carried the title of director of congregation services. She promptly told the tribunal that McCord had revealed to her that his vision was growing "blurry" because of the ripening cataracts, and he had once asked her to suggest an eye specialist in Terre Haute. After the cataract was removed from McCord's right eye in October 2000, Sister Mary recalled that the eye "looked just terrible . . . seemed half closed . . . looked puffy and bloodshot and discolored, red in the eye and sort of brownish under and around the eye."

"Do you know if there were risks involved with the [transplant], and what those were?" Bonke asked.

"Well, I heard there was a risk of even death . . . and he could go blind if it didn't work," Sister Mary testified.

"What was Phil's reaction that he had to have a risky operation for the cornea transplant?"

"He was scared," the nun said, "and very discouraged . . . I was told by Phil that he was walking down the hallway and went into the church by the tomb of Mother Théodore and prayed to her, stating he was not a Catholic and he would like her help if at all possible, so he could continue his work."

"And why," Bonke asked, "did he think to invoke Mother Théodore?"

"Well, our employees are very aware of Mother Théodore, and now," she testified, "we are praying for a second miracle."

Would she be willing to swear, Bonke asked, that McCord's visual revival was made possible by Mother Théodore's intercession?

"To my knowledge," Sister Mary responded, "I would."

That question—and that moment—had to feel surreal to the seventy-two-year-old nun. Sister Mary Dempsey had entered the Sisters of Providence congregation in 1949—nine years after Marie Kevin first stepped onto the campus. Sister Mary had, in fact, spent three-quarters of her life hearing about—and praying for—the possible sanctification of Mother Théodore. Now her own words, she realized, might help the founder achieve that titanic goal.

But even if the alleged McCord miracle was finally approved in Rome, and even if that validation ultimately sparked a splashy ceremony in St. Peter's Square, Sister Mary would never see it.

Five months to the day after she delivered her testimony, Sister Mary died in a bed in Karcher Hall, the Woods' round-the-clock nursing facility. Her death served as another reminder of the deep urgency felt by dozens of the community's oldest sisters. Many had waited a lifetime to savor the climax to their crusade. They hungered to see Mother Théodore canonized before—as the nuns phrased it—they, too, were "called home."

†   †   †

The second of Phil and Debbie McCord's three children, thirty-five-year-old Philip Todd McCord, was a full-time soldier in the Indiana Army National Guard. Several years after the trial, he would serve with the American forces waging war in Afghanistan.

During the closing months of 2000, however, Philip Todd was living at his parents' home outside Terre Haute while his father helped him remodel his own house in town, near the Indiana State University campus. Day after day, as Thanksgiving gave way to Christmas, the son had winced at the blistering deterioration of his dad's right eye.

Philip Todd always had considered his father's eyesight to be "horrible," he told the tribunal. And he described his father's eyeglasses as "actually quite disturbing" because the lenses were so massive and so thick. But following the second cataract surgery, the right eye's appearance had grown beyond disturbing, he said. It looked wounded. "He told me it was like somebody stuck him in the eye with a thumb," he testified. It was "watery and red . . . There was a lot of blinking. . . . He would dab at it with a Kleenex. . . . It was obvious he was in discomfort." But after his father's prayer in the church, the son quickly recognized, he said, a soothing of the eye's searing rawness. "It was clear," he testified. "It was an amazing transformation."

Describing the before-and-after picture? That was the simple part of the testimony for Philip Todd. Talking about Catholic theology? That made him somewhat uneasy. Phil McCord had raised his son as a Baptist. Saints and intercessory cures were not part of the family vocabulary, not concepts with which Philip Todd felt comfortable. To be sure, the young man was an American patriot with strong beliefs. But a God-given miracle occurring inside his father's eyeball? Philip Todd knew that his own father—a man of practicality and technology—might struggle with that core question.

"Was he completely convinced that he was recovered?" Bonke asked.

"I don't know that he was completely convinced because he is an engineer. So he has that scientific mind. So he's always questioning everything. So I don't know," Philip Todd testified.

The son was aware, too, that his father's vision had not totally cleared until he underwent a laser procedure to remove residual scar tissue fifty-six days after his prayer to Mother Théodore.

"He's an engineer," the son repeated. "So he lives by science. He's the kind of person that [believes one] should prove it."

But if his father's recovery indeed defied science, Bonke asked, "can you attribute it to the supernatural intercession of the Blessed Théodore Guérin?"

"I was raised a Baptist, so I'm not sure I even understand the whole nature of intercession. I know what I was told," Philip Todd answered. "I believe in the power of prayer to heal. So if he asked Mother Guérin for help, yes. I would say yes."

"It's hard to talk about this," the son admitted to the tribunal. "It makes me kind of squirm. Like I said, I was raised a Baptist. [But] yes, I would say Mother Théodore probably had something to do with it. And I believe it so much that my wife's great-uncle has cancer [and] they've got these little [Mother Théodore] prayer slips that the Sisters [of Providence] give out, so I asked to get one for him. I don't know what he's done with it. But I actually told him my father's story. I do believe it."

As did Philip Todd's mother. Debbie McCord, raised on an Indiana sheep farm, had been hardened by more than twenty years of nursing sickly babies in neonatal units and broken people in post-surgical wards. She had seen scores of patients inexplicably elude a deadly diagnosis. One of her quiet thrills: "Watching the people get well and walk out the door." Still, she described her own spiritual faith as "moderate." And as a healer herself, she was engulfed daily by the beeping monitors, beam-emitting tools, and bags of dripping drugs that were the common trappings of modern medicine. She observed, charted, and recorded the life-saving potency of everyday science. She also had noted, with frustration, the failure of medicine to fix her husband.

Bonke first wanted to hear exactly what Debbie McCord—as a wife and as a nurse—had witnessed in the man who nightly shared her dinner table in the kitchen nook.

"That evening [after the second cataract surgery on October 12] is when the pain and discomfort started," she testified. "He said it just ached. And when I took the bandage off the next day, there was bruising."

Her husband had made at least seven visits to Dr. Jeffrey Jungers's office over the next six weeks, she testified, and had been administered a range of different eye drops to relieve the swelling.

"What were the effects of this therapy?" Bonke asked.

"No change . . . in the morning [his eye] would be pink and by evening it would be bright red. . . . His right eyelid would be drooping . . . would almost cover half his eye."

Finally the tribunal moved into the area of the supernatural. What had Phil McCord shared with his wife about his unplanned visit to the Church of the Immaculate Conception? Had he known about the sacred practice of intercession? Many months later the theologians in Rome would sift through every word in Debbie's responses—particularly how Mother Théodore came to be mentioned in her husband's startling appeal.

"Does Philip pray or practice his faith when he needs something?"

"Phil feels that you should take care of yourself and then only in real big problems should you go ask God for help."

"Do you know why he thought to invoke Blessed Mother Théodore?"

"All I can tell you is what he told me at the supper table that night," Debbie testified. "He said, 'I went to church. I was walking down the hall and I just thought I would go in and sit down for a minute. And I went in and sat down and the sun was coming through the [stained-glass] window. And I thought, well, this is kind of a peaceful place to be. And I was calmed down a little. I just sat there and said, 'Mother Théodore, this is your house.' . . . I thought," Debbie continued, "'OK, Phil is a Baptist and he's used to praying directly to God,' and this kind of surprised me a little bit. . . . The next morning, when he woke up, I looked at him and said, 'Phil, how are you feeling? OK?' And he said, 'Yes.' And I said, 'Well your eye isn't swollen anymore.'"

"Can you give me a percentage?" Barker asked. "Was it completely not swollen? Or seventy-five percent better?"

"Oh, more than that," Debbie said. "The edema was gone!"

"Did he say anything about his vision on that day, the fourth of January?" Barker asked.

"He could see better. Yes, he said it wasn't as blurry as it had been."

But he didn't think, Debbie added, that he was fully cured—yet.

"What was keeping him from understanding—if he could see normally again?"

"Just his own skepticism," she said. "When you are sick, you always think you feel better in a short period of time. Hopefully you do. But in truth, he was. His eye looked better. I [soon] noticed he was starting to read more. So I think he was [eventually] starting to accept that, gosh, maybe this has healed."

Debbie, too, believed the eye had healed permanently—and supernaturally—that Mother Théodore had indeed interceded in her husband's life, she told the tribunal.

Then she revealed one more thing. During the ordeal, she had prayed for Phil every day. But like Phil's simple plea for peace, Debbie had never asked God to mend her husband's mangled eye.

Her quiet request came not from a place of medicine, but from a place of love: "Protect him."

CHAPTER ELEVEN

The Doctors

Before stepping into the archdiocese library to deliver the miracle trial's most decisive medical testimony, Dr. Nick Rader pondered two scraps of evidence that, so far, had not been mentioned in court. Two pepper-sized dots of human flesh laced with proteins and sugars. Rader knew that the entire case—perhaps even Mother Théodore's sanctification cause—likely teetered on those two tiny bits of optical refuse. He also knew that one of Phil McCord's two doctors had detected them, while the other had missed them entirely.

In all, five doctors had been summoned by the Church tribunal to share their thoughts and theories. Four had agreed to come. Two Indianapolis physicians—Robert Gregory and James McCallum—had been asked by the panel to separately examine McCord, squint into his right eye, peruse his medical file, and then report their observations. Two more doctors had been handpicked as formal witnesses. The first to arrive would be Dr. Jeffrey Jungers, who had removed McCord's cataracts and then prescribed seven varieties of drops in an unsuccessful bid to reverse the right eye's runaway deterioration. Jungers felt compelled to cooperate, pointing to the sisters' strong community presence—and to the Mother Théodore statue just outside his office window. He eventually would be followed by Rader, who had happily agreed to testify after reviewing McCord's case file as a favor to former Sister of Providence Kathy Fleming—his eye patient, his friend, and the former principal of his daughter's Catholic school. Rader also felt an obligation to come, prompted by his Catholic faith.

The fifth medical invitee would not appear before the tribunal, despite pleas from Rader and Sister Marie Kevin. Dr. Stephen Johnson, the Indiana ophthalmologist who in 2001 had once planned to snip out McCord's diseased cornea and stitch in a patch of donor tissue, never gave a formal reason for rejecting the overtures. His curious absence, however, would have to be addressed by Monsignor Easton in some manner before he bundled up the voluminous box of notarized transcripts, then sent the package off to Rome. One obvious question hung over the trial: Would the alleged miracle case hold together without Johnson's testimony?

The tribunal would be quizzing the four doctors in an attempt to establish four fundamental facts about McCord's cure: that it was definitive, instantaneous, perfect, and inexplicable to the laws of science. Those, according to the Vatican, were the four cornerstones of a medical miracle. For the pope to deem the recovery supernatural, it would have to pass each of those four tests.

As Jungers recited the oath of secrecy before Easton, Father Jim Bonke, Dr. John Barker, and the two notaries, he remained privately stymied by the cause of his patient's rapid decline two years earlier, and equally confounded by how McCord had suddenly reclaimed his vision. There were odd instances, he understood, when doctors simply could not solve the mysterious ebb and flow that sometimes occurred inside their patients. For the Terre Haute ophthalmologist, the McCord case had offered one of those rare moments. So Jungers simply decided to field each of the panel's questions with complete candor. If he didn't know the answer, he would tell them so. Only one of their questions would leave Jungers without a clear-cut reply.

During the early minutes of his testimony, Jungers patiently summarized the minuscule incisions and sonic bursts he had used to smash McCord's cataracts during a pair of fifteen-minute procedures at the Wabash Valley Surgery Center in Terre Haute. The first procedure,

completed on McCord's left eye on September 21, 2000, "was uneventful, a normal case," Jungers told the tribunal. The second, performed on the right eye on October 12, 2000, was equally "routine"
and "uneventful," he said. On October 13, when McCord had arrived
at Jungers's office for a post-op exam, the doctor noted "elevated
intraocular pressure and mild cornea edema" in the right eye, which,
he testified, he found "a little unexpected"—although such complications were "not infrequent" following cataract extraction. He prescribed glaucoma medication for McCord. That didn't soothe the
eye, nor did subsequent drips of different solutions. Twenty-five days
after the operation on his right eye, McCord visited Jungers again,
the ophthalmologist testified, reading from his medical notes. At
that stage, Jungers still "didn't think there was any primary corneal
decompensation," he testified. He suspected that McCord's right cornea was swollen because pressure was building inside the eye. More
drops were tried. And while those drugs finally eased the pressure,
they didn't fix the eye. In fact, Jungers testified, "the corneal edema
was getting worse." Sixty-three days after the right-eye surgery—on
December 14—Jungers had recommended that McCord go see
Johnson, the transplant specialist in Indianapolis.

McCord had followed his doctor's orders and allowed Johnson
to inspect his right eye on December 27, Jungers said. According
to a letter Johnson later sent to Jungers, the transplant surgeon
had diagnosed McCord with pseudophakic bullous keratopathy—a
swollen cornea caused by the cataract removal. Again referring
to the letter he received from Johnson, Jungers testified that the
Indianapolis surgeon had recommended a corneal transplant for
McCord. "If he did not have it," Jungers told the tribunal, "the
prognosis would have been very poor for recovering vision."
Jungers said he heard nothing further about the McCord case until
Johnson wrote him a second letter—composed just after Johnson's
examination of McCord on January 26, 2001.

"What was the result of his eye exam performed on January 26?" Bonke asked.

"The cornea had cleared almost completely," Jungers testified. "There was much improvement."

The only abnormality Johnson had spotted in the right eye was some scar tissue near the implanted silicone lens, Jungers said, adding that this filmy buildup—known medically as "posterior capsule opacificaiton"—was "a common occurrence" after a diseased lens was replaced with an artificial one. A simple, painless laser zap typically peeled away the scar tissue for good. Before ending his letter to Jungers, Johnson announced the most stunning development of all: a cornea transplant on Phil McCord was no longer necessary.

Jungers's next opportunity to examine McCord came on February 28. Using his own instruments, Jungers that day confirmed that the symptoms were "almost all totally clear," he testified. With McCord eager to clear out the remaining haze caused by the scar tissue, Jungers had that day performed the laser capsulotomy procedure. He scheduled McCord for a return visit about three weeks later.

"What was the result of [your] eye examination . . . on March 22, 2001?" Bonke asked.

"His vision was twenty-thirty," Jungers testified. "The cornea was virtually normal."

"Can we consider Mr. Philip McCord cured today?" Bonke asked.

"Yes," Jungers said.

"Did he definitely recover?"

"Yes."

"Do you think," Bonke continued, "the following events are . . . scientifically explainable? A: the fact that the edema disappeared in the right eye the morning after he prayed?"

"That's very unusual to occur that quickly. Highly unusual," Jungers said.

"B: the fact that the corneal transplant suddenly became unnecessary after Dr. Johnson had said it was the only solution to Mr. McCord's eye condition?"

"I mean, it's possible that he would have gotten better on his own. We don't know that for sure. But the rather suddenness [of] his recovery is unusual. I think the transplant became unnecessary because he spontaneously resolved the problem on his own without medical intervention," Jungers said.

"You said there was a chance that he could have possibly improved on his own. Do you know what those chances would be?"

"In my experience, when corneal edema has persisted that long after surgery, it would be very unlikely to improve without surgery."

"Do you think these two events make this recovery extremely extraordinary, really unusual?"

"Yes."

"If this recovery can be considered scientifically difficult, can you attribute it to the supernatural intercession of Blessed Théodore Guérin?"

Jungers, who thought of himself as "not a religious person at all," looked squarely at the priest sitting across the table. He knew what the tribunal needed to hear. He knew what the sisters at the Woods would want him to say. Jungers listened to his conscience.

"I don't know," he said.

† † †

Dr. Nick Rader had never met Phil McCord, had never explored the delicate surface or tender insides of his once-wasted right eye. Everything Rader knew about the convent engineer he had learned by digesting stacks of medical reports on the man's strange case and by asking a few vital questions of Dr. Johnson. But Rader, an ophthalmologist who often saw ninety patients a day in his suburban Indianapolis clinic, believed he had a firm grasp on the peculiar sequence of microscopic events that had transpired inside McCord's head. On Thursday, January 20, 2003—a hazy, 27-degree afternoon—Rader came to the basement of the Indianapolis Archdiocese headquarters, prepared to confer on medicine and converse about faith.

"Before I went in, I knew what my views were. I did not know what they were going to ask me," Rader recalled later. "When you are talking about what is science, and what constitutes a miracle, that is a very thought-provoking moment."

Speaking in a calm, hypnotic voice that was often just a few notches above a whisper, Rader initially walked the panel through the technically sophisticated yet now-familiar maneuvers required in performing cataract removals: the precise phacoemulsification times and the implantation of intraocular lenses into the capsular bags of McCord's eyes. Regurgitating the numbers and notations that filled Jungers's reports, Rader recounted how a pressure-packed storm had bloomed inside McCord's right eye, how it had unleashed a gush of excessive fluid, stretched and strained his transparent cornea, clouded his vision, and caused the convent caretaker to look like he'd been blindsided by a left hook. Rader repeated the list of eye drops that Jungers had prescribed to McCord and, finally, he mentioned the patient's last-ditch referral to see Johnson and discuss the benefits and risks of a corneal transplant.

Then the bombshell fell.

"I did note an additional finding that I had not seen in Dr. Jungers's records," Rader said, "namely the presence of nuclear material, which are basically the remnants of cataracts, in the front of the eye."

Barker leaped on the reference to "nuclear material." Days earlier he had leafed through the written findings of Dr. McCallum, one of the independent physicians tapped by the tribunal to check out McCord's medical file. McCallum, too, had highlighted the stray mention in Johnson's charts of cataract scraps in McCord's right eye. McCallum, a retired ophthalmologist, had even jotted that citation into his own letter to the tribunal. Barker had found the discovery of cataract chips "significant," he said later. He bored into Rader's findings, into those infinitesimal nuclear leftovers, and on the inconsistencies between the medical reports of Johnson and Jungers.

"Was this in Dr. Johnson's records and not Dr. Jungers's records?" Barker asked.

"That is correct."

"Was there some information saying that this retained material can sometimes cause the difficulty [McCord] was having?"

"Yes, sir."

For the first time the tribunal had been given some testimony that offered a potential explanation for McCord's eye complications. But exactly how did these remnants typically behave? Could they move within the eye, sloshing and pinballing against the optic tissues, creating the kind of havoc McCord was feeling? And why had they been detected by Johnson but not by Jungers?

Barker noted, for the record, that the panel had received a letter from another ophthalmologist (McCallum, he later confirmed) suggesting that such fragments—lingering pieces of the cataract's pit—may spark corneal problems if left inside the eye following surgery.

"Most definitely," Rader agreed. "Remnants of the nucleus, which is the hard part of the lens, can sometimes hide during surgery, behind the iris or at an angle at the front of the eye where they can't be seen. If they are retained, they will sometimes rattle around in the front of the eye and bump against the inside lining of the cornea, which . . . can be a cause for corneal edema."

"What is the usual outcome of that?"

"In my experience," Rader said, "the eye continues to become worse."

Then the eye doctor divulged a crucial fact: "Rarely, they can become walled off or encapsulated and the eye can get better."

With that remark, the trial reached a tipping point. A possible explanation for McCord's spontaneous recovery now lay on the table, ready for further scrutiny. Had his alleged miracle been a matter of destructive eye floaters finally coming to rest? Had the remaining grains of the old cataract—hidden from Jungers's view by their initial positioning—drifted into some inner wall of eye tissue where they had become stuck in place, allowing the cornea to mend? That occurred only "rarely," Rader had testified, but it was known to happen. The notion of a supernatural cure seemed to flutter between light and darkness, between logic and implausibility. Either way, the fragments held the answer.

Rader told the tribunal that he, too, had been curious about those bits of old lens. He had contacted Dr. Johnson to investigate deeper. Rader testified that Johnson, in turn, had explained to him that on December 27, 2000, he indeed had seen two cataract fragments, and that they were situated in a lower part of the front of McCord's right eye.

"My question to Dr. Johnson was, 'Where did they go, and why did you not recommend that they be removed at that point?' He said he thought that they were not moving around, meaning they were stuck in position. Then I asked him where they were when he looked [again] on January 26, [2001]," Rader testified. "He told me he thought maybe they had gone behind the pupil."

"How," Barker asked, "did they get behind the pupil?"

"If they are freely moveable, they can slosh around with [sudden, rapid head] movement and . . . they could go through the pupil.

Generally, however, even if they get behind the pupil, they continue to cause chronic inflammation within the eye."

With that response, Rader again seemed to fan the embers of the inexplicable, of the miraculous. He explained, "If they were fixed and not moving in December and didn't need to be removed, I don't understand how, without some sort of intervention, they could go away."

But Barker kept probing, searching for a possible medical sequence that might explain the missing fragments and the overnight disappearance of McCord's symptoms. The family doctor next asked perhaps the most critical question of the trial, and simultaneously suggested a scientific scenario to account for McCord's nonsurgical recovery.

"Would the retained nuclear lens fragments," Barker asked, "be absorbed over a period of time?"

"That's possible," Rader acknowledged.

Again, the tribunal hung on what Rader was about to say.

"Some will absorb," Rader said. "But it . . . takes a good deal of time. Although I may be answering more than you are asking at this point, that's another issue because I don't believe they absorb overnight. I don't believe they can stay around for two months and then suddenly go away."

Once more, Rader's viewpoint reinforced the mystery and sustained, for the moment, the possibility of an alleged miracle. He could not explain why the two cataract fragments were seen on December 27 and, without corresponding medical aid, were not visible to the same doctor on January 26. Equipped with all the known facts and with a handle on all the known variables, Rader remained baffled by how Phil McCord ever got better on his own.

Barker had been convinced.

"You can't have it both ways," Barker said later. "You can't have them walled off or encapsulated and not moving and then say, 'Well, they moved out of the way.' It doesn't make any sense to me. If they are freely moveable, they are freely able to cause problems, OK? And then, if the problem is suddenly gone and we can't find them, it sort of speaks to another possibility that's less scientific or less intellectually acceptable. . . . It does seem like this is the part where something occurred that was very special for Phil."

The tribunal members now possessed a more complete time-line: seven days after Johnson had identified the two cataract bits, McCord had prayed to Mother Théodore. And roughly twenty hours after saying his prayer, McCord noticed that his symptoms had waned. Yet Johnson had diagnosed the two chips as being lodged in place, and eight days was not medically long enough for them to have dissolved.

Rader felt his testimony had, in effect, proved a negative, had substantiated the unsolvable. He had led the panel to a place where reason gave way to belief.

"As I saw it, only two things could happen: the remnants dissolved or became sequestered," Rader would say years later. "If it's dissolved, that takes a great deal of time and it didn't fit the clinical picture here. If it's sequestered, there was no usual activity [by McCord], bumping the eye or anything [to cause the fragments to move to a new location where they stopped irritating the cornea]. But even if it is sequestered, then the real question becomes, why now, after his prayer? What caused them to move? That's where you're either a believer or not."

As he did for all the formal witnesses, Bonke read Rader question number fifty-one.

"If this recovery can be considered scientifically difficult, can you attribute it to the supernatural intercession of Blessed Mother Théodore Guérin?"

"Yes," Rader said. "I believe I could."

† † †

Long after the trial ended, Dr. Jeffrey Jungers flipped open a medical journal and happened to catch a particularly poignant paper published in 2006 by the American Academy of Ophthalmology. Its pensive title: "Retained Nuclear Fragments in the Anterior Chamber after Phacoemulsification with an Intact Posterior Capsule." Dry reading for non–eye doctors, surely, but Jungers often applied phacoemulsification to his patients' eyes to break up cataracts. And a bad complication from one such procedure had yanked him inside a Catholic miracle investigation. Jungers devoured the five-page study with great interest. And when he finished, he saw the Phil McCord case in an entirely new way.

Compiled by doctors at the Bascom Palmer Eye Institute in Miami, Florida, the study was a retrospective review of sixteen patients who had been diagnosed with leftover shreds of cataracts in a quadrant of their inner eyes known as the anterior chamber—an area just in front of the pupil. Most of those patients suffered from swollen corneas, but—unlike McCord—all required surgical extraction of the fragments to relieve their symptoms. The researchers concluded that stray flecks of shattered cataract nucleus were more likely to "hide" in the "posterior chamber, or behind the iris" of myopic patients with "long" eyes—ophthalmological jargon for nearsighted people. McCord had been extremely nearsighted.

When healthy, the eye is filled with a clear fluid that flows outward through the pupil toward the front of the eye. That small trickle of fluid is then absorbed into the body's bloodstream via the eye's drainage system. In McCord's right eye, however, the endothelium had been damaged—perhaps by the cataract chips—and its fluid-pumping ability had been compromised. That subsequently caused the buildup of fluid, the elevated eye pressure measured by Jungers, and an interruption of the eye's normal liquid flow.

Johnson had told Rader he suspected the cataract chips had essentially moved backward, had possibly floated behind the pupil. And according to the Bascom Palmer study, in myopic eyes such fragments were often concealed from the doctors' view when they moved behind and above the pupils.

"Had I seen that article a little earlier, I would have pulled it out [at the tribunal] and suggested it as a possible explanation," Jungers said in a 2009 interview. "I'm sure there are chips in a lot of people which we never see that just dissolve on their own. I'm surprised that [Dr. Johnson] wouldn't have said, 'Just take them out.'"

Still, Jungers acknowledged that the Bascom Palmer study didn't address if or how those fragments may ultimately dissolve—or how long that process may take. "But I do follow people with tiny little chips that just do go away," he said. "They can float around, get behind the iris [and become hidden]. In retrospect, I could have looked for the chips a little more. . . .

"When I read that article, looking back a few years, I said, 'Oh, I bet you that's what that was'" in the McCord case, Jungers added. "I can't prove that, and that's kind of what I told [the tribunal] at the time: 'I think there's some medical reason for this, I just can't give you the exact reason why this cornea became cloudy and then cleared up on its own.' . . . Had that article come out before, I would have said, 'Well, I'm sure this is what it is. If we look long enough [in McCord's eye] we'll find a chip.' . . .

"It seemed to me, they [the tribunal leaders] just seemed to really, really want this [miracle] badly. I felt like I was going to be honest when I testified. But I didn't want to skew my answers to hurt their chances, I guess."

In comparison, Jungers said he was keenly aware that Dr. Rader fully intended to come down on the side of the supernatural when delivering his perspective to the panel.

"Now, it's interesting—there was a Dr. Rader. Boy, he was

all, 'Oh, this is a miracle, blah, blah, blah,'" Jungers said. "Now, I know he's very big in the Catholic Church. But I remember that. He [said he] had reviewed everything, and [had concluded], 'Well, there's just no explanation.' I found that interesting. . . . He had an agenda."

In response, Rader said his testimonial opinions were forged only through long study of the McCord case, and he believed his role as a medical witness was to explain the facts as he saw them. But he acknowledged he also was influenced by the larger goals of the Sisters of Providence. "I was fairly neutral initially," Rader said later. "I got involved really doing this as a favor for Kathy Fleming. The more I had learned, and the more I learned about Sister Marie Kevin and the whole group, the more I learned of the story [about Mother Théodore], the more of a believer and a supporter of this [I became]. But initially, I was just acting as a doctor acts, providing and sharing my medical knowledge with this group. . . . I was a little surprised when I got that last question because I didn't feel like my opinion [on whether a miracle had occurred] was very important. . . .

"But there are two questions I couldn't answer in my own mind. One: why did [the fragments] choose that time [apparently after McCord's prayer] to move back there? And two: why did the cornea clear so suddenly? And, of course, there's no evidence that there is something [like a cataract chip] back there. . . . [So] he prays for intercession. And if there were remnants of the lens that were irritating the cornea that jumped through the pupil into the back of the eye, to me, that's a miracle."

Moreover, his dissection and defense of a purported miracle made him, Rader believed, a better doctor and a better person. "You become much more humble. You realize when something wonderful happens for a patient, you're happy for the patient, and you appreciate any praise or gratitude you get. But you understand, very clearly, that you could have taken the exact same actions with that patient and, for reasons we don't understand, it could have turned out completely different," he said. "The converse is true [as well]: if you practice long enough, you realize you do everything just right and things don't go the way you want.

"Humility comes with understanding that things are out of your hands."

† † †

One in a million. Tall odds. Slim chances. Those were the breezy buzzwords often used to give context to the sweetest victories of the everyday world: the "Miracle on Ice," the "Miracle Mets," the "Miracle on the Hudson." Longshots and underdogs. Such surprising achievements and narrow escapes tended to be measured in terms of their mathematical implausibility: once in a lifetime.

What was the probability of a suspension of nature's laws—the definition of a supernatural miracle? Philosopher David Hume felt the chances were too infinitesimal to even be calculated because we collectively witnessed—all the time—the perpetual effects of those accepted scientific maxims; they were constant.

What was the likelihood of an alleged miracle being approved by the Vatican? That equation was far easier to tabulate. Each year, on average, about twenty-five to forty purported medical miracles were presented for study to the Holy See's panel of doctors. Among those candidate cases, the Consulta Medica almost always found a scientific explanation. Franco de Rosa, a professor at the University of Rome and a member of the Consulta Medica, said in a 2000 interview with *Newsweek* writer Kenneth L. Woodward that the panel uncovered rational medical explanations for purported supernatural cures "ninety-nine percent" of the time. The Roman doctors were a tough sell.

But the odds also were stacked against a case ever reaching

Rome's skeptical eyes. Dozens, if not hundreds, of medically mysterious cures and recoveries were politely vetoed in their earliest stages, labeled unworthy of a local Church trial by the Vatican, by archdiocese officials, or by cause advocates. In making that sort of initial rejection, a postulator or promoter or canon lawyer might simply have judged the available evidence as being too flimsy, or might have decided the sick person had received just enough medical care to have been saved.

Although the tribunal in Indianapolis still had two doctors and a star witness to cross-examine, the McCord case had already outlasted and outdistanced so many other sincere Catholic claims of heavenly intercession—gripping miracle allegations that initially flashed, then fizzled in places like Lackawanna, New York, and Denver, Colorado, and River Edge, New Jersey—the hometown of Ryan Blute.

On the western bank of the Hackensack River in northeastern New Jersey, Ryan had blossomed by 2009 into one of the top hitters on the River Dell High School baseball team. But it wasn't Ryan's sweet stroke that turned his father into a cheerleader. Two years earlier, on his fourteenth birthday, Ryan had been diagnosed with melanoma. The cancer had spread to some of his lymph nodes— which surgeons later removed, along with a malignant mole. When the disease was discovered, Anne Blute, Ryan's grandmother, handed the teenager a special badge to wear. Anne belonged to a Father Solanus Casey prayer group in Yonkers, New York— where Casey, a Capuchin friar, had served from 1904 to 1918. The badge contained a Father Solanus relic. Ryan's family simultaneously began praying to Casey. During his life, the friar had earned a reputation for offering prayers for the ill that allegedly led to miraculous healings. After his death in 1957, more claims of Father Solanus's supernatural intercession were made by people who had prayed to the late priest. Pope John Paul II decreed in 2005 that

Casey had lived a life of heroic virtue, declaring him "Venerable." Four years later a website for the Father Solanus Guild in Detroit, Michigan (where he spent his final years), tracked some of the allegedly miraculous "favors" attributed to their namesake. Seven such "favors" were mentioned on the web page in late 2009, including restored vision and a mended heart. The Blute family believed Ryan belonged on that mystical list.

Three days after the teenager's 2007 surgery, intricate scans of his body showed no evidence of cancer, and he was still healthy in 2009. Whenever he went for follow-up scans—and when he took his college entrance exam—Ryan carried the Father Solanus relic in his wallet. His father, Kevin, felt he owed Father Solanus a debt. Kevin Blute belonged to a local chapter of the Ancient Order of Hibernians, a Catholic service group. At Kevin Blute's urging, the Hibernians held charity fundraisers and marched in parades in Yonkers, New York, and Bergenfield, New Jersey, while hoisting a large banner proclaiming Casey's name. But Brother Leo Wollenweber, a friar in Detroit who knew Father Solanus and who became the vice-postulator of his beatification cause, had immediate doubts that Ryan Blute's recovery would ever be examined by a local Church tribunal. "That's not a real clear case. There was an operation. It likely wouldn't go through," Wollenweber said. "We get a lot of reports where people are very hopeful, and we try to follow every report. . . . We've had a number of cases that looked promising and that would seem to be miraculous. But on close investigation, the doctors were not able to make that definite declaration [that the cure was inexplicable or permanent]. And today it becomes rather difficult to find a case like that—especially here in the U.S., where there are so many medical procedures. And if there's an operation, it wouldn't count.

"So," Wollenweber said, "we are still looking."

As they were in Oakland, California. In that city was the headquarters of the Santa Barbara Province of Franciscan Friars—formal sponsors of the petition to canonize Blessed Junipero Serra. An eighteenth-century Franciscan from Spain, Serra founded a series of Catholic missions throughout California, including San Juan Capistrano. Serra was beatified by John Paul II in 1988 after the Vatican approved an alleged miracle in his name—the full recovery of a nun with lupus. In 1993 a pregnant woman in Denver learned from doctors that her fetus had stopped growing and would likely be born with severe mental or physical defects, or both. She was offered an abortion. As a strong Catholic, she declined. The mother's parents lived in California and were familiar with Serra and his cause. They prayed to Serra to intercede on behalf of their unborn grandchild. When the woman eventually gave birth to her daughter, doctors immediately diagnosed Kayla Rebecca Kellog as completely healthy.

In the spring of 2007, the Archdiocese of Denver completed its seven-month investigation of the alleged Kayla Kellog miracle. Just as Easton and his tribunal had done in Indianapolis, priests in Denver collected medical documents on the pregnancy, interviewed members of the mother's obstetrical team, and pulled in independent doctors to assess the case. Their four-inch-thick file of transcripts and hospital reports was sealed in a cardboard box and handed to Father Ken Laverone, a canon lawyer associated with the Franciscan friars in Oakland. Laverone carried the box onto a Rome-bound flight, stowing it in an overhead bin above his seat in an emergency-exit row. After landing in Italy, Laverone retrieved the box, stepped off the plane, and headed for the Vatican. In May 2007 he handed the box to an official at the Congregation for the Causes of Saints. In 2008 Laverone heard the verdict.

"The Vatican has ruled that there was insufficient scientific evidence to authentically declare that some extraordinary event occurred regarding Kayla Kellog and [the] intercession of Blessed Junipero Serra," Laverone said. "So we are back to square one."

That feeling of frustration was shared by many Catholics in Lackawanna, New York. Located near the shore of Lake Erie, on the outskirts of Buffalo, Lackawanna seemed to be a town rich with alleged miracles—all swirling around a long-dead priest, Father Nelson Baker. Nearly thirty miracle claims had been ascribed to Baker, including the 1999 discovery of three seemingly fresh vials of Baker's blood originally siphoned from his body following his 1936 death, and the sudden reawakening in 2005 of a local firefighter who had been comatose for a decade. Yet Lackawanna also was a place where such mystical assertions suffered short lifespans.

Baker was a Buffalo native and a Civil War veteran who had fought at the Battle of Gettysburg. He was of small stature and had a fat bank account—built through his grain and feed business. He also had a spiritual yearning. In 1876 Baker swapped merchantry for ministering and was ordained a Catholic priest. He was immediately dispatched to serve at a Lackawanna orphanage that was wheezing in debt. Baker tapped his own fortune to pay off the home's bills and to expand the orphanage. Then he laced together a comprehensive web of help for the locals: a school, a hospital, and a "protectory" for wayward children. After learning that the bones of intentionally drowned babies were sometimes found during an annual summer dredging of the Buffalo River, Baker established a home for unwed mothers. As immigrants streamed into Buffalo to take jobs at the steel factories and shipyards, Baker catered to the workers and their families, growing his Lackawanna parish and earning the nickname "Padre of the Poor." Before his death in 1936 at age ninety-five, he raised money to construct a massive marble basilica in Lackawanna, Our Lady of Victory. A half-million people were said to have attended Baker's funeral. His sanctification cause seemed inevitable. In 1987 Pope John Paul II named Baker a "Servant of God." Purported miracles in his name surfaced

in bunches—so many, in fact, that two books were written exploring Baker's alleged supernatural touch: *The Father Baker Code* and
The Mysteries of Father Baker. Claimants included Mary Timm, a
former employee in the basilica gift shop, who said Father Baker's
apparition had once appeared there and spooked away a would-be
robber. Baker's beatification campaign even boasted one of the best
postulators in Rome: Andrea Ambrosi.

In 1999 the Vatican suggested that Baker's body be moved from
its cemetery plot to a sarcophagus inside the basilica, where visitors
could pray for his intercession. Near his grave, in a concrete vault,
workers also found three jars of Baker's blood—saved by parish
officials who had anticipated a future canonization push. The blood
in the vials was soon tested by a panel of Buffalo doctors and university experts who called the retained fluid "unexplainably fresh,"
Buffalo Bishop Henry Mansell said in 2000. There was talk in Buffalo and Lackawanna that Father Baker's first miracle had been
found. But Vatican theologians ruled that the blood was essentially
inadmissible because "the quote-unquote miracle has to happen for
someone else," Monsignor Robert Wurtz, the chief local advocate
for Baker's cause, told the *New York Times* in 2005. "In this case, the
Congregation [for the Causes of Saints] did not see it happening for
someone, but for Father Baker himself."

By then, though, Wurtz held hopes that a new possible miracle
loomed in Baker's name. On April 30, 2005, brain-damaged Buffalo firefighter Donny Herbert awoke from his deep, ten-year sleep,
sat up, and spoke three clear words. Herbert, then a resident of a
long-term-care facility called Father Baker Manor, had been in a
coma since a burning roof collapsed onto him on December 29,
1995. "Where's my wife?" Herbert abruptly asked a startled aide.
That question unleashed a sixteen-hour torrent of animated chats
between Herbert and his family, his friends, and the firefighters
with whom he once worked. About a week later, Herbert began

drifting back toward semiconsciousness, fluctuating between lucidity and unresponsiveness.

At the Father Baker nursing home, other patients had occasionally reported seeing an apparition of Baker entering their rooms, and Herbert's wife, Linda, said that Donny, too, told her he had spotted the priest, according to the book *The Day Donny Herbert Woke Up* by Rich Blake. In several interviews with local media members, Monsignor Wurtz said he wanted to speak with Linda Herbert about her husband's case—and perhaps prompt a miracle investigation. According to Vatican rules, however, Linda had to contact the diocese, not the other way around. Linda heard about Wurtz's overture, but ultimately decided not to initiate that conversation with the monsignor. "What could she tell him anyway?" Blake wrote in his book on the events. "She knew God was at work. But who was she to say if it was or wasn't a Father Baker miracle?" And there was still another theological complication: Herbert's doctors had infused him with an experimental drug cocktail that might have aided his temporary awakening. On February 21, 2006, less than ten months after he unexpectedly stirred from his coma, Donny Herbert died of pneumonia.

Since 1987 the Our Lady of Victory parish had submitted almost thirty alleged miracles tied to Father Baker—purported supernatural events "that we thought had legs," said parish spokeswoman Beth Donovan. "All were turned down."

Monsignor Wurtz kept hunting, continuing his vigil for a provable miracle to finally nudge Father Baker's cause forward. He also maintained a sacred ritual. Each morning the white-haired priest in black clothing knelt before Father Baker's marble tomb in the Our Lady of Victory Basilica and posed a single, desperate question to the late priest: "What's the holdup?"

The answer never came for Wurtz. Less than ten months after

Herbert's passing, the monsignor died of cardiac arrest at age seventy-four.

But the sanctification crusade lived on. For years afterward, inside a neighborhood tavern not far from the Lake Erie shore, a local rock band belted out its rendition of the house favorite: "Make Father Baker a Saint."

† † †

The day of Phil McCord's testimony had finally dawned. Snowflakes fluttered in Terre Haute on Thursday, February 6, 2003. McCord felt just a bit jittery about his day of testimony, about the unknown questions he would face from the priests. But he knew that Monsignor Easton and Father Bonke were even more nervous. They had told him so.

"They were concerned that they do everything properly and according to canon law; they felt this was an opportunity for Mother Théodore, and if this actually, truly was a miracle, then they didn't want to mess it up," McCord recalled.

"I've never done this before," McCord had once said, half joking, to Easton. "I hope I do it right."

"Me too!" Easton had replied.

One of the sharpest ironies of the alleged miracle involved the faith of the man at the core of Catholic investigation. McCord was not merely a non-Catholic. He was a Baptist and the son of a Baptist lay minister.

The modern tensions or outright disdain between some Baptists and some Catholics transcended oceans and centuries, coiling back to seventeenth-century Europe, where Baptists were persecuted by Roman Catholics, in part for their belief in adult baptism and their rejection of infant baptism. This strain between the two religions was old stuff. And the bad blood seemed to go beyond the disagreements in Baptist and Catholic doctrines, or differences between their Sunday services. Sometimes, like in McCord's own childhood house, the contempt seemed downright personal.

Perhaps nobody on the tribunal panel understood that religious divide more than Dr. John Barker, a Catholic. Barker's grandfather had been a Baptist minister who had raised John Barker's father "with fire and brimstone," Barker said.

"So Baptists and Catholics are not favorite friends or anything. They don't mix well," Barker recalled long after the trial.

"And here comes Phil. Very nice fellow, nice family. But this is a Baptist guy. You know, a *Baptist* guy! Here's this *Baptist* guy coming in."

CHAPTER TWELVE

The Star Witness

They rode mostly in silence. During their eighty-minute drive from Terre Haute to Indianapolis—cruising east on Interstate 70 through a light curtain of snow flurries—Phil and Debbie McCord never once discussed the purpose of their trip. Exhausted from her long stretch of days nursing the ill and elderly, Debbie napped in the passenger seat. When she awoke, the quiet chatter between husband and wife meandered between mundane snippets of community news and the latest headlines from the morning paper. They spoke nothing of miracles.

They pulled into the Archdiocese of Indianapolis parking lot around 9:00 a.m., locked their car, and entered the downtown building through a rear glass door. In the basement, two priests and a Catholic doctor waited expectantly for the quiet Baptist caretaker who had strayed into one of their religion's holiest moments.

That morning, McCord had no intention of overhyping his healing. That wasn't his style, anyway. He felt no undue pressure to deliver—much less aggrandize—a miracle for his bosses at the Woods. He would freely admit to the tribunal his unfamiliarity with the nuances of Catholic intercession. If asked, he could not list the basic ingredients his prayer had to contain in order for the Vatican to label his healing a supernatural favor. He knew only that his unrehearsed appeal in the basilica had come from a place of pure misery, that his side chat with Mother Théodore—almost an afterthought—had been prompted by the humble recognition that he was, in a sense, her employee.

He had only a loose grasp of the Catholic belief that the faithful on Earth, the souls in purgatory, and the saints in heaven all were bound in spiritual solidarity, were organically unified in the same mystical body under Christ—or, as Catholics called it, "the communion of saints." That world was uneasy ground for a man of science. Strolling through the local Catholic headquarters that day, McCord leaned on the simple notion that he would not be asked to rationally explain or spiritually justify his cure. He could do neither of those things, anyway. His only task was to tell the truth. And the truth was that he now possessed essentially perfect eyesight.

"I don't even know who my patron saint is," McCord acknowledged years after the trial. "I know that if you're having trouble selling the house, you bury a Saint Joseph statue in the backyard.

"And my prayer? Not only was it not elegant," he added. "It was not coherent."

The priests—in Indianapolis and, later, in Rome—would listen vigilantly for a few precious theological code words from McCord. They would want to hear that he had exhausted all his available options when he asked God and Mother Théodore—and exclusively God and Mother Théodore—for help. They would pay close scrutiny to whether McCord had prayed, as Catholics sometimes say, "with a pure heart," meaning that he held no expectations of a cure. And, of course, they would be curious to learn exactly how McCord had stumbled into begging a would-be saint to intercede in his life.

The priests and doctors together—in Indiana and, finally, in Italy—would cull his testimony for certain medical cues: that McCord's eye was diagnosed as being unfixable without the transplant, that his cure came soon after his prayer, and that his vision remained vivid and clear all those years later. They already had ascertained each of those ophthalmological points from two eye specialists and a heap of medical reports. Now they needed to hear it from the patient.

McCord walked into a conference room crammed with

canon-law books and suffused with tension. He recited the oath of secrecy with one palm pressed against the Bible, then took the customary witness chair at the center of the long table. He looked into the somber faces of Monsignor Fred Easton, Father Jim Bonke, and Dr. John Barker, and immediately felt the sobriety of the moment, not to mention the silent anxiety of the priests who prayed that they wouldn't make a single mistake.

Then it began, with questions and answers establishing his existence, his place, his identity, and his oldest physical defect. He rattled off his birthdate, birthplace, and home address, and called himself an "engineer." He synopsized his family's health history as "good" and listed his own chronic ailments: hypertension, asthma, and, until 2001, horrendous vision. "I have worn glasses since I was six years old," McCord testified. "It has just been part of my life, increasingly poor eyesight. . . . I was wearing glasses that were very, very thick and they corrected my vision to about twenty-fifty."

His eyesight hazed further, he said, as cataracts grew fat on his natural lenses. He wasn't certain why his eyes had fogged at the early age of fifty-two, but perhaps, he speculated, it was due to the steroids he took to treat his asthma. The left eye, always the worst of the two, was the first to undergo cataract removal surgery. He described his post-op emotions with glee: "I was delighted. I could read things and see things. I had peripheral vision that I never had. . . . My wife would drive and I would go down the street and I would read streets signs to her. . . . Here I had one perfectly good eye and this other very thick lens. I pushed . . . to do [the right eye] as quickly as we could."

"In what did the operation consist?" Bonke asked, reading verbatim from the prepared questions, reflecting their stilted translation to English from Andrea Ambrosi's Italian.

"Exactly the same procedure," McCord answered. "There was really no difference in the surgery. . . . His [Jungers's] comments were exactly the same. He thought I would be happy with this."

"After how many days did you take off your bandages?"

"Two days . . . I didn't have the same vision. . . . I was a little concerned about that."

"If there were differences . . . can you say how many days from the operation on the twelfth they began?"

"There was a heaviness in the eye, and an ache that hadn't been there before. I noticed my right eyelid was drooping fairly significantly, about halfway down. And the whole side of my face felt pulled. . . . After four to five days, it really wasn't progressing. The sight wasn't coming back. It was blurry. The light wasn't the same. The colors weren't quite the same."

"What did Dr. Jungers think?"

"He just wasn't sure as to the cause. . . . He exhausted what he could do for it and referred me to Dr. Johnson."

"What was his diagnosis?"

"That I would be a good candidate for the transplant. I asked him specifically if there were other treatments available. . . . He said no."

"What were the risks?"

"Everything from hemorrhage in the eye [to] loss of vision . . . loss of the eye, death as a reaction to anesthesia."

"What was your reaction?"

"I was very upset."

"You had a lot of anxiety?"

"Anxiety would probably be the least way I would describe it. Fearful. Depressed . . . It was such a complete shock."

"How many days after you received this news . . . did you go inside the church to pray to Mother Théodore?"

"About a week . . . It had preyed on my mind through New Year's."

"Do you usually pray . . . when you need something?"

"I would like to tell you yes, but I'm not very observant of my religious faith."

"Are you Catholic?"

"No."

"What religion do you profess?"

"Baptist. American Baptist."

McCord, privately, noted the trial's easy tone and, with some surprise, its gentle feel. "Actually, I was kind of waiting for the Devil's Advocate to come forth, but actually the whole process was very respectful," he later recalled. "I never got a sense at all that they were trying to trap me. It was, as Monsignor Easton said, a search for the truth." Engineers had a nickname for data that had been purposely massaged or manipulated to fit a hoped-for conclusion; they called those findings "rubber coordinates." McCord did not see or hear anything that looked or sounded like rubber coordinates during the secret trial. "I wouldn't say it was adversarial," he said later. "But there wasn't any opportunity to fudge things to get the outcome."

Father Bonke liked McCord's lack of pretension, his sheer absence of awe, he said later. He admired the man's sincerity, his straight-ahead manner. And he felt his being a non-Catholic injected the case with extra merit, infused the tale with an honest detachment. But amid his contemplation of a cure that allegedly defied logic, the priest still needed to hear the Baptist man explain how he logically had come to put his faith in a pre–Civil War mother superior. The pope would ultimately ask the same question. Bonke started dredging through McCord's intercessory plea.

"Were other servants of God, blesseds or saints, prayed to or invoked?" Bonke asked.

"She was the only one," McCord replied.

"Why did you think to invoke Blessed Mother Théodore?"

"I'm not really sure. . . . I remember saying that I normally like to handle things myself. I figure God is busy with other things. . . . I sat down and said, 'This is not something I can get through on my

own. I can't deal with this.' . . . But I really didn't have the courage
to go through with that procedure. . . . And it occurred to me that
here was Mother Théodore. And not being Catholic, I really wasn't
sure how intercession worked. But I heard about it. I said, 'Mother
Théodore, this is your house and I'm your servant.' "

"What kind of prayers or formulas did you use to ask?"

"I really had not intended to pray as such. At times, when I'm
bothered with things, I can just walk in the church. . . . It's quiet, a
place of solace, and I can just reflect. But this time, I felt I needed
to pray and just say . . . 'I don't like to ask for a lot of things but I
need help with this.' . . . And that was basically it. I just sat there for
several minutes longer. . . . But I really felt, at that point, a sense of
peacefulness. That was what I had gone in to pray for—being able
to have the fortitude to face this."

The panel's lone doctor sized up the witness across the table.
He appreciated McCord's calmness, the precision of his answers,
and the fact that he was not overtly hawking sainthood for Mother
Théodore, Barker said later. He glanced at McCord's healthy right
eye. The family physician wanted to know what McCord had felt
in that eye the first dawn after his prayer and, equally, what he had
been able to see. In short: When, exactly, did McCord believe he
was cured? Had that moment come nearly two months later, when
a laser-surgery session at Dr. Jungers's office knocked out a stubborn batch of scar tissue on McCord's implanted right lens? The
tribunal was headed there next—although via something of a leading question, scripted by Ambrosi.

"Is it true that the morning after you prayed, you did not feel
heaviness in the eye?" Bonke asked.

"Yes, I woke up . . . and the first thing I noticed . . . [was] that
the droopiness in my eye was gone," McCord said.

Barker leaned forward. He wanted to walk once more through
the medical timeline of McCord's case. The doctor asked McCord

to confirm that his eye symptoms had—before the morning of January 4, 2001—persisted for more than two months.

"Yes . . . There had been kind of a downward droop at the outside of my eye, and that was gone. Blinking, I thought, 'I think that's better.' Now, it wasn't a thing that I woke up and my sight was restored. But . . . I felt like I could see better light. . . . And there was a little better clarity. . . . I just remember thinking, 'This is much better.' This is as far as it went then."

"On that same morning," Bonke asked, "did you tell your wife?"

"Yes . . . and she looked at it, and said, 'I think it's better.'"

"Were you, at that time, convinced that you were completely recovered?"

"No," McCord said. "I wasn't convinced . . . I still had the blurriness."

"What," Barker pressed, "was keeping you from feeling like you were completely recovered?"

"One of the side effects of cataract surgery is that the eye can notice the [implanted] lens as a foreign body and can encapsulate it. I'm told it is like a protein buildup. . . . I assumed that was what it was."

"What was the result of your eye exam [on January 26, 2001] with Dr. Johnson?" Bonke continued.

"He asked me how it was. I said, 'I think it's better!'. . . . He said, 'Oh, what did you do?' I said, 'I said a prayer.' That's about the only thing I can think of that I did. So he just kind of looked at me. He looked and I remember he sat back from the microscope and he looked over at the chart and he looked at the chart and he looked back at the microscope, [then said], 'You're right. It is better. . . . You don't need the surgery.' . . . The weight of the world had lifted. . . . I was kind of euphoric and I really don't remember much of our conversation after that."

"What was the result of your eye exam with Dr. Jungers [on February 28, 2001]?"

"He looked at the eye and confirmed the edema was gone. He saw that there was a buildup on the lens . . . and said that we can take care of that."

"Was the vision immediately better?" Barker asked.

"It was. . . . At that point, I said, 'Now I have sight.'"

McCord watched Barker lean back in his chair. The engineer read the doctor's body language. "He seemed satisfied," McCord later recalled.

Would Rome be satisfied? Given McCord's admission that he didn't "have sight" until fifty-six days after his prayer—and that a laser beam ultimately had restored his full vision—would the Vatican's medical experts, its theologians and cardinals, and the pope himself, consider McCord's cure to be truly instantaneous or swift? Did that lag time chop a gaping hole into his allegedly supernatural recovery?

"I didn't think so at all," Barker said years later. "It would have been really cool if he woke up that morning [and] his vision was better in his eye, and the remnants were gone, but we just don't know the timing. By the time he did get checked, his vision was as good as it was going to get. . . . It would have been really cool if he had been [examined by a doctor on January 4]. But since he wasn't, I was trying to estimate what the healing time was. The thing was, all these medications that were supposed to help all failed. There was no improvement with the drops and the steroids. And then suddenly, the next morning after his intercession, he is improved. It seemed pretty impressive."

Five questions now remained for McCord to field. They were the most treacherous to answer—especially for the star witness.

The tribunal's priests and its doctor had no hint that McCord was still quietly grinding to fathom and find the reasons for his allegedly mystical healing. When the final questions came, would the engineer deconstruct his own medical case and tell the panel he truly saw something supernatural? Would the man who requested help from Mother Théodore actually swear — on the Bible — that a French immigrant, dead for nearly 150 years, had fixed his eye?

Did Phil McCord believe in miracles?

The closing scenes of Stanley Kubrick's film *2001: A Space Odyssey* whisk viewers through a silent metaphysical morphology. An astronaut watches himself briskly age and die, to be reborn as a floating, interstellar fetus — a "godling" or "starchild," as some movie critics have interpreted it, born to oversee new worlds. Throughout the science fiction spectacle, Christian mythology drapes the narrative: human creation, damnation, atonement, and deliverance. That overlay — faint churchly brushstrokes atop a larger canvas of space and technology — is the voice of Arthur C. Clarke, the screenplay's coauthor.

Born on December 16, 1917, the son of an English farming family, Clarke was part scientist, part artist, and all futurist. In 1945 the British magazine *Wireless World* published his watershed paper "Extraterrestrial Relays," a treatise that first set out the precepts of worldwide communication using artificial satellites. He also predicted space stations and flights to the moon. But Clarke, who died in 2008, is most remembered for more than seventy science fiction stories, including *The Nine Billion Names of God*. His tales often burrowed into the epic collision between rationalism and faith, although Clarke himself was not a religious man. "Any path to knowledge is a path to God — or Reality, whichever word you prefer," he once said. His obituary in *The Times* of London said Clarke's words "gave man's journey a mystical significance and a quasi-religious intensity." "I don't believe in God," he once said, "but I am very interested in her."

Clarke formulated three principles of prediction. His first: "When a distinguished but elderly scientist states that something is possible, he is almost certainly right. When he states that something is impossible, he is very probably wrong." With his mind so entwined with days and discoveries yet to come, Clarke chewed on great human unknowns and spewed out his glimpses of what might be. If slivers of our modern existence still defied explanation—were deemed inexplicable—Clarke knew we merely needed to wait a century or two for the solutions to become visible.

On a small swath of Indiana land that cradled a college campus, farm fields, and a convent, the property's bearded caretaker considered his own physical mystery and quoted verbatim another of Clarke's three laws of prediction: "Any sufficiently advanced technology is indistinguishable from magic."

"You can take someone from the twelfth century and try to explain electricity to them, but it would be indistinguishable from magic," McCord said in 2009. "Maybe one hundred years from now somebody will explain this [eye healing] was triggered by an endorphin [released from my brain while I prayed]. Maybe at some point there will be some scientific, rational explanation. I don't know."

McCord had relied on higher beings. But he would still give science a toehold in his purported miracle. Of course, McCord was hardly alone in taking that sort of split view—a dual belief in the wizardry of natural healing and in the immeasurable potency of faith. And the quest to bridge those two worlds was under way in certain laboratories and hospital rooms in the United States, where researchers aimed to methodically gauge the power of prayer—or, in a more earthly sense, the neurological voltage that came with putting one's trust in God. In one clinical example, a radiological expert compared the brain scans of praying nuns and meditating monks. Dr. Andrew Newberg, an assistant professor in the Department of Radiology at the Hospital of the University of Pennsylvania, found that their frontal lobes—the portions of their brains that helped them focus—were more active during their prayers.

Simultaneously, Newberg saw that sections of their brains tied to fear reactions—their amygdalas—were quieter than normal when they spoke to God. Those findings were published in his 2009 book *How God Changes Your Brain*, coauthored with Mark Robert Waldman, echoing McCord's suggestion that his own prayer might someday be shown to have stirred his brain's healing juices. "Faith is equivalent with hope, optimism and the belief that a positive future awaits us," Newberg wrote. "Faith can also be defined as the ability to trust in our beliefs, even when we have no proof that such beliefs are accurate or true."

One year prior to the release of Newberg's observation, scientists at the Johns Hopkins School of Medicine also peered inside some busy brains. They hoped to understand the neurological fireworks that ignited when jazz musicians created chords on the spot—when they improvised new melodic concoctions. During those minutes of pure creation, the musicians typically closed their eyes and appeared almost trancelike, similar to when the faithful pray or meditate. The Hopkins team recruited six jazz pianists and crafted small keyboards so they could play as they reclined inside a functional magnetic resonance imaging (fMRI) tube. Such diagnostic gadgets can distinguish which regions of the brain respond to various types of stimuli. The researchers spotted eerily similar patterns in the heads of each artist. According to the fMRI scans, the jamming musicians all exhibited a slowdown in a swath of their brains known to aid planned actions and self-censoring—the dorsolateral prefrontal cortex. At the same time, the musicians more actively plugged into a brain area known to convey individuality and self-expression—the medial prefrontal cortex.

How much of human healing came spontaneously from within, particularly through the streams of hormones churned out by the brain? Thousands of doctors have admitted that they've tried to harness that murky brain chemistry to soothe some patients. In a survey of nearly seven hundred U.S. internists and rheumatologists conducted in 2008 by the National Institutes of Health, as many as 58 percent of the physicians said they regularly prescribed placebos to their patients. Those included vitamins, over-the-counter pain-killers, and sugar pills. And only 5 percent of the doctors said they revealed to patients that their prescribed formulas were placebos — inert tablets or solutions scientifically thought to carry no therapeu-tic value but which were theorized to raise the recipient's positive expectations, thereby becoming a curative remedy. The modern notion of the "placebo effect" was fanned by Henry K. Beecher, a medical ethicist and researcher at the Harvard Medical School. Beecher didn't introduce the possible benefits of doctors adminis-tering mock medicines, but his 1955 paper "The Powerful Placebo" certainly boosted the concept. In evaluating fifteen clinical trials involving more than one thousand patients with various ailments, Beecher found that 35 percent got better by taking only placebos. A 2001 article in the *New England Journal of Medicine* again clouded the issue, however: the authors' meta-analysis of 114 different studies revealed that "compared with no treatment, [the] placebo had no significant effect on binary outcomes."

Of course, the prayerful typically didn't think of their divine pleas as physiological antidotes per se. They generally communed with their chosen higher powers in sincere gasps of hope and faith — often, like McCord, asking for peace and strength, if not for mend-ing or miracles. Forty-three percent of Americans prayed for their own health, according to a 2004 survey conducted by the federal government. In fact, prayers for maintaining or regaining physi-cal vigor vastly outstripped all other so-called alternative forms of medicine, the poll found. "This is the most ancient, widely practiced therapy on the face of the Earth," said Dr. Mitchell Krucoff, a Duke University Medical Center professor of medicine and cardiology. "We need to . . . understand it better."

Yet it was within that unfathomable gap that faith dwelled. Prayers came from faith, inherently bathed in the vapors of the unknown, dispatched from people on Earth to unseen yet all-seeing authorities, transcending the bounds of the here and now. Those sacred communications were meant to somehow touch the inexplicable. "The only way of discovering the limits of the possible," Arthur C. Clarke wrote in his third and final law, "is to venture a little way past them into the impossible."

The time had come for Phil McCord to venture into the impossible.

† † †

Father Bonke had reached the finale of his gentle interrogation. His closing queries, written by a Roman saint-maker, were meant to test faith and assign a profound meaning to McCord's visual restoration. The same mystically flavored questions were posed to each material witness, including two doctors, two nuns, an administrative assistant, a nurse, and a soldier.

Now an engineer would contemplate them.

"Do you think," Bonke asked, "the following events are scientifically explainable? A: the fact that the edema disappeared in the right eye the morning after you prayed?"

"Not to my knowledge," McCord answered. "From everything that the doctors have told me, there is no scientific explanation for that to have occurred."

"B: the fact that the corneal transplant suddenly became useless?"

"Not to my knowledge," McCord said, again carefully couching his response in a way that was true to his beliefs. According to his comprehension of the events—down to the cellular level—he did not think science could explain how he no longer required a new cornea.

"C: the fact that you had no therapy?"

"That there was a result with no therapy, that was not explainable to me," McCord said.

"Do you think these ... events make this recovery extraordinary?"

"Yes, yes, yes, very extraordinary."

"Extraordinary" was a somewhat safe word for McCord—by definition, it meant beyond the ordinary, exceptional. What had happened to him was truly exceptional, and anything but ordinary.

Then, however, he confronted the last question—the very conundrum that had boggled McCord since a nun had first suggested to him in the basilica that his healing was a miracle. His testimonial response could advance the possible sainthood of the woman to whom he had prayed—or it could deflate her canonization cause for good.

"Can you attribute this recovery," Bonke asked, "to the intercession of Mother Théodore Guérin?"

The Catholic trial's judge, prosecutor, and appointed doctor watched the healed man form his words, heard him speak with his usual, matter-of-fact exactitude.

"That's the only answer available to me," McCord said. "I think that is the only thing that happened. That is the only cause of the cure."

† † †

The tribunal wasn't quite done with its star witness. The man who had bared his faith before the priests still had to open his eyes for a pair of visiting physicians, or, as the Vatican called them, *ab inspectione*. And those two doctors then had to testify as to what they saw.

Dr. James McCallum, the retired Indianapolis ophthalmologist who had served as an eye doctor to both Monsignor Easton and Father Bonke, performed a rigorous perusal of McCord's eyes on

Tuesday, February 25, 2003. They met in a clinic at St. Vincent Hospital in Indianapolis. There, Dr. McCallum measured the vision in each of McCord's eyes as 20/25, nearly normal and the common range for a post-cataract patient. He checked the pressure inside each eye, and again both registered as healthy—10 millimeters of mercury in the left and 12 in the right. As his cornea deteriorated following cataract surgery, the pressure in McCord's eye had reached 38 millimeters of mercury.

The second exam, on Friday, February 28, took place at the Woods campus in Providence Hall, the old building where Sister Mary Theodosia Mug had awakened on Halloween Day 1908 seemingly free of the cancer that had painfully bloated her torso for months. Not far from the stairwell Mary Theodosia had hastily climbed following her tomb-side prayer, McCord met Dr. Robert Gregory, a retired Indianapolis internist. Because Kathy Fleming had asked Dr. Gregory several years earlier to review the McCord case for her, he was familiar with the tiny and strange events that had occurred in McCord's right eye. Gregory was a diabetes specialist, not an optical expert. Still, he took the opportunity to leaf through McCord's medical records and to casually quiz the engineer about the promptness of his cure.

After lunch on Thursday, March 6, 2003, McCallum and Gregory came to the Indianapolis Archdiocese offices and descended to the basement library to present their findings. But on the miracle trial's final afternoon of testimony, talk once more would turn to those minuscule nuggets of cataract that once had been detected in McCord's right eye.

Gregory was sworn in first, telling the tribunal he had practiced medicine for thirty-seven years on the city's east side, similar to Dr. Barker's longtime practice in that area. He testified that during his meeting with the convent engineer, McCord had described his eyesight as "very good" on both sides. Gregory next revealed what he believed to be his chief duty: to determine whether McCord's eye had rebounded quickly after his prayer, or whether it had improved progressively.

"I'm convinced," Gregory testified, "that there was a change that occurred within the twenty-four-hour period."

McCallum soon followed Gregory to the witness chair, saying that he had been an ophthalmologist in private practice at St. Vincent Hospital before his retirement. He opened his testimony by divulging that after his in-person check of McCord's eyes, he had also interviewed Dr. Stephen Johnson "briefly."

"What did you learn from Stephen Johnson in this conversation?" Bonke asked.

"In Dr. Johnson's first examination [of McCord], he said there were nuclear remnants in the eye," McCallum testified. "And if, indeed, these are nuclear remnants, they can cause a lot of inflammation in the eye. If they are close enough to the cornea, they can cause corneal edema. They can cause an elevated pressure in the eye and inflammation. . . . Dr. Johnson related all these things on his previous chart [from his December 27, 2000, exam of McCord]. The inflammation, the corneal edema, all of that, were [also] mentioned by Dr. Jungers. But the nuclear remnants were not. So I asked Dr. Johnson about that."

Again, that shadow of discrepancy in the records of the two doctors had puzzled an outside physician. It had also persuaded McCallum to do his extra legwork. For vital context, he further explained to the panel that if leftover cataract bits were small enough, they were more easily absorbed by the internal eye tissue. Was Johnson familiar with that phenomenon? McCallum had asked Johnson that very question. According to McCallum, Johnson had told him, "Yes, and sometimes they stay around and you have to remove them. [But] sometimes it is just a matter of time and the cornea can clear."

In measuring this alleged miracle, timing was everything. Because McCallum had raised the issue, however, size now mattered. The dimensions of each cataract crumb might offer still another coherent theory to explain McCord's nonsurgical cure. Had they been puny enough to presume that they had suddenly melted away? Barker launched his forensic follow-up on that point.

"Now, I realize we can't ascertain the size of these remnants," Barker said. "However, is it reasonable to consider that in a month these remnants could disappear on their own, given that they were causing all of this inflammation in the eye?"

Barker's citation of "a month" carried meaning: one month had passed between the day Johnson first saw the fragments in McCord's eye and the day in late January when the chips no longer were apparent to him.

"You hit it right on the head," McCallum said. "If the size is small enough, yes, they could, they could be absorbed over the period of a month."

"Even though they had not been absorbed over the previous four months?" Barker asked.

"Right," McCallum said. "Unfortunately medicine is not always a really precise science."

Just as unfortunate for the fact-finding tribunal was that Johnson had not noted the sizes of the two remnants in his examination records. Like other elements in the McCord cure, their proportions would remain a permanent mystery. Yet, McCallum theorized for the tribunal, they could have been relatively large. And, he said, they could have been tucked behind McCord's iris—concealed from Jungers's view—throughout the autumn of 2000, when Jungers had feverishly foraged for the cause of McCord's eye ailment. Finally, McCallum added, both fragments could have flowed forward through McCord's pupil to the front of the eye sometime in December, lodging just where Johnson had viewed them.

"Maybe that is why they weren't seen before," McCallum said. "That is a tough question I cannot answer. If the remnants were small enough at the time they were first seen, they could be absorbed over that period of time. However, it usually takes a little longer."

"From your professional knowledge and expertise, do you think there is a scientific explanation for his recovery?" Bonke asked.

"I can't explain what happened overnight. I can't explain the immediate effect that he had noticed," McCallum said.

In short, he believed the recovery was indeed instant.

"I have seen people who have had corneal edema and have had nuclear remnants or inflammation or elevated intraocular pressure in the eye that, with treatment for the pressure with steroids, have cleared [in two to six months]," McCallum said. "So yes . . . he could have responded to the treatment he was given. But does that answer the immediate effect that he noticed?"

Simply put, the eye doctor considered the sequence of McCord's cure to be inexplicable.

"On the basis of your examination of him . . . do you feel he had recovered?"

"Right. And if anything," McCallum said, "when I looked at him, I was somewhat surprised that there were no signs of previous . . . edema. Because when we talk about this corneal edema, it is like getting a blister on your skin. And many times . . . once that blister goes down or pops or is removed, that leaves a very linear scar. . . . But there were no signs of such a scar at all."

In other words, McCord's eye looked perfect.

CHAPTER THIRTEEN

The Jury

T
he final testimonies were tucked away. The trial rested. More than five hundred questions had been posed by the archdiocese tribunal during its secret Thursday gatherings. Each word uttered by the ten sworn visitors had been recorded, transcribed in English, translated into Italian, printed, signed by the corresponding witnesses, and then notarized. The case was closed. The miracle file now had to be bundled and properly sealed for transport to Rome—the Vatican even had ancient norms for how to ship a book.

Monsignor Fred Easton, the trial's judge, also was entrusted with the sacred wrapping duties. Stacked neatly in triplicate, bound beneath a mottled gray cover, the transcript pages had the heft and thickness of three city phone books. In saint-making terminology, the compendium of affidavits and medical reports was formally known as "the acts." A long sheet of plain brown paper was draped, folded, and taped around the bound pages. With notaries Catherine Fislar and Karen Clement observing, Easton looped two red grosgrain ribbons around the length and width of the parcel and fixed them in place on the front. Following Vatican protocol, he poured a dollop of hot red wax out of a yellow mug onto the spot where the two ribbons intersected. Then he stamped the blob of hot wax with the emblem of Indianapolis archbishop Daniel Buechlein. The traditional sealing was done to assure the Vatican that all the documentation inside was authentic. As an extra measure of security, every step of the package assembly was photographed by an archdiocese employee to prove that the Holy See's strict preparation fundamentals had been followed.

Finally, Easton placed the acts into a white baker's box filled with foam peanuts, and that container was similarly wrapped and taped with brown paper. The monsignor vowed to preserve the chain of custody by keeping the acts in his sight until he hand-delivered them to the Vatican's diplomatic headquarters in Washington, D.C. In May 2003 he rested the box on the passenger seat of his Nissan Sentra and set out for a solo, six-hundred-mile drive from Indianapolis eastward to the nation's capital—about a ten-hour trek. Plenty of time to mull over all that had occurred in his tribunal room since late January, to once more pick apart the case, and to consider how the conversations in the basement library had left a permanent imprint on the man at the wheel.

"It was, in some ways, a life-changing event," Easton later reflected. "It's not like I didn't believe in miracles before, but seeing it firsthand is a whole bunch different. I called this a 'quiet miracle.' It was not flashy. But it made you a believer. You're just sitting there [listening to the witnesses], and if you didn't believe in miracles before, you did now. . . . What I experienced was arriving at the certitude of a miracle."

Reaching "moral certitude" was the prime directive for Catholic tribunal judges, as etched into canon law by Pope Pius XII in 1942. During routine tribunal matters, such as marriage annulments, Church judges were expected to find moral certitude by hearing and viewing presented testimony. In the case of the alleged eye miracle, Easton's certitude would not be sought by Rome. They only wanted the evidence. But when objectively dissected, the evidence was pocked with a few potential dents—possible soft spots for the Vatican's doctors and theologians to ponder. The Consulta Medica—notorious for vetoing a vast preponderance of the purported miracles it reviewed—would be the harshest critic of the case. Ushering the alleged miracle past the Vatican's medical experts was expected to be Andrea Ambrosi's most challenging task.

Four questions lingered about Phil McCord's recovery—all of them medical in nature.

First, had the two cataract fragments naturally dissolved between December 27, 2000, when Dr. Stephen Johnson first observed them, and January 26, 2001, when Johnson could no longer locate them? Between those two dates, McCord had, of course, offered his prayer, gaining an instant mental breather and some next-day physical relief. According to the trial record, some patients with retained nuclear chips and identical symptoms eventually responded to treatment with steroid drops, as McCord had received. And if the size of cataract bits was relatively small, such remnants could, in theory, be absorbed by the eye in roughly one month, testimony showed. Had enough evidence been offered in Indianapolis to prove that the remnants had not merely melted away naturally inside McCord's eye?

Second, had the two cataract scraps broken free after Johnson first detected them, floating backward through the pupil where they eventually became wedged again in the rear of the eye chamber—in a place where they no longer created havoc? The trial had raised that theory as well. And was it possible that those two fragments were still stuck somewhere in the back of McCord's eye? At least privately—and long after the tribunal ended—Dr. Jeffrey Jungers speculated about that scenario. But again, had there been ample testimony to allow Rome to even answer that question?

Third, was McCord cured when he woke up the morning after his prayer without the face-swelling, lid-drooping, red-eyed "anger" that he had exhibited for more than two months? Or did he actually recover fifty-six days later, when a doctor's laser beam blasted away scar tissue on his implanted lens? It was on that day in late February that McCord had finally declared, "Now I have sight."

Fourth, would the Vatican evaluators be negatively influenced by Dr. Johnson's refusal to participate in the trial? He had been the last doctor to look deeply into McCord's right eye before the engineer's prayer (seven days prior), and the first doctor to assess the eye's improvement after the prayer. He was a central player in the McCord drama, an essential link in the healing sequence. Why had he been unwilling to appear? In short, did he know something that could spoil the possible miracle?

Before sealing the acts in red wax, Easton had, for the record, addressed Johnson's void. Within his bundle of papers, he had included one piece of correspondence dated January 29, 2003, written to Monsignor Easton from Sister Marie Kevin Tighe. It read, in part, "The purpose of this letter is to explain the lack of participation by Dr. Johnson in giving testimony. I wrote to Dr. Stephen Johnson on February 8, 2002, asking him to meet with . . . Andrea Ambrosi and me at the Adam's Mark Hotel on March 9, 2002. Dr. Johnson sent a reply indicating an unwillingness to meet with us. On February 22, 2002, I sent Dr. Johnson a letter asking if I could meet with him simply to explain the purpose of my original request. He agreed to have me meet with him in his office on March 1, 2002. I told him briefly about the history of the cause and showed him the official *positio* on the miracle approved for the beatification. He was very cordial and interested but did not show any sign of being ready to accept the invitation offered previously."

Johnson's refusal to testify had elicited some guesswork at the Indianapolis Archdiocese offices, but Easton never learned the reason for the doctor's decision. "Maybe it is bad form for a doctor to have a miracle happen on his watch," Easton said years later. "It was a disappointment. But we just figured we had enough [evidence] with the others who testified." Besides, the Vatican surely would understand, Easton figured, that some doctors were offended by the implicit mystery of alleged medical miracles. Perhaps Johnson was one of those. "It bugs them because their whole reason for being is to find an explanation for a phenomenon," the monsignor said later. "It's what they do. It's their stock in trade. But that's why you want them in the process." Johnson's absence didn't worry him.

Likewise, the discovery of the cataract remnants—and their subsequent disappearance—did not cause Easton to fret that the Vatican might boot the case. The way he figured it, "The prayer activated another physical process that maybe would not have occurred, a process that allowed the cornea to heal."

Back at archdiocese headquarters, however, there were some quiet doubts whether the case would survive the critical buzz saw of the Vatican's medical and theological panels. "I just was uncertain as to maybe how strong the evidence was, whether this was a real miracle, if there was some possible medical, scientific explanation for what happened," Father Jim Bonke later acknowledged. "Even though the doctors all said virtually the same thing—they could not say, from their knowledge or experience, there was any medical or scientific reason for what had happened. But I just didn't know if the Congregation [for the Causes of Saints] in Rome wanted to hear [from the doctors], 'Yes, we think this is a miracle.' I didn't know if they wanted it that strongly affirmative. I just didn't know what to expect."

Upon arriving in Washington at the Apostolic Nunciature—the Holy See's U.S. embassy, Easton was greeted at the front door by a brown-haired nun wearing a dark blue habit and a broad smile. She accepted from Easton the heavily wrapped package—an alleged miracle in a box. The monsignor also snapped a photo of the nun holding the bundle in her arms as final documentation that the chain of evidence had been preserved. Pope John Paul II's American ambassador at the time, Colombian-born Archbishop Gabriel Montalvo, soon placed the box in a diplomatic pouch, flew it to Rome, and delivered it to the Congregation for the Causes of Saints in St. Peter's Square. On June 7, 2003, Sister Marie Kevin received word from Rome that the acts had arrived safely and that Congregation officials had verified that Easton had properly followed the ancient document-sealing norms. For all those who were pulling for a miracle—including the nuns at the Woods and the postulator in Rome—the next stop would be the most treacherous.

The curious cure of Phil McCord—synthesized into a bulky book, tied with a red ribbon, and sealed with a wax stamp—was placed in the summer of 2003 at the bottom of a stack of alleged supernatural healings, just one of the dozens of peculiar cures awaiting scrutiny from the Vatican's pool of Catholic doctors.

More often than not, the Consulta Medica was where purported miracles went to die.

† † †

Once or twice each year, in his private study near the Tiber River, Dr. Francesco Santori cracked open a hefty volume of secret medical evidence and searched for physical aberrations and freakish anomalies—human recoveries that somehow slipped between the rigid planks from which the house of science was constructed. He looked for the unsolvable. He hunted for the wondrous.

Usually—by his count, 85 percent of the time—the Roman orthopedic surgeon saw within those pages an irrefutable, mortal reason for the patient's recovery. When it came to alleged miracles, Dr. Santori was a hard man to convince. But as one of the roughly one hundred Italian doctors who made up the Vatican's Consulta Medica, he felt the job required deep leeriness, a duty to be dubious. "I am Catholic, but not so particularly fond [or devout]," Santori said in a heavy Italian accent, often pausing to find the proper English word. "When I can't explain something, I want to use my eyes [to look harder]." Santori was a thorough skeptic. But among the thirty cases that he had been asked by the Holy See to inspect since 1986, he immediately recalled three that had stumped his analytical mind.

One involved a patient with a malignant tumor in a femur that had healed spontaneously. Another concerned a patient with chronic typhoid lesions so painful they inhibited physical movement; yet the sores had suddenly vanished, allowing the patient not only to walk again, but to return to work the day after the cure. And then, Santori remembered, there was the little boy who, with his father, had gone fishing for piranhas.

"The boy put his hand inside a container where the piranhas [he had reeled in] were still alive. And one piranha take off completely one of his fingers," Santori said. "So his hand was bleeding a lot and the father went to the little village [nearby]. He found someone, probably not a doctor, and the man asked, 'What about the finger? Where is the finger?' The father said, 'The finger is inside the piranha!' And so he went back and he take the finger out from the belly of the piranha, and they put the finger back on the boy's hand, and they fix it with just a needle. They used the needle to attach and then they put the finger in a splint. It healed. Completely unexplainable. And the little boy was moving the finger after. He was moving the finger and he had the control."

The fish story, Santori believed, was a miracle. And miracles, he contended, were possible. He just didn't see one in every case that came across his desk. Like the rest of the doctors in the Consulta Medica, he had been recruited by the Vatican for his medical specialty. He was a bone doctor, noted in a 2000 medical journal for his performing "cementless femoral revision operations with long collarless distally fixed stems"—or hip replacements. (He was not one of the Vatican doctors who would consider the McCord healing.) The members of the Consulta represented nearly every branch of medicine, from cardiology to tropical diseases. More than half were department chiefs at medical facilities in Rome or medical professors at Roman universities. All were Catholic. The cardinal prefect atop the Congregation for the Causes of Saints assigned small teams of doctors to examine the alleged miracles, matching the doctors with cases that fell into their specific fields. But connections also mattered when it came to gaining a coveted seat on the Consulta. Santori, who had earned his medical degree from the University of Rome in 1960, had tight ties with the Vatican. His father—"a very Catholic man," he said—was a dermatologist and served as a personal doctor to Pope Paul VI, who died in 1978. The younger Santori served as an orthopedic surgeon for Vatican personnel, operating on some of them. "Probably they asked me [to join the Consulta] for these reasons." He agreed, he said, because "I was believing in miracles but I wanted to check if really there were miracles or not."

After alleged miracle cases arrived at the Vatican—as the massive McCord book had done in June 2003—staff members at the Congregation for the Causes of Saints eventually sent selected doctors copies of the *Positio Super Miraculo* plus the sworn testimonies collected by local tribunals and, often, duplicates of X-rays, MRIs, biopsy results, and other medical charts. The Vatican generally would not accept recoveries from diseases that typically carried high rates of natural healing or remission, such as certain lymphomas or renal-cell cancer, and mental illnesses were not admissible.

"I am only called for cases of orthopedics," Santori said. "They send me this printed book, which is normally [in total] between one hundred and two hundred pages. And then I write my consideration."

For the first medical test of any alleged miracle, each case was initially handed to just two consultants (in saint-making jargon, those doctors were referred to as *ex officio*). They studied the materials and checked to see if the cure was instant, complete, lasting and, most important, if it was scientifically inexplicable. Each *ex officio* doctor was not told the identity of the other doctor, to prevent any collaboration. What's more, all Consulta doctors were barred by the Vatican from discussing alleged miracles with any person outside the Congregation until either the cases were dismissed or the pope had rendered his decision. Later, if they chose, the doctors could write about the odd recoveries in medical journals, although that rarely happened.

Digesting the avalanche of facts, charts, and testimonial opinions attached to purported miracles could take a doctor one full month. After that task was completed, each *ex officio* doctor wrote up a four- or five-page opinion. If one or both of those opinions were "positive," meaning that the expert believed the cure had defied known medical principles, the case moved on. Two negative opinions snuffed an alleged miracle. During Ambrosi's decades of experience, he found that those two votes usually were split. Backed by at least one "positive" opinion, the case next was presented to three additional doctors who read the thick files as well as the opinions offered by the two *ex officio* consultants. In time, all five doctors met in a private room on the third floor of the Congregation for the Causes of Saints—just down the hall from the office of Monsignor Robert Sarno.

The teams gathered about two or three times a month at the Vatican to brood over the proposed cases.

Behind a closed door, all five doctors took turns reciting the pieces of medical logic that went into their final judgments. Sometimes the debates were rigorous. Sometimes opinions were swayed. "Only when we meet [do] we find that others have a different diagnosis, and sometimes . . . others change their minds," Dr. Franco de Rosa, a Consulta member and internal medicine expert, once told a Spanish website. The Holy See paid its doctors between one hundred and two hundred Euros (about $150 to $300) for each case they analyzed—a meager amount for the hours the Italian physicians and professors invested. Santori said he earned that same amount of money in a single twenty-minute outpatient exam. Moreover, Vatican leaders never attempted to coax their doctors into choosing whether they ultimately supported or opposed an alleged miracle, said Dr. Raffaello Cortesini, an organ-transplant surgeon who served as president of the Consulta Medica from 1983 to 2002. Cortesini also was among the five doctors who had approved the first miracle attributed to Mother Teresa. "We never received any kind of pressure. . . . We work with complete freedom," Cortesini once told a journalist. During another interview, Cortesini added, "There is skepticism about miracles, I know, even in the Catholic Church. I myself, if I did not do these consultations, would never believe what I read. You don't understand how fantastic, how incredible—and how well documented—these cases are. They are more incredible than historical romances. Science fiction is nothing by comparison."

Dr. Santori, meanwhile, seemed to be one of the Consulta's most persuasive members, perhaps because he was not so easily convinced of supernatural cures. Among the thirty cases he had contemplated, he believed science could not explain just six. The purported miracles he had vetoed involved people with acute back pain, dangerously high fevers, infections, and fractures that had allegedly healed quickly after they prayed. In each instance, however, Santori had spotted a medical reason for the recovery. "They were exceptional cases, but not totally unexplainable."

"So we discuss and we decide," Santori added. "Each one is giving his opinion and then at the end, if we are not in accord, we discuss again. Normally, [in] the cases which I [said] were not explainable, the [others] were in accord with me."

After all the talking was finished, the five doctors voted openly. In casting their verbal ballots, the doctors didn't use the word "miracle." They merely indicated whether they thought the cure on the table was "natural" or "inexplicable." Unanimity was not required.

A simple majority—three votes—ruled and sent the case on to the Vatican's theological panel for its next intense phase of exploration and judgment. Among the cases found to be medically inexplicable, Dr. Raffaello Cortesini once estimated that only about half received unanimous votes. The Consulta Medica's historic rejection rate was somewhat cloudy, however, and seemed to vary with whichever doctor was being interviewed on the topic. While Dr. Franco de Rosa had once estimated that 99 percent of the cases presented to the Consulta later were rejected as "natural," Cortesini once told *The Times* of London only that "most" miracle submissions failed.

"I do this [work]," Santori said, "first, because I am curious, second, because sometimes there are really very interesting cases, and, third, because I believe that I am not so particularly religious. I am objective. I think these things must not be done by people very near to religion and the Vatican. Some of the [other] consultants are not as strict as I am. This is why I continue to take part in this. I am not linked to any type of religious community. I believe I am a good test."

† † †

The Sisters of Providence had waited ninety-four years for not one but two proven miracles. Patience was one of their learned virtues. So, as the summer of 2003 turned to autumn and then to winter without any fresh dispatches from Rome, the mood on campus remained one of "joyful anticipation," Sister Marie Kevin later recalled, although she admitted feeling twinges of suspense: "It was a very slow process." She made it a point to keep Phil McCord informed, even if her smiling briefings were devoid of details.

"I haven't heard anything," she would tell him, "but I just wanted to let you know."

Finally, on February 17, 2004, Ambrosi notified Monsignor Easton of some intelligence he had gathered inside the Vatican.

Officials at the Congregation for the Causes of Saints had stamped the McCord case with a "decree of validity"—a critical finding. Easton subsequently told Marie Kevin: "This current decree says essentially that the contents [of the acts] were juridically correct, that is, that the procedures [of the Indianapolis tribunal] were followed correctly. As a consequence, now they can move on to the substance of the issue, namely, does the evidence sufficiently demonstrate that the miracle was authentic?"

Positive, yes, but the bulletin only fanned the sisters' rising anticipation. As it turned out, they would have to nibble on that lone nugget of good news for a long time.

Throughout 2004 the sisters made no public comments about their alleged miracle under the Vatican microscope. "We had been so well schooled in being advised not to talk about it a lot until it had been examined," said Sister Denise Wilkinson, who was then two years away from assuming the top nun position at the convent. On campus, however, many sisters held animated sidewalk or hallway chats with McCord about his healing. "Being here every day, and thinking, 'So he went into that church where we go every day, and talked to Mother Théodore,' it was just remarkable," Sister Denise said. "A lot of the sisters talked with Phil about it. To know someone to whom it had happened made all of us consider how God works in our lives."

"It was fun," McCord said years later. "I didn't care for me. Basically I got more out of it than I ever hoped to anyway, because my eye had healed. The rest of it would be frosting on the cake. But it meant a lot to me that it meant so much to the sisters. They had invested so much of their time and money. But the wheels grind slowly, very slowly."

Each month Sister Marie Kevin published a community newsletter, *The Founding Spirit*. She used it to report on other purported healings made in Mother Théodore's name, to recount small episodes from Mother Théodore's life, and to share the latest word on the canonization cause. In August 2004 Marie Kevin decided to reprint an overview from the 1992 Vatican theological panel convened to assess the 1,300-page *positio* authored by Sister Joseph Eleanor Ryan. Ultimately the eight theological consultants voted unanimously that Mother Théodore had lived a life of heroic virtue worthy of Catholic veneration, and they wrote long opinions to support their ballots. In her newsletter, Marie Kevin published excerpts of the eight opinions, but she boldfaced a selected section from "Consultant #7," perhaps as a quiet pep talk to offset the long slog the modern sisters were also enduring. "The Cause . . . despite its merit so widely recognized has been, nonetheless, difficult even to the point of anguish," the seventh theologian had written in 1992. "The reason for the slow progress of the Cause seems to have been brought on by extraneous circumstances, beginning with locale (the various places where the Servant of God resided), and with the availability of extraneous personnel. It is a matter of accidents along the way that were later most brilliantly overcome."

As 2004 rolled into a new year, Marie Kevin continued her promotional work while keeping an eye on her e-mail in-box, hoping for any sunny updates from Ambrosi or Easton. In early 2005 she gave one of her typically beaming presentations on the founder to students at Seton High School in Richmond, Indiana. At the same time, her associate promoter, Sister Mary Ann Phelan, spoke about Mother Théodore to Sunday parishioners at Saint Elizabeth Catholic Church in Rockville, Maryland. Meanwhile, the nuns at the Woods continued welcoming dozens of tourists who wanted to wander their tranquil campus, the place of one Vatican-validated miracle and perhaps, soon, a second. All the while, the sisters listened for any hints of movement in Italy.

Then, on February 1, 2005, an ominous bulletin was flashed by news agencies in Vatican City: Pope John Paul II had been rushed by ambulance to Gemelli Hospital in Rome. The eighty-four-year-old pontiff had spiked a high fever and was reportedly gasping for breath. Two years earlier, the Vatican had confirmed that John Paul was dealing with Parkinson's disease, a degenerative condition that had slowly hushed his once-powerful voice. At Gemelli late that Tuesday night, doctors diagnosed the pope with influenza and determined his larynx had become so inflamed that it had momentarily closed, temporarily blocking his ability to get air to his lungs. One week later, John Paul remained in bed at Gemelli—the hospital to which he also had been whisked immediately after the 1981 shooting in St. Peter's Square. Following the assassination attempt, John Paul stayed at Gemelli for twenty days. In his later years, the increasingly frail pope had returned to Gemelli so often that the medical center reserved a special bank of rooms for him on its tenth floor. The suite included a chapel, a kitchen, and sleeping quarters for his longtime aide. The Italian press had dubbed the hospital "the third Vatican," after the seat at the Holy See and the pope's summer home in Castel Gandolfo. On February 6, 2005, Dr. Corrado Manni, the pope's anesthesiologist, told the Italian newspaper *La Repubblica* that "even if, as certain, the Holy Father overcomes this crisis, in the future there could be similar relapses. . . . Unfortunately, Parkinson's can't be cured—at the most it can be slowed down. And this entails a series of risks, including those that we have seen these days." John Paul was driven back to the Vatican after a nine-day hospital stay.

The most prolific pope in Catholic history—the man who had used canonization as an evangelical hammer, earning the Vatican its "saint factory" nickname—seemed to be teetering toward his final days. For the dozens of congregations and parishes around the world with beatification and canonization causes in the Vatican pipeline, two obvious questions arose: What will become of our saintly crusade if John Paul dies? And if he passes away, will the next pope clamp down on canonizations and halt our cause?

Having waited nearly a century to see their founder sainted, those precise questions ricocheted between the snow-covered buildings at Saint Mary-of-the-Woods, as well as in the hallways at archdiocese headquarters in Indianapolis.

"The pope's health was beginning to fail and I just thought, *Oh my gosh, this is going to delay it, delay it, delay it,*" recalled Father Bonke. "I was anxious. So I would often e-mail or call Sister Marie Kevin and ask, 'Have you heard anything? Have you heard anything?'"

Then another news alert rocked Rome—and Indiana—on February 24, 2005: the pope had again been placed in a private ambulance, had again been dashed to Gemelli. His fever and the breathing troubles were back. Attendants had carried the pontiff, conscious but lying on a gurney, into the hospital. This time, however, news agencies reported that doctors had been forced to perform a tracheotomy, cutting a hole into his windpipe to allow air to reach his lungs. John Paul, the grand canonizer, was dying.

CHAPTER FOURTEEN

The Verdict

After the final prayers of morning Mass, the Providence Hall cafeteria filled with the low murmur of sisters chatting over their lunch trays and the tinny jangle of forks and knives. The room swirled with a delicious medley of aromas—steaming soups and stews, freshly prepared fish and meats, hot coffee and warm pie. The nuns sat in clusters of four or five at cozy circular tables. Many had graying hair, or locks as white as the snowdrifts outside. Some arrived on canes, some on walkers, some in wheelchairs. Several tables sat entirely empty. Most conspicuous was the sparse sprinkling of young nuns who lunched alongside their elders.

Sister Marie Kevin was acutely aware of the convent's aging demographic. By the late winter of 2005, she was eighty years old herself—and mindful of her community's diminishing lifespan. The Sisters of Providence had faded from a thriving, one-thousand-woman order in the 1960s to barely more than four hundred nuns. With each passing year, the order lost more sisters to age and disease than it replaced through its novitiate—an attrition rate that, some sisters estimated, would cause Mother Théodore's beloved Catholic home to wither and perish sometime around the year 2035.

Across America, many communities of religious women were similarly wasting away. In Chicago, the last remaining Oblate Sisters of Providence—an order for Catholic women of African descent—had been forced to shutter their lone elementary school and leave town in 2002 due to dwindling ranks. In New York State, three shrinking congregations had merged in 2004—strictly as a matter of survival—to form a single new order, the Sisters of St. Francis. The following year, the Archdiocese of Baltimore announced closure of the Visitation Monastery. A Baltimore landmark since the 1820s, Visitation Monastery was, by 2005, occupied by just three elderly sisters. Nationally, the number of nuns had thinned from a peak of 180,000 in the mid-1960s to some 66,000 by 2005—a population erosion of nearly three thousand sisters per year. In explaining the fall-off, some congregation leaders pointed to the fact that American couples were having fewer children while modern U.S. women were reaping more lucrative career opportunities. What's more, the Second Vatican Ecumenical Council—the historic "Vatican II" meetings of the early 1960s—had emphasized and applauded the rising importance of lay Catholics. That, in turn, had influenced many devout women to dedicate themselves to the Church while also marrying and having families. Meanwhile, some nuns blamed their national numerical decline on their own lack of visibility: most orders, like the Sisters of Providence, had abandoned the practice of wearing habits. The dress-code change was made, in part, because many sisters worried that their habits conveyed the false impression that they were somehow above the laity. Oddly, members of one of the few modern orders that continued to flourish—the Dominican Sisters of St. Cecilia in Nashville, Tennessee—still draped themselves in long white habits with black veils and white headbands. Marie Kevin had last donned her habit in 1969, the year the Sisters of Providence had voted to make the uniform optional.

In blue jeans and sweaters, the Sisters of Providence lugged their various ministries and messages into dozens of neighborhoods where they offered food banks, adult literacy programs, and bilingual counseling, or where they publicly protested against the war in Iraq and against capital punishment. Unlike monastic cloisters of nuns, the Sisters of Providence were an "apostolic" community—by definition, they searched for people in need, as the twelve Apostles did. For the sisters, that meant heading into low-income housing projects, crowded suburbs, or city high-rises. While working outside their hushed compound, however, some sisters eventually absorbed certain secular traits. One internal survey taken in the mid-2000s asked the Sisters of Providence to name any negatives they associated with their community. In response, two words often were cited: "individualism" and "consumerism"—ripple effects, Marie Kevin contended, of the nuns' apostolic work. Yet she also believed such an honest moment of self-reflection could be crucial to stemming the community's fatal attrition rate. In that same survey, the nuns were asked to list what qualities they savored about being a Sister of Providence. The answer for many: Mother Théodore's lingering charism, her divine charisma—her indomitable trust in providence, and her steadfast conviction that God would see her through ocean storms, fiery attacks on her outpost by anti-Catholic locals, even her turbulent clashes with the local bishop. That charism had for decades been the sisters' collective personality. In some ways, however, Marie Kevin believed the apostolic nuns had lost some of their self-image along with some of their public identity. "We used to own twenty-two schools. We don't own them now. We decided in the early 1970s we had to divest because they were too costly to maintain," Marie Kevin said. "We're big into justice issues and have been for some time . . . [but] we're not as recognizable to the public." To attract more postulants and boost the ranks of younger sisters—to help salvage the congregation's future—Marie Kevin felt the order needed to reclaim its own vision, and the view the outside world held of the Woods. One pathway there, she suggested, followed a re-embracing of the founder's charism—her rugged story, her earthly values, and her utter trust in divine providence. "It was her charism which brought this Congregation to birth," Marie Kevin once wrote for the Sisters of Providence website. "It is our living of that charism, in all aspects of human and world need, that will carry us into the future."

The haven's traditional allure and its singular woodsy character could be globally rekindled through Mother Théodore's successful canonization cause, Marie Kevin believed. The destiny of her cherished congregation might even rest on the founder's sanctification — and on the healed cornea of its blue-eyed Baptist caretaker.

But as spring loomed in 2005, the sisters' happy anticipation carried a sharper edge: the pro-miracle pope was deteriorating sadly, publicly, and rapidly. On Palm Sunday, March 20, tens of thousands of pilgrims crushed into sunny St. Peter's Square with hopes of seeing John Paul II offer the Mass to launch the Catholic Holy Week. Just three weeks earlier, the Catholic world had read or heard that doctors had inserted a tube into the pope's throat to help him breathe. They cheered on March 20 when he appeared at his third-story window wearing a braided palm frond. They smiled when he waved an olive branch. They grew more silent when he put his hand to his face, then pounded his lectern in apparent frustration. He did not speak a word. Finally the white curtains that dangled at the edges of the pope's window were snapped shut.

One week later, another throng gathered atop the sea of cobblestones and travertine below the papal quarters. Again the pope was wheeled to the window of his study. Next, an aide placed a microphone in front of John Paul's mouth. He coughed spasmodically. He pressed his fingers against his temples. He tried to speak. He grimaced. The pilgrims heard him utter only a few rasps. He silently traced the sign of the cross. For the first time in his twenty-six-year reign, John Paul was too sick to preside over the Easter service. Twelve minutes after he appeared, he was wheeled back and away from the window. The curtain was drawn. In the crowd below, some people cried.

Six days later, as his kidneys failed, John Paul prayed with his aides and doctors in his personal quarters. His heartbeat slowed, his blood pressure dropped, and his breathing grew shallow. No ambulance was called. John Paul had asked to remain in his papal home. The vicar of Vatican City, Angelo Comastri, told candle-holding worshippers in St. Peter's Square, "This evening or tonight, Christ will open the gates to the pope." The curtains on the papal apartment remained closed. Around the fringes of the window, however, the pilgrims could see lamplight burning inside. On Saturday, April 2, 2005, at 9:37 p.m., John Paul died. Several news agencies reported that his final whispered word was "Amen." For the record, however, the pope's physician, Dr. Renato Buzzonetti, told *La Repubblica* that the pope was ultimately silenced by his ailments and had "passed away slowly, with pain and suffering which he endured with great human dignity." Vatican TV broadcast a simple message: "The angels welcome you."

During the four months preceding the pope's death, the usual chatter and speculation about a successor had buzzed in Rome, gaining volume each time he was hospitalized. One name that often topped the papal guess lists was Cardinal Joseph Ratzinger, a German who led the powerful Congregation for the Doctrine of the Faith — a four-centuries-old wing of the Roman Curia that globally promoted and safeguarded Catholic beliefs and canons. Vatican insiders believed the voting cardinals would purposely pick a transitional figure, a short-term leader whose philosophies echoed the conservative teachings of John Paul. At seventy-seven years old, the hard-line Ratzinger appeared to fit both qualifications perfectly. Like John Paul, he was known to oppose the ordination of women priests and the use of contraception, and he had stood against any loosening of the celibacy rules for priests. Moreover, as dean of the College of Cardinals, he would govern the selection of the next pope.

Dr. Andrea Ambrosi had long been acquainted with Ratzinger, sharing his company at meeting tables and at other formal occasions in Vatican City. Ratzinger's name was bandied about at the Woods as the sisters wondered aloud who would next control Catholic saint-naming. If Ratzinger were chosen, the sisters wondered, would Mother Théodore's canonization bid stall—or worse? "I know he is much more severe [than John Paul] in everything he does," Ambrosi acknowledged. "He thinks you should study things, and that things should take much longer." The sisters braced for another potential slowdown in the cause—while outside the Vatican, the faithful expected, and demanded, saintly speed. At John Paul's public funeral on Friday, April 8, mourners in St. Peter's Square lifted banners that read *Santo Subito!* ("Saint at Once!"), and chanted, *"Santo! Santo!"*

By April 12, 2005, as the cardinals prepared to assemble in seclusion to vote for a new Roman Catholic leader, news leaked from the Vatican that a petition already had been circulated among the electorate seeking signatures in support of a fast-track canonization for John Paul. That push carried the strong scent of politics and pre-conclave maneuvering, some Vatican insiders believed; they interpreted the quick-sanctification campaign as a bid to build an alliance among like-minded cardinals, and perhaps to boost one candidate out of John Paul's inner circle. Perhaps someone like Ratzinger, who had closed his eulogy at John Paul's funeral with the words, "We can be sure that our beloved pope is standing today at the window of the Father's house."

On Sunday, April 18, during the Mass at St. Peter's Basilica dedicated to electing the next pope, Ratzinger used his homily to admonish the faithful—and his fellow cardinals—about some encroaching ideologies he deemed as menacing: liberalism,

Marxism, agnosticism, atheism, and the concept that there were
no absolute truths, also known as relativism. Journalists dubbed it
Ratzinger's final "stump speech" for the papacy. The next day, he
and the other 114 cardinals sequestered themselves in the Sistine
Chapel to cast their votes. They remained there through one night
and four ballots. At 5:50 p.m. on Tuesday, April 19, white smoke
puffed from the frescoed chimney atop the Sistine Chapel, and
twenty-five minutes later, the bells chimed above St. Peter's Square:
signals of a decision. The conclave had elected Ratzinger. Taking
the name Benedict XVI, he became the 265th pope of the Roman
Catholic Church.

One of Benedict's early directives to the Congregation for the
Causes of Saints was, according to Ambrosi, to "look more carefully" at the alleged miracles they were handed. "He's never told
them to slow down . . . but to take your lens and make it bigger so
you are looking at everything, so that nothing passes by you," the
postulator recalled later. "He is a very rigorous man who looks at
things very diligently. He is much more rigorous, the new *papa* [as
Italians called the pope]. He's not so willing to push things forward
as maybe John Paul was." Eventually, Benedict also urged the
Congregation to pay "maximum attention" to its assessment of the
documents supporting each cause, and to give "scrupulous observation" to ecclesiastical norms. Archbishop Michele Di Ruberto, the
Congregation's secretary, revealed as well that the new pope would
read every cause file, page by page, seeking a personal conviction
that the miracles attributed to would-be saints truly fell outside the
bounds of science.

Via e-mail or in phone calls, Ambrosi reassured the nuns at the
Woods that their cause was in no danger of skidding to a halt. But
he also prepared them emotionally for the new era of tenacious
scrutiny at the Vatican.

"We are not sure of things because this new pope has a new way of doing things," Ambrosi's translator, Francesca Lorenzetti, told the sisters in one e-mail.

"We had a new Holy Father. There were, I guess, rumors or opinions that Benedict XVI was not going to have, or didn't have, the same position on canonizations," recalled Sister Denise Wilkinson, who was then on the cusp of becoming general superior. "I don't know if it's true or not, but that's what the big opinion was. That was the guess—probably it wouldn't happen."

† † †

Less than two months into Benedict's papacy, Ambrosi was tipped off that the alleged miracle of Phil McCord was about to undergo its first—and most arduous—Vatican referendum. Selected doctors from the Consulta Medica had plumbed and pondered the tribunal transcripts as well as the attached reports on phacoemulsification times, dispensed drug amounts, visual measurements, and pressure readings. They were poised to vote whether they believed science could explain the healing that had happened inside the eye of the man from Indiana. Through his own painstaking edits and revisions of the *positio*, Ambrosi had tried to distill the essence of the case into one persuasive peculiarity: the baffling behavior of those two tiny scraps of cataract that had temporarily wedged in the front of McCord's right eye. "The remnants," Ambrosi said, recalling his emphasis to the panel, "could have been removed only surgically— the *only* way. And they went away spontaneously without this operation. I reinforced that idea."

Everything rested on those two chips, Ambrosi believed. Their vanishing act, he maintained, was purely supernatural—not an optical illusion. He had been firmly and finally convinced that their disappearance was miraculous during a private chat he had held with Dr. Nick Rader in an Indianapolis hotel room shortly after the 2003 tribunal had closed.

"Sister Marie Kevin was keeping me updated that things were moving forward and that Dr. Ambrosi liked the case," Rader said later. "Then she called me out of the blue. She said, 'Dr. Ambrosi's in town. Can you meet with him downtown? He'll be at the Hilton.' So I go on a really cold night. I pull into the parking garage. Sister Marie Kevin meets me in the lobby. It reminded me of *The Da Vinci Code*."

The doctor and the nun rode an elevator to an upper floor in the hotel. They entered Ambrosi's suite and gathered around a coffee table in a sitting chamber. Rader sat in a chair across from the postulator, who took his place on the couch, with his interpreter to his left. Marie Kevin nestled into a chair to Rader's right. The room was warm and smelled stuffy, as if many conversations had been held there that day. Ambrosi seemed focused but tired from a long workday, Rader recalled. The Italian's suit looked rumpled, and his tie had been loosened.

The twenty-minute meeting had one purpose: Ambrosi wanted to better comprehend the inner landscape of the eye, where the cataract bits had been spotted, how those remnants had reacted with the cornea, and how they could have suddenly moved. "He didn't have a lot of questions, and it almost appeared as if he just wanted to hear it directly," Rader said later. The doctor leaned forward and, on a piece of notebook paper atop the coffee table, began to sketch the anatomy of the human eye. As Rader spoke and roughed out some lines and dots, Ambrosi's interpreter repeated the optical technicalities in Italian. Ambrosi nodded silently. "So I draw some models out for him, trying to explain what I am thinking, where the particles go. It seemed almost clandestine."

After leaving Ambrosi with his ballpoint-pen pictures, Rader departed the Hilton. Years later, Ambrosi could still conjure Rader's hand-rendered reference when he fed those same microscopic highlights to the Consulta Medica. "The remnants," Ambrosi said, "that is where the miracle occurred."

The first test, as always, would come from the two *ex officio* doctors. If one of the two Roman medical experts gave an affirmative vote, the McCord case would roll before the full, five-member Consulta Medica. "Usually one [vote] is positive and one is negative," Ambrosi said years later. "In this case, both gave positive votes."

In the early days of June 2005, Ambrosi rushed off a brief e-mail to Sister Ann Margaret O'Hara, then the convent's general superior: the case was at the medical commission, and the doctors soon would cast their ballots. At the convent, the tension spiked.

Following the postulator's alert, Sister Ann Margaret started every day by eagerly scanning her e-mail—first in her personal quarters and then again at her Woods office.

"We knew they were meeting," Ann Margaret said.

"They were waiting," Ambrosi said.

Through June 8, 2005, Ann Margaret's in-box flashed no further updates from Rome.

On Thursday morning, June 9, Ambrosi staked out a third-floor room at the Congregation for the Causes of Saints. Inside, the five doctors were voting. His heart pumped a few ticks faster. "I was the one who convinced the sisters to spend the money and go forward," he said. "All that convincing. If it went badly, I would throw myself into the river."

Suddenly the big doors were shoved open. Then Monsignor Michele Di Ruberto, the Congregation's undersecretary at that time, emerged and waved Ambrosi over.

"Listen," Di Ruberto said in Italian, "this is how it happened."

Ninety-seven years of investigations and exhumations, of hope, prayers, and sisterly yearning—everything—hung on the monsignor's next words.

The doctors, he told Ambrosi, all had viewed McCord's recovery in the same way. The five votes were unanimous.

"Inexplicable."

"Fantastic," Ambrosi said. To the veteran postulator, the moment felt "like a personal victory."

Still beaming, Ambrosi left Vatican City, recrossed the bridge spanning the Tiber River, and reached his office near Piazza Navona. He tapped out a short e-mail and sent it halfway around the world to Ann Margaret's computer. Nearly noon in Rome, it was barely dawn at the convent. When the general superior reached her desk in Owens Hall, on the east side of campus, she immediately glanced at her screen. She saw the note from Ambrosi. She opened it.

"The medical committee found no scientific reason for the cure," the e-mail read.

She stared at the words. She felt the palpable potency of the news, the history of the moment, the sweet joy of the positive vote. But amid a purported miracle about restored vision, she almost could not believe her eyes. She typed a response and sent it to Rome.

"Are you sure?"

Ambrosi quickly wrote back.

"Yes," his e-mail read. "It has gone on."

This is really going to move forward, Ann Margaret thought.

She summoned to her office the other five women on the Woods leadership council and shared the happy bulletin with them. She phoned across campus to inform Sister Diane Ris, the previous general superior who, at the 1998 beatification ceremony, had presented John Paul II with a box containing one of Mother Théodore's rib bones. After the nuns had gathered for their 11:30 a.m. Mass in the Church of the Immaculate Conception—before the prayers began—the headline was announced. At the same time, Ann Margaret sent out a mass e-mail to the more than two hundred Sisters of Providence who were scattered in other states and in lands abroad. And she called Marie Kevin.

"It was the culmination," Marie Kevin recalled later, "of a long wait. Although the community had waited a lot longer than I did. I was working on the cause, all together, eleven years. But my great-est joy, still, was the day I received the letter from Sister Nancy Nolan in 1996 asking me to take over the cause. I didn't know what I was doing. I was just doing what I knew needed to be done. But [when one is assigned to find a miracle, and help escort your hero to sainthood], they don't really give you a clear blueprint. You do all you can to make her better known. I did that by making presenta-tions everywhere."

This time no speeches were made. Publicly, Marie Kevin and Ann Margaret said very little about the Consulta decision. Ann Margaret gave the Indianapolis Archdiocese website a brief state-ment about the latest development: "We all breathed a sigh of relief." The sisters still were bound by Vatican-mandated silence. More important, three primary obstacles remained for the alleged miracle, including the Vatican's seven-member panel of theologians. That was where the McCord case would go next. The theologians would need to be convinced that the convent's own caretaker—a Baptist man raised by a Baptist lay minister and a Christian Scientist mother—had prayed properly for the intercession of a Catholic nun.

Four days after the Consulta Medica ruled that McCord's recovery had, in their opinion, eluded the laws of science, Marie Kevin wrote the man at the center of the alleged miracle a one-page letter about the vote. "We now await the discussion of the theo-logical commission, which will convene in the autumn. . . . I asked Monsignor Easton what the emphasis of this second review might be, and in part he replied, 'I think it seems to be heavily a pre-cautionary check, but there might also be . . . the question of what message [Mother Théodore] has in her life and writings [and if that message] is needed for our times.' . . . We will continue to keep you informed as an expression of gratitude for all that you have done to assist us."

In November, seven theologians repeated the late spring

examination performed by the five Vatican doctors. Again, after Ambrosi received word that a vote loomed, he stood in a marble corridor at the Congregation headquarters. On November 20, 2005, he watched for the doors to open. And once more, a Congregation official exited the confidential session and whispered the verdict: "None of the theologians had any problem with this particular miracle," the postulator recalled later. As he had done in June, Ambrosi alerted Ann Margaret via e-mail. He also typed a brief note to Monsignor Easton, who, in turn, revealed on the archdiocese website that the theologians had "decided there was nothing contrary to faith or morals in the miracle and life of the Blessed."

"It's feeling very much," Marie Kevin said at the time, "like we're coming to the conclusion of this."

The *positio* remained at the Vatican, poised for a February 2006 assessment by the third and final commission—in Italian, the Congresso—fifteen cardinals and archbishops from the Congregation for the Causes of Saints. That group, which included the Congregation's prefect, secretary, and undersecretary, would "not necessarily give it a bad vote," Ambrosi said. "If they see something they don't think seems right, they will ask me for clarifications." But if the Congresso saw something supernatural in McCord's cure, every Catholic cardinal and archbishop scattered around the world would be asked to review the cause—barely more than a formality. If that august body raised no objections, the *positio* finally would land in Benedict's papal study. And if it reached the pope's desk, carrying a mandate from the College of Cardinals, the nuns knew that their case—and Mother Théodore's cause—almost certainly would earn papal approval. A February 21 endorsement from the Congresso would unleash musical revelry and gleeful prayers of thanks at the Woods. The sisters already sensed rising momentum in Rome, and they had heard Ambrosi's surging confidence. "I was sure it would continue passing," the postulator said. "I had absolutely no doubts."

On February 1, 2006, Ann Margaret drafted an excited letter to update every Sister of Providence at home and abroad, asking them to "keep [this] confidential. . . . Dr. Ambrosi, our postulator, has informed us that the meeting will be held on February 21 in Rome. We should receive word later that day of their decision. . . . Let us continue to draw on the hopes we have for each other and for the Congregation because of this moment in our history."

Twenty-four hours before the Congresso met, Ann Margaret dashed off an angst-tinged cyber-note to Ambrosi's interpreter: "Dear Francesca . . . we are all anxiously awaiting your e-mail tomorrow with — we hope — positive news."

The Congresso assembled, as scheduled, in an apostolic palace — a publicly off-limits complex adjoining St. Peter's Basilica that included the pope's residence. Ambrosi was not allowed to wait there to receive the first word. Instead, he nervously watched the clock in his office across the river. When he assumed enough time had passed for the cardinals to decide the matter, he restlessly pressed a series of three phone numbers — repeatedly ringing the offices of the Congregation prefect, secretary, and undersecretary. "I keep calling until one of them picks up," Ambrosi said. One finally did.

The McCord case, Ambrosi was told, had been decided. The Congresso agreed that the engineer's corneal restoration defied all natural explanation — that it was a miracle. Ambrosi shouted the news from his office to Lorenzetti's desk next door. The translator typed a short e-mail to the Woods and pressed Send. In Rome it was 2:25 p.m., and in Indiana, 8:25 a.m.

"The congress of the cardinals went well! . . . Love, Francesca."

Ann Margaret stared at her computer screen. Once more she read the sweet words from Rome and felt a duty to double-check.

"Francesca," she typed, "does this mean that the miracle has passed? . . . May we begin our celebration? . . . Love, Ann Margaret."

The reply came within seven minutes: "Yes, of course!"

Ann Margaret immediately phoned Providence Hall and spilled the news to Marie Kevin, who hung up and instantly dialed McCord at his desk. "There's going to be an announcement," Marie Kevin said. "Keep this under your hat, but you ought to know, this has been approved."

† † †

The eleven bells that hung in the tower of the Church of the Immaculate Conception once were hand-pulled to tell the sisters when to wake, when to pray, and when to turn out their lights and sleep. By the twenty-first century, the bells were computer-operated, but they still chimed on Sundays to accompany Mass, and they tolled whenever a sister died. They were tuned to the key of D, once dubbed "the key of glory," and the primary key in which the "Hallelujah Chorus" from Handel's *Messiah* is written.

On Tuesday, February 21, 2005, at precisely 1:15 p.m., beneath a deep blue sky that had been drearily overcast only a few hours earlier, the bells rang high above the same church where the convent caretaker had prayed in anguish five years before, and where Mother Théodore's body still rested. Amid the enclave's brick dormitories, above its creaky motherhouse and throughout the leafless walnut trees that gave the place its rustic name, the rhythmic tolls echoed for exactly fifteen minutes, signifying the jubilant end to an epic wait.

"Smiles were broader. Feet were quicker. Pictures of Mother Théodore were observed in a new way. Hugs were plentiful," read an article in *The Founding Spirit*, describing the day. Ann Margaret e-mailed the original Sisters of Providence in France with the news. And regional journalists were invited to come to the Woods the next day for a press conference at Providence Center, the campus welcoming hub. Now they could speak freely.

The next day, standing beneath a painted portrait of Mother Théodore, Ann Margaret told the reporters and photographers, "The way is now open for canonization of our foundress." Marie Kevin followed and took the opportunity to do some teaching on Catholic dogma and miracles: "We do not believe Mother Théodore can reverse the laws of nature, but we do believe that because she is close to God, she has what is called intercessory power. When we ask her help, we are asking her to intercede with God for us and our needs."

And the man who once had asked Mother Théodore to intercede finally was introduced. Wearing a suit and tie, he looked out at the faces before him. He was not comfortable with the attention. McCord's identity had never been publicly revealed by the sisters before that day. In his typically soft tones, McCord explained the nasty soreness and swelling that had half blinded and disfigured him following his cataract surgery. He mentioned how a doctor had told him he would require a corneal transplant to regain full sight. "I was stunned to say the least," he told the journalists. He repeated the tale of his prayer, his sudden cure, and how doctors later had told him they could not explain his restored vision. His eyesight, he said, was now nearly perfect—he needed glasses only to read small print. Before McCord surrendered the microphone, a reporter asked how it felt to be the recipient of a miracle. McCord paused at the very question that had privately dogged him for four years.

The cure, McCord answered, "has had a profound effect on my life. I went through a long period thinking, 'What did I do to deserve this?'"

Sister Denise Wilkinson, then five months away from becoming the convent's leading nun, never forgot McCord's wide-eyed demeanor at the press briefing. "He was sort of amazed, sort of dazed, at a loss almost," she recalled. "He was still trying to figure it out."

Two months later, Pope Benedict XVI put his conclusive stamp on the case. On April 28, 2006, he held a private audience with Cardinal José Saraiva Martins, then-prefect of the Congregation for the Causes of Saints. There, Benedict authorized the publication of seven decrees that approved seven separate miracles, including the healing of Phil McCord—now officially, according to the Roman Catholic Church, a divine cure.

Marie Kevin jetted back to Rome in late June accompanied by Sister Mary Ann Phelan, the associate promoter of the cause. In Vatican City, the two nuns planned to conduct the first piece of business for a looming Vatican celebration that once had seemed like a hazy, distant dream.

On July 1, 2006, Pope Benedict led a consistory, a special meeting, of about thirty cardinals. Their agenda included picking a date for the next round of Catholic canonizations. That morning, Marie Kevin and Sister Mary Ann were ushered into a snug, ornate room at the Vatican. The doors were framed in old dark wood. The walls were adorned in a faint pattern of pink roses. A choir sang. Worshippers recited prayers. The nuns sat two-thirds of the way back, sharing the space with the representatives for three other causes also on the cusp of completion. One section of the crowd had come to support Rafael Guizar Valencia, an early-twentieth-century Mexican bishop who, as a result of religious persecution in his homeland, spent much of his life on the run, disguising himself as a street vendor, a musician, and a homeopathic doctor—all so he could console the sick and administer the Catholic sacraments to the dying. Another cluster in the room backed the campaign for Sister Rosa Venerini, an Italian nun who devoted her life to educating and promoting women, opening more than forty schools throughout Italy. At her school in Rome, she once received a surprise visit from Pope Clement XI and eight cardinals. They had arrived on October 24, 1716, to watch this famous teacher of girls. At the end of her lessons, Pope Clement had told the nun, "Signora Rosa, you are doing that which we cannot do. We thank you very much because with these schools you will sanctify Rome." The third group sitting near Marie Kevin and Sister Mary Ann had come to cheer the cause of Filippo Smaldone, an Italian priest who aided people who could not hear or speak. In 1885, in Lecce, Italy, Father Smaldone had founded an institute for the hearing-impaired, training a cadre of nuns to patiently deliver a specialized form of care. Eventually the group of nuns in Lecce evolved into the Salesian Sisters of the Sacred Hearts. All around Marie Kevin, the chairs were filled with hopeful, expectant people. Then Pope Benedict entered, followed closely by Cardinal Martins. They silently stood at the front. All the visitors listened for the chosen date.

In Italian, Martins read short descriptions of the four candidates for sainthood. Mother Théodore's official Vatican biography portrayed her as a "fragile" yet "steadfast" French missionary who had carved a Catholic niche in the densely forested and often unfriendly American frontier, and it quoted from her journals—a line she had written about one of her many chats with God. That snippet referred specifically to one of the hurricanes that had battered her U.S.-bound ship, yet her words seemed to foreshadow Phil McCord's own tale: "What strength the soul draws from prayer! In the midst of a storm, how sweet is the calm it finds."

Then the date of the canonizations was announced. The two nuns from Indiana stepped outside the crowded room. Sister Mary Ann turned on her cell phone and dialed Sister Ann Margaret. At about 4:00 a.m., the general superior's phone buzzed in her quarters. She had gone to sleep expecting the wake-up call from Rome. She received the news. Five hours later, Ann Margaret faced about three hundred sisters—those who lived at the Woods and those who had flocked back home from their teaching jobs or from their far-flung ministries. They jammed into O'Shaughnessy Dining Hall for the convent's prescheduled "chapter," a convergence of all sisters held every five years to discuss governance matters and to elect a fresh leadership council. This chapter would be altogether different from any other convened over the past century. O'Shaughnessy, bedecked with arched windows, soaring white pillars, chandeliers, and a cathedral-like ceiling, crackled with happy tension before Ann Margaret spoke. As she opened her mouth, the room fell silent.

"It is," she said, "October fifteen!"

The sisters instantly roared with cheers and applause, and one nun shouted, "Go, girl!"

The sanctification moment would mesh perfectly with the community's most hallowed month: Mother Théodore's birthday was October 2, her Catholic feast day was October 3, and the anniversary of her arrival at the Woods — Founder's Day — was October 22.

When the fanfare ebbed, some sisters flipped through their 2006 calendars and measured what precious little time they had to pull together one of the biggest Catholic parties among all the religion's solemn festivities, a canonization. Thousands of pilgrims would fly from Indiana to Rome for the occasion. More would stream into Italy from other countries, including many from France. Every last inch of St. Peter's Square would be filled with faith-frenzied folks. From the morning they first heard the date, the Sisters of Providence had 106 days to prepare. Relics and papal gifts had to be selected and arranged. Flights and hotels had to be coordinated and booked. The chores were many. And nobody grasped that short span better than Marie Kevin. She had a thick list of planning tasks to cross off before the day of sainthood dawned.

After flying back to the Woods on July 2, Marie Kevin immediately returned to work. By the middle of that month, she was composing a mass informational mailing to about 350 people who would be traveling to Italy alone, and not with the scheduled tour groups that were being organized. Her letters would tell the independent pilgrims when and where in Rome they could pick up their canonization tickets. She hustled to beat the daily postal deadline at the convent's post office. She missed the last mail pickup, however, and was forced to drive about eight miles into Terre Haute to send the stack of envelopes. Later, with that errand completed, she strolled again into Providence Hall. Suddenly she felt a piercing jolt in her abdomen. She looked for a chair and sat. A nurse walked past and saw the nun holding her midsection—below the spot on her body where doctors had removed a cancerous mass twelve years earlier.

"What's the matter?" the nurse asked.

"I don't know," Marie Kevin gasped. "I'm just having terrible pain."

By that evening, the eighty-one-year-old sister was lying in a hospital bed. Droplets of morphine flowed into her veins to quell the deep ache in her belly. The next day, doctors would conduct a battery of diagnostic tests.

Well, that's it, thought the woman who had tirelessly toured, preached, and crusaded for Mother Théodore's sanctification, leading it to the fringe of reality—her life's work. *I'm not going to get to go to the canonization.*

CHAPTER FIFTEEN

The Third Miracle

From the splashy sea of red-robed cardinals to the throaty shouts of blissful pilgrims to the constant stares of saintly statues atop St. Peter's Square, Roman Catholic canonizations delivered a sumptuous sensory banquet, all bathed in time-worn ritual. With tens of thousands of faithful typically crammed into seats below the basilica's gleaming dome, popes usually entered the piazza behind a parade of green-clad bishops. They sat on a gold-trimmed throne, theatrically flanked at the altar by Swiss guards in red-plumed helmets. On the basilica's façade, huge tapestries depicted the honorees. Popes said canonization Masses in Latin and, at the climax of the service, they formally added the blesseds to the roll call of saints—the highest honor in Catholicism.

On an October Sunday in Vatican City, one of the banners fluttering between the grand columns of St. Peter's would portray the face of Mother Théodore Guérin, part French, part Italian, part Indiana trailblazer. Pope Benedict XVI would name her the eighth American saint while scores of her fans—sisters, campus employees, and college alumnae—would wave scarves of sky blue, the school color at Saint Mary-of-the-Woods College. The convent's maintenance chief would enjoy a front-row view, soaking in the majestic spectacle with his crisp, clear vision. The Roman postulator of the aged cause would blaze his bright smile over the festivities and kneel before the pope. The attendees would even include some ancestors of Joseph Thralls, the farmer who had sheltered Mother Théodore and her five fellow nuns in 1840 when they wearily arrived at their assigned place in the forest. But in mid-July 2006, flat on her back in a Terre Haute hospital, Sister Marie Kevin Tighe could only imagine the delirious celebration she would be missing in Italy.

Doctors spent a full day scanning and testing her body. At night, they operated. They discovered that a small patch of surgical mesh—implanted in her small intestine during a 1995 hernia surgery—had become blocked "like concrete," she said later. They could not remove the mesh, so they resected a portion of her intestines to restore her digestive tract. When she awoke again, a doctor told Marie Kevin he was worried the obstruction might recur. When she heard the severity of her case, she figured there was no chance she would be able to travel in the fall. Yet she never stressed, never panicked, and never felt agitated about missing the moment, she said. It was as if her work was done. "I can't explain the peaceful feeling I had," she recalled. "I was never upset about not going." That sudden, soothing calmness would have been quite familiar to Phil McCord.

"That was a special grace from God," Marie Kevin said later. She spent about one week in Union Hospital and then several more days in an infirmary bed at the Woods.

As she had so often before during extreme sickness, Marie Kevin rallied.

"I recuperated well."

"I think," McCord said later, "she is the miracle."

Soon she was back at her desk in Providence Hall, organizing and mobilizing.

On Wednesday, October 11, 2006, under damp, cloudy skies, Marie Kevin departed the Woods with a group of fellow sisters—the first wave of pilgrims to embark. In Indianapolis, she clicked her seatbelt on a jumbo jet bound for Rome, her sixth trip to the Eternal City.

Later that same day, Phil and Debbie McCord took a different plane to Newark Liberty International Airport, then transferred to an Alitalia flight to Italy. The other passengers included several Sisters of Providence plus a news crew from the British Broadcasting Company. The BBC would document almost every step of McCord's excursion for a documentary on miracles. A cameraman filmed McCord as he boarded and settled into his seat. In Rome the attention would inflate and explode into rock-star-like adulation — all for a shy engineer who was delighted to rejoice with the nuns yet wholly uncomfortable with the limelight, and still uneasy with his so-called miracle. His private creed for the Italian adventure: "Don't let me screw this up for the sisters."

The McCords checked into a hotel miles away from hoopla, in a quiet, industrial section of Rome. On Friday the Vatican invited representatives of all four causes to come to St. Peter's Square for a canonization rehearsal. Hurrying to his designated spot, Phil McCord barely had time to see and savor the ancient grandeur of the place — the gold cupola atop the basilica, the massive Tuscan colonnades that beckoned people to enter the church, and the slim, towering obelisk of red granite in the center of the piazza that radiated lines of travertine in every direction. Touristy snapshots would have to wait. Directions, sequences, and ceremonial stations had to be learned and practiced. The participants were given copies of the program to study. Amid the walkthrough, several Vatican priests huddled on the dais and talked quietly. Sister Ann Margaret O'Hara, now the ex-general superior, sought to ask them a brief procedural question. She stepped up and onto the stage. One of the priests snapped his head around and angrily rushed toward the nun. He raised his hand high as if to say "Stop!" From below, the Sisters of Providence, including general superior Sister Dennis Wilkinson, watched in disbelief. They instantly recognized that the Italian man was ordering the startled American woman off the platform. "The visual was that he pushed her away," Sister Denise said later. McCord's eyes narrowed. He grew furious as the priest stood above, seeing that Ann Margaret indeed returned to her assigned level. The clear message the priest meant to convey, McCord believed, was "this is for men only." As he recounted that brush-off years later, McCord balled his right fist and pounded it into his left palm with a loud slap while revealing the words that flared in his mind that morning in Vatican City: "Little shit, I'm going to smack him! Who the hell do you think you are?"

The emotional clash served as a clear, sad symbol for McCord and some of the sisters—a quick-flash representation of the subordinate and limited place women still held within the ranks of the Catholic Church. The irony was almost laughable: they had crossed an ocean to attend the canonization of their founder, a woman who was being sainted—in part—because she had the guts to stand up to chauvinistic, overbearing priests and local businessmen. "The people who were coordinating the ceremonies, the fathers, were basically just kind of jerks," McCord said. "They treated the sisters like second-class citizens. I mean it was just like we weren't honored guests. At the Vatican it was like, 'Yeah, we're putting on this big show and you guys are the props.' . . . Frankly, the sisters are the backbone of the Church, and they treat them like maids and servants. They make a great deal out of women [gaining] priesthood. They'd settle for just being treated like people—affirmed and appreciated."

"Overall, it was an experience that had its highs and lows," Sister Denise recalled. "Its lows were very, very low, and its highs were very, very high. We all just concentrated on the highs: we and our friends are there to celebrate."

As canonization Sunday neared, McCord's mere presence in the streets unleashed staccato clicks of camera shutters and whispers of "the miracle man" or *l'uomo di miracolo*. Wherever he strolled, necks craned in his direction. His wife laughingly said, "It was like he was [American rocker Jon] Bon Jovi or something." In public, the BBC crew kept their cameras and microphones constantly trained on the reluctant celebrity. A producer from *The Montel Williams Show* eventually called and asked if McCord would come to New York to appear on the program. "Do I have to?" he wincingly asked the sisters. "No, you've done your part," they said. He didn't go there. But throughout Rome that weekend, strangers gawked. Some suddenly hugged him. Some grabbed his hands. A few asked, "Can I touch someone who has been touched by God?" One woman pleaded, "Can you pray for my uncle?" McCord devised a scripted response for those aching requests: "Look, something very special has happened to me. It doesn't make me special. I'm not special. The event is special. You might want to pray to Mother Théodore."

"Yeah," he later recounted, "I'm just not used to that. I'm not a very outgoing guy."

"Phil was embarrassed," Debbie said. "It was as if they thought Phil had a direct conduit to Mother Théodore."

"I thought, *I guess this is my fifteen minutes. God, help me not to embarrass the sisters. This too shall pass.* But to see what it brought to the sisters, and to Marie Kevin," McCord said, "that was enormous to me. It wasn't until I got there that I understood what a big deal it was. It began to sink in."

The day of sanctification had, for years, seemed to McCord "like a fairytale." But now the Baptist man from an anti-Catholic family was about to greet the pope in front of the entire Catholic command structure on the religion's most hallowed ground while tens of thousands of the most fervent Catholics watched in awe. It was becoming quite real.

"I like to say, 'I'm just a guy—just a guy that this happened to.' But if people feel like, 'Jeez, it happened to him, it could happen to anybody,' if I am a reaffirmation of what people like to believe, that is a good thing."

Slowly the engineer was digging out and grabbing his own dark mystery, and he was holding it up to inspect in the light of day. He was beginning to scrape away the mud and touch the truth. He was building his own road to acceptance.

The queue—about twenty thousand people from first in line to last—shoved and jostled in the chilly darkness outside the closed Vatican gate. By 6:00 a.m. the nuns from Mexico were growing restless. The throng of eager Italians spanned all ages, peering ahead, waiting for the big doors to move. There were some French sisters. There were diehard Catholics from Taiwan, Madagascar, and Sri Lanka. And there was a pack of sleepy-eyed Hoosiers. Dawn would break at 7:20.

At precisely 8:00 a.m. on October 15, 2006, the entrance to St. Peter's Square slowly opened and the human crush swarmed forward, squeezing through a single, narrow portal, racing to grab the seats closest to the raised altar. A low, vocal din built then rose into a collective shout—mostly in ecstasy, but partly in fear. Inside the surge, some worried about their safety. A group of line standers physically tried to thwart some of the Italians in the back from cutting ahead. The BBC later described it as a "scrum."

"I wasn't expecting them to wave pond fronds and lead us to our seats," McCord said later. "But actually having to fight with the Mexican nuns to get into the gate? . . . I've been battered black and blue by a group of Mexican nuns."

The McCords and many of the Sisters of Providence had assigned spots at the front of the audience, about fifty feet from the pope. Once they emerged from the deluge at the door, they stepped through the piazza. The seats in the square quickly filled before the start of the 10:00 a.m. Mass. Journalists estimated that about fifty thousand people had wedged into St. Peter's. Some 1,200 of them wore blue scarves, identifying them as Mother Théodore supporters. Among the spectators were Monsignor Fred Easton, Father Jim Bonke, and Dr. Andrea Ambrosi, who took deep pride in having ushered an American cause to the edge of canonization. Nearby sat Dr. William Dugan, the oncologist who had removed a cancerous growth from Sister Marie Kevin's gastroesophageal tract in 1994. Dugan was not Catholic, but he had told Marie Kevin he "felt called" to be present in Rome because he had never before seen a patient survive her type of disease. The pilgrims also included teenagers like Miguel Salazar and Michael Puza, students from Blessed Théodore Guérin High School in Noblesville, Indiana, who had worked summer jobs to raise $2,450 to cover their travel costs— Salazar picking apples and Puza lifeguarding. During the Mass, each would serve as candle bearers. The Mother Théodore corps also included sixty-five-year-old Marilyn Wheeler, a Terre Haute resident who had gone into her 1999 breast cancer operation with a Mother Théodore relic—a patch of fabric—pinned to her surgical cap. Seven years later, on a cool, blue-skied Italian morning, Wheeler wore that same patch over her breast.

Pope Benedict, draped in a bright green robe, entered behind the train of bishops. The dais was lined with cardinals in red and lower-level Church officials in purple. Four choirs—one consisting of Sisters of Providence and Woods students and alumnae— harmonized hymns beside the pontiff.

Sister Diane Ris, the convent's general superior on the morning McCord had prayed in the basilica, sat next to the engineer and watched him try to absorb the historic weight of the moment and the full, five-course feast of Catholic glitter and protocol. "He was in awe of all that was happening. He could hardly believe it was happening to him," Ris recalled. "You could see it in his body language, in his facial expressions. I leaned over once and said, 'It's going to be just fine.'"

What am I doing here? McCord thought. *A Baptist kid from Indiana, about to meet the pope.*

He looked down to collect himself. He glanced at his arms, then his legs. He felt his heart thump. *My pants!* he thought. They were blue. When he and Debbie had awakened early that morning, he had dressed in such a rush to get to St. Peter's that he had pulled on a pair of plain blue dress pants to wear with his pinstripe jacket. *That's great, Phil,* he thought, *when I get up there, the pope is going to say, "Oh, you're from Indiana—you couldn't afford the whole suit?"* He stuffed down his embarrassment and hoped nobody would notice.

Benedict began the Mass, speaking in Latin. Soon the pope brought the service to the traditional offering of gifts. Three former general superiors—Sisters Ann Margaret O'Hara, Diane Ris, and Nancy Nolan—stood and began a long climb up the steep marble stairs toward the pope and the awning-covered altar. Sisters Diane and Nancy held candles while Ann Margaret clutched a reliquary that encased several of Mother Théodore's hand bones. Ann Margaret had choreographed their short journey. "It was like carrying her body and her presence forward into the celebration of her life and her witness," Ann Margaret said later. As Ann Margaret ascended higher, she looked out over the Indiana pilgrims and spotted a banner held aloft by students from Blessed Théodore Guérin High School. It read, ST. THEODORE ROCKS. The ex–general superior smiled. The sisters placed the candles and the relics on a gold stand near the altar. They each knelt before the pope, who told them, "Ah, Mother Théodore. God bless. God bless your work."

The next offertory procession also numbered three. Scaling the same stairs, Marie Kevin gently cupped a Eucharist plate, Sister Denise Wilkinson clasped a communion chalice, and Phil McCord nervously held a silver tray containing a papal gift: a $5,000 check.

This is the end, Marie Kevin thought to herself. *It was all so worth it.*

McCord had always been taken with Marie Kevin's chipper fortitude and resolute spirit, her resurgence from two cancers, and how she had stubbornly trudged the cause forward when other sisters at the Woods had openly chastised her life's work. He watched the nun gleam as she made eye contact with Benedict. This was her time.

"All the setbacks and delays and bureaucracy and dissension among the sisters, to get knocked down and to feel so motivated again, to go back, to believe that this was so right, that this was the right thing to do," McCord said later. "I learned a lot from Marie Kevin—that it's OK to throw yourself wholeheartedly into something you believe, but that other people might think isn't right. Her constancy of purpose overwhelmed me."

McCord bent down and knelt in front of Benedict, presenting him with the tray. The pope touched the gift and accepted it. Benedict looked into the eyes of the healed man and then blessed him.

As McCord prepared to stand, he felt a twinge of pain in his right knee—the aftermath of a high-school football injury. The knee locked. He immediately tried to push himself upright using only his left knee. That wasn't going to hold him, either. With what felt like the entire Catholic world watching, McCord began to pitch forward. He was about to tumble headfirst into Pope Benedict XVI. *Great,* McCord instantly thought, *I'm gonna end up right in his lap.* His mind blazed with the two words he imagined television stations around the globe later would broadcast: "Pope mugging!" McCord swiftly shot one hand forward and grabbed a golden arm on Benedict's throne just as the pope simultaneously reached out to brace McCord from collapsing.

"Beg your pardon!" McCord gasped.

Benedict grinned widely. His eyes twinkled and he warmly waved his hand as if to say, "Had you the whole time."

McCord, known as a klutz among friends and family, laughed

it off as well. But one tactile sliver of that awkward moment stuck with him for good. When the pope caught McCord, their two hands gripped firmly. The pope's hand, he sensed, was strong, firm, and rough, like a farmer's hand. Benedict was a man who had apparently done some physical work in his lifetime, who had maybe used tools and grimed up his palms. He was someone, perhaps, like McCord. He was real, the engineer thought. *Real* in the best sense of the word. Genuine. Authentic. That realness meant something to McCord. He respected all the day's pomp and pageantry, to be sure. But McCord was a nuts-and-bolts guy from Indiana who, more than anything, appreciated substance. He believed what he saw and what he felt. The coarseness of the pope's hands — that was important to McCord. And it surpassed any sermon that he would hear that day.

Back in his seat among the crowd, McCord shook off his papal faux pas and listened to Benedict conduct the day's primary business — the Catholic immortalization of Sister Rosa Venerini, Father Filippo Smaldone, Bishop Rafael Guizar Valencia, and of a resilient French transplant who had made a name and cut fresh history in the American frontier. In Latin, the pope said, "We today determine and find that [they] and Théodore Guérin are saints, and we inscribe them into the catalog of saints of the Universal Church, and say that they must be remembered with pious devotion."

The sheer permanency of that designation resonated with McCord.

"Marie Kevin was the last one in line among all the people who had worked on this for one hundred years," McCord mused. "The Church goes on. And Mother Théodore is a saint forever: the constancy of purpose."

† † †

Miles above the ceaseless blue water, bound for home and half dozing. There and then, Phil McCord finally found peace.

When packing for his Italian trip, all the old, stubborn questions had become just part of his baggage: "Of all the people in the world with sickness and trouble, why me?" "What have I done to deserve a miracle?" "If God mended my eye, how am I ever supposed to pay back this favor?" In Rome, McCord had warmed to the notion of his own visual symbolism—if something wondrous could happen to an ordinary man, not even a particularly religious man, perhaps others could draw hope from that, maybe reaffirm their own beliefs. But the rest of it? It had all remained dim, distorted, and murky. Sort of like his eyesight before the prayer.

He looked forward to returning to Indiana and the Woods, and to regaining the old rhythms and regularity of his life.

"No," he corrected himself, "nothing will be the way it was before. This has come to pass."

Always the engineer, he remembered his sole, self-assigned blueprint for Vatican success: "Don't embarrass the sisters." Aside from almost taking out the pope with his near spill, McCord felt he had delivered on that mission. *I didn't screw up too badly,* he thought. *Task completed.*

He then smirked at the magnitude of the media coverage, at the worldwide interest in what had gone on inside his right eye. He had been interviewed by CNN and the BBC and by dozens of newspaper writers and radio reporters. *I don't know that it will get me any free drinks at the bar,* he thought, *but it is an interesting story.*

His mind fell quiet again. Rome—an exhausting whirlwind of cameras and crowds and rituals—had offered him no time for reflection. But with no one tugging at him or talking to him, with just the soothing drone of the jet engines in his ears, McCord had the space to breathe and ponder. His mind returned to a special dinner held for the Woods sisters and pilgrims Sunday night after the canonization. The group had boarded a bus that took them into hilly country thirty miles north of the city, to a farmhouse restaurant. Everything on the autumn menu was raised on the farm or grown in the soil: pumpkin, mushrooms, and rabbit. The room, gently lit by candles, was loud and festive. Woods alumnae belted out school songs. Ambrosi shined, as always, embracing and chatting with the Americans. A long file of people approached McCord and asked if he was happy that the event was now done, if he was content to be off camera. He was glad, he told them. He was drained.

As he sipped a glass of red wine, Sister Jenny Howard stepped near his table. The worldly and outdoorsy nun, with her short gray hair and palpable human warmth, leaned down to check on her friend. At the Woods, they had talked often about the hard questions that had perplexed him.

"How are you doing, Phil?"

"Well, I'm doing OK," he said.

"How are you dealing with the other issue? This has really changed your life, too. Have you accepted it now?"

"Pretty much."

His response was not definitive. Jenny knew he wasn't quite there. She knew how the convent caretaker thought. He accepted nothing at face value. When confronting conundrums, McCord never arrived at solutions until he first wandered every possible intellectual byway—no matter how outlandish the conjecture. He had two heroes: Arthur C. Clarke, who had entwined outer space with theology, and science fiction master Robert A. Heinlein, whose writings satirized organized religion while blending futuristic engineering with the themes of human freedom and self-reliance. Those two authors, in particular, had shaped McCord as a thinker, had taught him always to traverse alternative possibilities—even the theory that Earth perhaps hosted alien "visitors" shortly before the time of Jesus Christ. "Even those pathways, I explored," McCord said.

He almost always kept his thoughts and his woes to himself. He was hardly the kind of man who willingly shared his breathtaking tale. "I don't go around saying, 'Hi, I've had a miracle.'" If the topic did happen to arise in conversation, McCord was endlessly fascinated with how other people—particularly nonreligious people—processed his version of the events. Their puzzlement typically was not aimed at how it happened; instead they asked: Did it happen? Was it divinely inspired?

"They're always looking for some other explanation. And I suppose that's like me. I'm cynical, I guess," McCord said. "A lot of people, of course, just leave it there—they say, 'Well, there is no explanation, it is beyond our wisdom,' but they will not take the next step to say it was divinely inspired." For McCord, the next step—the final step—was to somehow believe he was worthy of God's help.

Accepting that he had merited God's attention would be, for McCord, another wonder. A third miracle.

"Did I do anything to deserve this?" Phil had often asked Jenny. "There are so many others who seem worthy of a miracle."

"There is no quid pro quo," Jenny said. "There are no expectations, Phil."

She had told him such things before.

"You know," she said, "sometimes it's hard when you receive a gift and you're not expecting it. You don't know how to act. You wish you had a gift to give back. It's kind of an awkward moment. But it's also a very humbling moment because the gift was given by someone out of care, out of love."

He listened.

"This was a gift of love, Phil, an act of love. And that's the thing about love: there are no strings attached. All you have to do is accept it."

Soaring above the Atlantic, McCord heard Jenny's words echo once more in his head. A profound gift, given purely: the definition of love. He had been searching so long for a justification of the cure, for an explanation. There it was.

Love was the reason.

Finally, he saw.

The Parting

The lonely thread of interstate that bent southwest out of Indianapolis was hemmed for almost seventy minutes by pine groves and tangled forest. Near the outskirts of Terre Haute, a billboard rose from the foliage. The sign for exit number three brandished the image of a habit-cloaked, nineteenth-century nun and the words, CAUTION! SAINT AT WORK.

If drivers took that off-ramp — just west of the Wabash River — and continued several miles north up a rising two-lane highway, they soon arrived at a brick gatehouse. Just beyond the entrance lay a living postcard of clipped lawns, thick-trunked oaks, a soccer field, a softball diamond, and a small lake spanned by an arched footbridge. Concrete pathways wound past a valley grotto. From the high limbs, bluebirds and chickadees chirped. From a tower, bells tolled. In the distance, horses and alpacas grazed in green fields. Along the main driveway, sporadically placed signs warned, THOU SHALT NOT PARK HERE. The grounds felt more like a country park than a college campus or convent. Quaint and cozy and charming — a scene painted from a past era. This was the place that had instantly enticed and later enchanted a bearded Baptist engineer.

But by the summer of 2009, some things had changed at Saint Mary-of-the-Woods. Requests for group tours of the motherhouse had nearly doubled, and drop-in visitors annually numbered tens of thousands. Sales of Mother Théodore trinkets at the gift shop shot up 600 percent. Mother Théodore's remains had been moved yet again, enshrined at the front of the Church of the Immaculate

Conception, just to the left of the altar, and encased in a simple
brown box hewn from campus walnut trees. Throughout the property, lightposts fluttered with blue banners emblazoned with the
face of the founder and carrying her new title: Saint.

In a brick courtyard outside the Church of the Immaculate
Conception, a new six-foot-tall bronze statue of Mother Théodore
extended her right palm skyward while her left hand cupped an
ever-present cross hanging from a necklace. The gleaming likeness
was poignant in three ways. It purposely stood off-center in the
courtyard because Mother Théodore fervently preached that only
God should occupy the center of people's lives. It was not elevated
above the red bricks because the founder had frequently admon-
ished her sisters never to put themselves on a pedestal over others.
And the statue had been dedicated—during a prayer service led
by Marie Kevin—to Larry Fleschner, a Terre Haute businessman
who had paid for the piece of art, saying he wanted Woods visitors
"to have a place to be with her so that they could breathe in her
strength and her comfort."

Fleschner had traveled with the sisters to Rome to watch and
celebrate the canonization. Like so many of the pilgrims who had
packed St. Peter's Square on October 15, he had felt a deep urge to
be present. At age fifty-three, Fleschner was diagnosed with colon
cancer. He had undergone surgery and chemotherapy. Near his
sickbed, he had situated a Mother Théodore statue. He would look
at her face and he would talk to the figure until she became, to him,
a living presence and a spark of hope. Less than a year after returning from Rome, on September 30, 2007, Fleschner died from the
cancer. He was fifty-five.

Some prayers were not answered. And some endings were not
perfect.

In late April 2008, about a month before his sixty-second
birthday—and less than two years after his cure had helped the

sisters fulfill a century-long journey—Phil McCord was told to pack up his belongings and mementos and vacate his office at the Woods.

"It was," he said, "a shock to me."

His abrupt and unexpected departure followed the completion of a $3-million campus boiler system. State permits for the project's various stages had been coming too slowly, in McCord's view. He pushed the construction ahead without the permits, drawing the convent a $25,000 fine from regulators at the Indiana Department of Environmental Management. His supervisor and the congregation's treasurer, Sister Nancy Reynolds, heard about the bill and demanded an explanation from McCord. He told her the fine had been "negotiated" into the building plans "as part of the cost of doing business," and that by finishing the boiler ahead of schedule he actually had saved the congregation "hundreds of thousands of dollars."

"Money-wise, it was a good decision," McCord said.

"You have destroyed our good name" with the state agency, Sister Nancy responded, according to McCord.

"They don't care about your good name," he said. "They're bureaucrats."

"Well, who's to blame?" she asked.

"Well, me," he said.

Soon after that exchange, the campus human resources director stood at McCord's desk and, he recalled, "we cleaned out my office, and that was it."

"There was," he added, "a little bit of vindictiveness in what happened. . . . Nancy and I were never really friendly. But she just didn't get [the business of] it; she never did get it. Had she come to me and said, 'We're going to have to part ways,' I would have said, 'OK, fine, I'll retire.' Maybe we could even have a party, and I would have gone away quietly. They didn't even let me say good-bye to my staff. Nothing. It could have been handled a lot differently."

Sister Nancy declined to elaborate on McCord's termination, saying, "That's a totally confidential matter. . . . Being a canonist, I have a very strong affinity to rights that people have within the Church, and one is the right to privacy and one is a right to a good reputation. I will preserve those for Phil as long as I live."

"It was an enigma to all of us," Marie Kevin said later. "He was dismissed. I don't know anything about it. But I don't begrudge him. He was chosen to receive the gift, and I'm happy about that."

The ultimate irony, however, was unmistakable. The sisters had weighed the staggering financial costs of their sanctification campaign and, over a century, had paid all the necessary bills while working through the Vatican's bureaucracy. That's how the saint-naming business worked. After they achieved their grand goal, the sisters had feted their caretaker. Two years later, McCord calculated that it would be far less expensive to incur a state fine by rushing a boiler project versus waiting months to wade through Indiana's governmental bureaucracy. That's how the construction business worked. After he got the job done at a cheaper cost, the sisters fired their caretaker.

One year after his final day at the Woods, McCord said he was "at peace" with the events. Around the time of his termination, he had been diagnosed with a chronic heart condition, including an arrhythmia and a leaking valve. He'd had a pacemaker implanted to help correct the problem. "It would have been hard for me to keep working. I would get tired and I always tried to push through it. We had a lot of projects going then. So, in my own way, I look at it, and say, 'It might end up saving my life. I feel better now.' My time there was nothing but a good experience."

Ever pragmatic, Phil and Debbie McCord decided to use his sudden retirement as an opportunity to rearrange their lives, as a moment, he said, "to achieve our dreams." They bought a new home near the Gulf Coast of central Florida, next to a lake in Citrus

County. They moved their boat and their belongings down from Indiana. Debbie raised a lush patch of melons and thought about planting a lemon tree so she could squeeze fresh lemonade for her husband. Sandhill cranes, adorned with bright red foreheads, sometimes strutted through their lawn. While watching them, McCord smiled.

"I don't wear my religion on my sleeve," he said. "But if you believe—even a little bit—that God has a plan for you, then whatever happens to you is the best thing that can happen to you."

Back on Blinn Court in Terre Haute, where Phil McCord awoke one January morning forever changed, a For Sale sign stood in the front yard outside the empty home—the place where, according to the Catholic Church, a miracle once took place.

Before leaving town, the McCords dug a small hole in the Indiana dirt next to their house. And for a little heavenly help with their sale, they buried—upside down and facing backward—a statue of Saint Joseph.

Acknowledgments

This book could not have been written, nor this story told, without help from and the cheerful cooperation of Phil McCord, Debbie McCord, Sister Marie Kevin Tighe, Dr. Andrea Ambrosi, Madelaine Kuns, Kathy Fleming, Monsignor Fred Easton, Father Jim Bonke, Dr. Nick Rader, Dr. Jeffrey Jungers, Dr. John Barker, Edward Mulkern, Dr. Richard Jantz, Sister Ann Margaret O'Hara, Sister Marianne Mader, Sister Nancy Nolan, Sister Diane Ris, Sister Denise Wilkinson, Sister Jenny Howard, Sister Charles Van Hoy, Brother Barry Donaghue, Sister Nancy Reynolds, Sister Stacy Pierce, Sister Marie Esther Sivertsen, Monsignor Robert Sarno, Dr. Francesco Santori, Michele Smits, Monsignor Richard Soseman, Brother Leo Wollenweber, Father Ken Kaucheck, Father Kenneth J. Laverone, Beth Donovan, Dave Cox, Dr. Robert D'Ambrosia, and Anthony Monta.

To Margaret Briggs and Robert Briggs, a heartfelt thank-you. Long ago, they nurtured my interest in journalism. And they were kind enough to read my unfinished manuscript and offer thoughtful and sage advice.

My wife, Nancy, has long believed in and intensely supported my passion for writing. She adored this book and supported my quest to author it. I'm proud to call her my partner and friend.

My literary agent, Frank Scatoni, enthusiastically embraced this project from my first mention of the idea, then doggedly found us a terrific publisher. Thank you, Frank. May all your long shots come in.

My editor, Charlie Conrad, served as a calm, smart, and insightful guide when I launched this project and, again, as I completed this book. I put my full trust in Charlie's instincts and he gently steered us home.

My research was informed by the work of these fellow journalists: Robert King, Kenneth L. Woodward, John F. Fink, Will Daugherty, Father William Saunders, Jennifer Del Vechio, Ari L. Goldman, Jacques Ellul, Cindy Wooden, Emma Stickgold, Jerry Davich, Elizabeth Holmes, Jeremy W. Peters, Micheline Maynard, Claudia J. Beresford, Tracy Wilkinson, Damon Adams, Usha Lee McFarling, Barbara Drake Boehm, Barbara Abou-El-Haj, Rachel Bellerby, Patrick J. Geary, Faye Flam, Sean Gallagher, Jack Wintz, O.F.M., Brandon A. Evans, William F. Tuohy, Robert Delaney, Jeff Israely, Mary Adamski, Laura Sessions Stepp, Norman Geisler, Sabrina Arena Ferressi, George W. Cornell, Richard Smoley, Walter V. Robinson, Michael Paulson, Stephen Kurkjian, Matt Carroll, Sacha Pfeiffer, Michael Rezendes, Michelle Boorstein, John L. Allen Jr., Richard Owen, Elaine Ganley, Molly Moore, Sarah Delaney, Deacon Keith Fournier, Tom Roberts, Michael Paulson, Megan Williams, Bob Simon, Christiane Amanpour, David Van Biema, John Thavis, Edward Pentin, Francis X. Rocca, Cathy Lynn Grossman, Monika Scislowska, Nicole Winfield, Monsignor Charles M. Mangan, Frank M. Rega, Jan Cienski, Frances D'Emilio, Mike Sullivan, Paul Heinrichs, Krittivas Mukherjee, Christopher Hitchens, Kristine M. Crane, Stacy Meichtry, Nicola Clark, Philip Pullella, Nigel Cawthorne, Kevin Sullivan, Satinder Bindra, Alan Cowell, Jennifer Lindberg, Massimo Pigliucci, Ashley Kindergan, Charity Vogel, David Harsanyi, Jean Torkelson, John Gleason, David Staba, John Barry, Alice Dembner, Jeremy Manier, Denise Gellene, Thomas H. Maugh II, Diane Cameron, Christen Brownlee, Stefania Falasca, Ernest Tucker, David Briggs, Nancy Hernandez, Renee K. Gadoua, Kristin E. Holmes, Victor L. Simpson, Daniel Williams, Liz Sly, Valentine Low, Tom Hundley, William J. Kole, John Phillips, Sue Loughlin, Robert L. Flott, Mark Bennett, and Ryan Lenz.

Notes

EPIGRAPH

The source of the Albert Einstein quote was ThinkExist.com.

CHAPTER ONE: THE WOODS

Descriptions of Sister Mary Theodosia Mug's illness, prayer in crypt, recovery, and biography came from materials at the Saint Mary-of-the-Woods archives and help from the archivists. Other sources included *The Path Marked Out: History of the Sisters of Saint Mary-of-the-Woods*, by Sister Mary Roger Madden, S.P.; numerous in-person, telephone, and e-mail interviews with Sister Marie Kevin Tighe in 2008 and 2009; a tour of the now-closed community crypt and a tour of Providence Hall; and the Sisters of Providence of Saint Mary-of-the-Woods website: www.spsmw.org. My sources for the biographical history of Mother Théodore Guérin and the early days of Saint Mary-of-the-Woods included *Mother Theodore Guerin: Journals and Letters*, edited by Sister Mary Theodosia Mug; *The Eighth American Saint*, by Katherine Burton; *Life and Life-work of Mother Theodore Guerin*, by Mary Theodosia Mug; the Franciscan website American-Catholic.org, specifically an article authored for that website by John F. Fink and published in November 2006; the Archdiocese of Indianapolis website and archives; phone and personal interviews with Kathy Fleming in 2008 and 2009; interviews with Sister Marie Kevin Tighe; an October 6, 2006, article by Robert King, published by the *Indianapolis Star*; and research at—and a great deal of help from—the Saint Mary-of-the-Woods archives and archivists.

CHAPTER TWO: THE QUEST

My sources for the early intercession requests on campus, the exhumation of Mother Théodore, and details on Mary Theodosia and her literary work included research at the Saint Mary-of-the-Woods archives and help from the archivists, *The Path Marked Out: History of the Sisters of Saint Mary-of-the-Woods*, and *Life and Life-work of Mother Théodore Guérin*. Information on Saint Philomena came from the Saint Philomena Foundation, at www.philomena.us; from the Vatican website, www.vatican.va; and from St. Patrick Catholic Church in Washington, D.C. The section on Catholic doctrine regarding relics was taken from the website "Catholic Answers," www.catholic.com, which bills itself as "one of the nation's largest lay-run apostolates." In this chapter, my sources for the history and rules of the Catholic canonization process and on the core concepts of intercession and miracles included the Catholic news website Catholic. org; the Vatican website; an undated essay, "The Process of Becoming a Saint," published in the *Arlington Catholic Herald* by Father William Saunders, dean of the Notre Dame Graduate School of Christendom College; the online Catholic Encyclopedia, www.newadvent.org; *Making Saints: How the Catholic Church Determines Who Becomes a Saint, Who Doesn't, and Why* by Kenneth L. Woodward; and from materials supplied by Sister Marie Kevin Tighe. An estimate on the modern cost of the canonization process was pulled from an October 19, 2003, *60 Minutes* interview with *National Catholic Register* correspondent John Allen. The Saint Mary-of-the-Woods archives provided Mother Théodore's journals. All references to weather were researched via the Vigo County Library archives department and 1907 and 1908 copies of *The Terre Haute Tribune*. My sources for passages on Bishop Francis Silas Chatard included *The Path Marked Out* and two non-bylined *New York Times* articles published December 19, 1883, and June 28, 1885.

CHAPTER THREE: THE VOICE

The scenes describing Mary Theodosia's prayer and healing included these sources: the Saint Mary-of-the-Woods archives; *The Path Marked Out*; a letter Sister Mary Theodosia Mug wrote to General Superior Mary Cleophas Foley on November 21, 1908; interviews with Sister Marie Kevin Tighe in 2008 and 2009; and a personal tour of the crypt and Providence Hall. Information for the passage on the "the faceless ghost" came from the Sisters of Providence website. The passages on Sister Marie Kevin Tighe came from my multiple interviews with her, from a 2009 interview with Sister Nancy Nolan, and from the website for Presentation Academy: www.presentationacademy.org. For Saint

Kevin of Glendalough, I consulted the online Catholic Encyclopedia, http://www.newadvent.org/cathen. Details on the milestones in the cause for Mother Théodore came from materials supplied by Sister Marie Kevin Tighe and the Sisters of Providence archives. Descriptions of the beatification ceremony came largely from a 2009 phone interview with former Saint Mary-of-the-Woods general superior Sister Diane Ris and from materials supplied by the Sisters of Providence. The passage on Phil McCord was pulled from my numerous personal, telephone, and e-mail interviews conducted with Phil and with his wife, Debbie, in 2008 and 2009, as well as from phone interviews with Sister Denise Wilkinson and Sister Jenny Howard in 2009, and from the Sisters of Providence website. Information on Sister Joseph Eleanor Ryan, her work, and details of that era of the cause, were provided by Sisters of Providence archives.

CHAPTER FOUR: THE MALADY

My reporting on the day of Phil McCord's prayer, January 3, 2001, involved multiple interviews with Phil and Debbie McCord, as well as their 2003 testimonies before the Archdiocese of Indianapolis tribunal. Terre Haute weather from that day came from the Weather Underground archives: www.wunderground.com. More help in describing that day came from my tours of the Providence Center and the Church of the Immaculate Conception, from a 2009 phone interview with Brother Barry Donaghue, and from information from the Congregation of Christian Brothers—Iona College website. Medical details on cataracts were provided by the University of Illinois Eye Center, the Vanderbilt Eye Center, and 2003 Indianapolis Archdiocese tribunal testimony of Dr. Jeffrey Jungers. For the section that describes events at the Woods in late 2000 and early 2001, I used the Sisters of Providence media kit and website, an April 12, 2002, article written by Jennifer Del Vechio for the Archdiocese of Indianapolis website, multiple interviews with Sister Marie Kevin Tighe, interviews with Sister Diane Ris and Kathy Fleming, and a 2009 phone interview with Sister Nancy Reynolds. Details on Allison Giesting were supplied by Sister Marie Kevin Tighe. Information on the general cost of a cause was pulled from an article posted at the Archdiocese of Indianapolis website April 22, 2005. My sources on the theology and canon rules of beatification included an October 13, 2006, article written by Monsignor Fred Easton for the Archdiocese of

Indianapolis website, and a non-bylined article published April 27, 2006, by the Catholic News Agency. In this chapter, my sources on feminism and sexism in the Catholic Church came from a June 22, 1991, *New York Times* article by Ari L. Goldman; from a September 1987 article in *The Other Side* by Jacques Ellul; from an undated 2005 article by Cindy Wooden, published by the Catholic News Service; and from the books *How to Save the Catholic Church*, by Andrew M. Greeley and Mary G. Durkin, and *Hollywood and Catholic Women*, by Kathryn Schleich. The passage about Edward Mulkern was drawn from a 2009 phone interview with, and several e-mails from, Edward Mulkern. A portion of Mulkern's medical records was supplied by the Sisters of Providence. Some of this passage was based on interviews with Sister Marie Kevin Tighe, from an Archdiocese of Indianapolis website publication on December 9, 2005 (about Sister Mary Eleanor Galvin), from the November 2002 issue of *The Founding Spirit*, a Sisters of Providence publication. Information on squamous-cell carcinoma came from the National Cancer Institute. Details on Dr. C. C. Wang came from an obituary found at MassGeneral.org and from a December 20, 2005, *Boston Globe* article by Emma Stickgold.

CHAPTER FIVE: THE PRAYER

The description of Phil McCord's prayer on January 3, 2001, came from my multiple interviews with Phil McCord in 2008 and 2009, and was helped by my own visits to the Church of the Immaculate Conception in 2008 and 2009. To write about the events of January 3, 2001, I also used interviews McCord gave to several media outlets. Those included an October 17, 2006, article by Jerry Davich, published in the *Chicago Sun-Times*; an undated, non-bylined article from the Sisters of Providence website; an episode of *Anderson Cooper 360* broadcast by CNN on December 20, 2006; a March 12, 2006, *Northwest Indiana Times* article by Elizabeth Holmes; and an interview McCord gave American Catholic Radio in 2006. The biographical passage on Phil McCord was drawn from my many interviews with Phil and Debbie McCord—and particularly from the interview conducted with Phil McCord at Providence Center at Saint Mary-of-the-Woods on May 21, 2008. The history of General Motors in Anderson, Indiana, was drawn from my interviews with Phil and Debbie McCord and from a February 20, 2006, *New York Times* article by Jeremy W. Peters and

Micheline Maynard. History about the Church of God was found on a website for the Church of God: www.chog.org. My sources for general information on eye anatomy, vision, and cataracts included the Mayo Clinic website at www. MayoClinic.com, the American Optometric Association, the Eye Surgery Education Council, Lighthouse International, and eMedicine.com. The passage on Dr. Jeffrey Jungers was drawn from my two interviews with Dr. Jungers conducted in 2008 and 2009 by phone and at his office in Terre Haute. The section describing Phil McCord's cataract surgeries was based on interviews with Phil McCord and Dr. Jungers, from a transcript of the Indianapolis Archdiocese trial, and from the detailed medical records that were included in the transcript file. For information about corneal donation, corneal transplants, and eye banks, I used the Eye Bank Association of America, Minnesota Lions Eye Bank, Indiana Lions Eye and Tissue Transplant Bank, National Institutes of Health, National Eye Institute, and the Mayo Clinic. My description of Dr. Stephen Johnson's office was drawn from my 2009 visit to that office. The scene describing the evening after McCord's prayer, January 3, 2003, was reported during my numerous interviews with Phil and Debbie McCord.

CHAPTER SIX: THE CURE

Descriptions of the events on January 4, 2003, were pulled from multiple interviews with Phil and Debbie McCord, particularly an interview at the McCords' former home on Blinn Court in Terre Haute on February 5, 2009, and from my two interviews with Sister Jenny Howard in 2009. I used U.S. Census results for the demographics on West Terre Haute, Indiana. To write about the events of January 4, I also plucked some details from the testimonies Phil and Debbie McCord gave to the Indianapolis Archdiocese tribunal as well as the tribunal testimony of Sharon Moore. Details about the morning newspaper were taken from the January 4, 2003, edition of the *Terre Haute Tribune-Star*. The passage on Phil McCord's exam on January 26, 2001, was based on multiple interviews with Phil McCord and on his tribunal testimony. Information on McCord's February 28, 2001, exam with Dr. Jeffrey Jungers was collected from two interviews with Dr. Jungers, and from Dr. Jungers's tribunal testimony. The pages detailing Jungers's thoughts about religion and medicine were drawn from my interviews with Jungers. The study Jungers cited was published in the April 2006 issue of the *American Heart Journal*. My sources for the interlaced history of faith and medicine included *Blind Faith: The Unholy Alliance of Religion and Medicine*, by Richard P. Sloan; *The New American Commentary: An Exegetical and Theological Exposition of the Holy Scripture*, by Daniel I. Block; "Ancient Egyptian Medicine in Sickness and in Health: Preventative and Curative Health Care," from http://nefertiti.iwebland.com/timelines/topics/medicine.htm; "Religious Influence in Ancient Greece, Life in a Time When Religion Was Law," by Claudia J. Beresford, dated September 19, 2009, found at http://greek-history.suite101.com; "Useful known and unknown views of the father of modern medicine, Hippocrates and his teacher Democritus," from U.S. National Library of Medicine; "Conclusions on Hippocratic Behavior in the Treatment of Wounds and Burns," by G. S. Polycratis, University of Athens, September 1987; "The History of Miracles," *U.S. News & World Report*, March 29, 1993; an October 15, 2003, *Los Angeles Times* article by Tracy Wilkinson; *The Old Testament* via http://scriptures.lds.org/ot/contents; "All the Miracles of the Bible," by Herbert Lockyer; the website AllAboutJesusChrist.org; *Making Saints: How the Catholic Church Determines Who Becomes a Saint, Who Doesn't, and Why*, by Kenneth L. Woodward; *The Faith Factor: Proof of the Healing Power of Prayer*, by Dr. Dale A. Matthews and Connie Clark; the website for Dr. Dale A. Matthews: http://awesomepower.net/matthews.htm; a December 23, 2004, article at the website "WorldNetDaily.com" titled "Poll: Doctors believe in miracles: 3 out of 4 physicians think supernatural events still happen"; a March 25, 2002, *AMN News* article by Damon Adams; a December 22, 1998, article written by Usha Lee McFarling, published by Knight Ridder/Tribune News Service. For the section on relics, my sources included an article by Barbara Drake Boehm, "Relics and Reliquaries in Medieval Christianity," written for the Metropolitan Museum of Art New York website; *The Medieval Cult of Saints: Formations and Transformations*, by Barbara Abou-El-Haj; an article by Rachel Bellerby, "The Importance of Medieval Religious Relics: The Trade in Real and Fake Christian Souvenirs in the Middle Ages," published by Suite101.com; an article at www.museumofhoaxes.com titled "The Medieval Relic Trade"; *Furta sacra: Thefts of relics in the central Middle Ages*, by Patrick J. Geary; and *Contemporary Sources for the Fourth Crusade*, by Alfred J. Andrea. For passages on the Consulta Medica and Vatican Observatory, my sources included a September 27, 2000, article by

Faye Flam, published by the *Philadelphia Inquirer*, and a website for the Vatican Observatory, http://www.vaticanobservatory.org. The final passage on Phil McCord's prayer and the first mention of a possible miracle was drawn from my interviews with Phil McCord, Sister Marie Kevin Tighe, Sister Charles Van Hoy, and Dr. Andrea Ambrosi.

CHAPTER SEVEN: THE SAINT-MAKER

The scenes describing the visit to Rome by Sister Marie Kevin Tighe and Kathy Fleming and the subsequent meeting with Dr. Ambrosi were drawn from my interview with Dr. Andrea Ambrosi and Madeline Kuns, at Ambrosi's office in Rome on March 30, 2009, and from my multiple interviews with Sister Marie Kevin Tighe and Kathy Fleming. My sources for the Saint Agnes passage included an article at www.sacred-destinations.com/Italy/Rome. The sources for my biographical sketches of Dr. Ambrosi in this chapter and in later chapters included my multiple interviews with Dr. Ambrosi in 2008 and 2009, conducted in person and via e-mail and telephone, translated by his assistant, Madelaine Kuns; my interviews with Sister Marie Kevin, Kathy Fleming, Sister Nancy Nolan, and Monsignor Robert Sarno, and information found at Dr. Andrea Ambrosi's website, www.beatificationprocess.com/index2.html; an October 20, 2006, article by Sean Gallagher, published by the Indianapolis Archdiocese website, www.Arch.Indy.org; the website for Father Patrick Peyton's cause, www.familyrosary.org as well as a June 1997 *St. Anthony Messenger* article by Jack Wintz, O.F.M.; the website for Father Nelson Baker's cause, www.OurLadyOfvictory.org; an article on Henriette DeLille at a Catholic health-care website, www.catholichealthcare.us/About/CalltoCare/delille .htm; a 2006 article by Brandon A. Evans, published by the Archdiocese of Indianapolis website; the website for the cause of Archbishop Fulton Sheen, www.archbishopsheencause.org; background materials provided by the Sisters of Providence and the convent archives, and information about Caprarola, was found at the website, www.italy.com. Historic information on the Congregation for the Causes of Saints, the Devil's Advocate, and Father Rafael Perez was pulled from the Vatican website, the United States Conference of Catholic Bishops, the website Catholic Online, www.catholic.org, the article "Promotor

Fidei" found at the online Catholic Encyclopedia www.newadvent.org, *Making Saints: How the Catholic Church Determines Who Becomes a Saint, Who Doesn't, and Why* by Kenneth L. Woodward, and a May 4, 1974, *Los Angeles Times* article by William F. Tuohy. My sources for the passage on Sister Maria Euthymia Üffing included the Vatican website, a 2001 article by the Catholic News Service found at http://newsaints.faithweb.com/biographies/Uffing.htm, and *Butler's Lives of the Saints: The Third Millennium* by Paul Burns and Alban Butler. Much of the section on Monsignor Robert Sarno, his work at the Congregation for the Causes of Saints, the miracle beliefs and statements of Pope John Paul II and Pope Benedict XVI, and the Catholic doctrine on miracles was pulled from my interview with Monsignor Sarno at the Vatican on March 31, 2009. My other sources included a CNN broadcast on June 16, 2002: "Padre Pio: The Path to Sainthood"; a December 16, 2003, CNN broadcast of *Anderson Cooper 360*; a March 2, 2007, article by Robert Delaney, published by the *Michigan Catholic*; a non-bylined January 27, 2008, article, published by Zenit.org; an April 25, 2008, *Time* magazine article by Jeff Israely; a February 19, 2008, non-bylined article by the Associated Press; an August 10, 1998, article by Mary Adamski in the *Honolulu Star-Bulletin*; a February 18, 2009, report by the BBC News titled "Vatican slows sainthood process"; a March 22, 1992, article by Laura Sessions Stepp, published by the *Washington Post*; a July 14, 2002, article by Norman Geisler, "Miracles and Modern Scientific Thought," retrieved from www.leaderu.com/truth/1truth19.html; an article by NASA researchers on the "Big Bang Theory," retrieved from http://map.gsfc.nasa.gov/universe/bb_theory.html; a May 9, 2008, article by Cindy Wooden, published by the Catholic News Service.

CHAPTER EIGHT: THE CHOICE

My primary sources for the opening passage were multiple interviews with Sister Marie Kevin Tighe and Kathy Fleming in 2008 and 2009, my 2009 interview with Sister Denise Wilkinson, my 2009 interview with Sister Nancy Nolan, my 2009 interview with Sister Ann Margaret O'Hara, and my 2009 interview with Monsignor Robert Sarno. For information on the vows, I used information found at the Sisters of Providence website, www.spsmw.org/Sistersof-Providence/Becomeasister/Discerningyourcall/Perpetualvows, and the website

"Ask a Catholic," www.cptryon.org/ask/ask/vows. The section on Catholic saints tapped numerous sources, including the interviews mentioned above. Other sources were a 2001 *National Catholic Register* article by Sabrina Arena Ferressi; the website for Catherine of Sienna Institute, which helps parishes form lay apostles, www.siena.org; *Making Saints* by Kenneth L. Woodward; an article called "Making Saints" retrieved from the website "Ask a Catholic," www.cptryon.org/ask/ask/beat.html; a January 18, 1992, article by George W. Cornell, published by the *Albany Times Union*; an undated article on the Protestant Reformation by Richard Smoley, published by *Gnosis Magazine, a Journal of Western Inner Traditions*; an article comparing Roman Catholicism and Protestantism, published by *Ontario Consultants on Religious Tolerance*; and a July 27, 2009, editorial published by *The Guardian*. For the passage on the preparation for Dr. Andrea Ambrosi's informal trial, I drew on my 2009 interview with Dr. Nick Rader, his 2003 testimony before the Indianapolis Archdiocese tribunal, Rader's biographical page at his professional website, www.indianaeyeclinic.com/our doctors.htm, my interviews with Sister Marie Kevin and Kathy Fleming, and my interviews with Dr. Jeffrey Jungers, both by telephone and in person at his Terre Haute clinic. The section on the informal trial at the Woods in March 2002 was reported through these sources: materials provided by the Sisters of Providence, including agendas and letters; my multiple interviews with Dr. Andrea Ambrosi; the "about us" section of the *Terre Haute Tribune-Star* website, http://www.tribstar.com/aboutus; my interviews with Sister Marie Kevin, Kathy Fleming, Dr. Jeffrey Jungers, and Eddie Mulkern; a series of 2002 articles published by the *Boston Globe* about the church sex-abuse scandal in the Boston archdiocese, dated August 17, 21, 22, 23, 30, September 1, 4, 7, 12, and October 31, authored by Walter V. Robinson, Michael Paulson, Stephen Kurkjian, Matt Carroll, Sacha Pfeiffer, and Michael Rezendes; a December 13, 2002, article posted on the BBC News website titled "Timeline: Boston sex scandal," http://news.bbc.co.uk/2/hi/americas/2573723.stm, and an October 30, 2003, report by NPR's program *All Things Considered*.

CHAPTER NINE: THE SAINT FACTORY

The opening scene and subsequent descriptions of the office for the cause of Pope John Paul II's beatification and canonization were drawn from my April

2, 2009, visit to the Basilica of St. John Lateran in Rome and the cause office, as well as from my in-person interview with Michele Smits. Other sources for this chapter included the October 2008, January/February 2009, and March/April 2009 editions of *Totus Tuus*; the Vatican website; a June 2, 2008, *Washington Post* article by Michelle Boorstein; an October 13, 2006, article by John L. Allen Jr., published by the *National Catholic Reporter*; a December 20, 2004, article by Richard Owen, published by *The Times* (London); a non-bylined January 31, 2006, article, published by Reuters; a March 30, 2007, Associated Press article by Elaine Ganley; a March 31, 2007, *Washington Post* article by Molly Moore and Sarah Delaney; a non-bylined April 1, 2008, article published by the Catholic News Service; a non-bylined March 19, 2009, article published by the Catholic News Agency; a March 20, 2009, article by Deacon Keith Fournier, published by *Catholic Online*; a January 25, 2002, article by John L. Allen Jr., published by the *National Catholic Reporter*; a June 1, 2009, article by Cindy Wooden, published by the Catholic News Service; a non-bylined June 2, 2009, article published by CatholicCulture.org; a June 3, 2009, article by Tom Roberts, published by the *National Catholic Reporter*; a July 12, 2009, *Boston Globe* article by Michael Paulson; an April 5, 2002, article by John L. Allen Jr., published by the *National Catholic Reporter*; a November 1, 2007, radio report by Megan Williams for the program *MarketPlace*; a non-bylined September 22, 2007, article published by the *Telegraph* (London); an October 9, 2003, report by Bob Simon, broadcast by the CBS program *60 Minutes*; a June 16, 2002, broadcast by Christiane Amanpour titled "Padre Pio: The Path to Sainthood," broadcast by CNN; a non-bylined June 24, 2008, article published by *The Independent* (London); a November 10, 2003, article by Richard Owen, published by *The Times* (London); a February 29, 2008, *Time* magazine article by David Van Biema; a September 25, 2007, article by Richard Owen, published by *The Times* (London); a non-bylined October 1, 2007, article published by CatholicIreland.net; a non-bylined May 14, 2005, article published by the Associated Press; an April 2009, article by John Thavis, published by the Catholic News Service; an April 19, 2009, article by Edward Pentin, published by the *National Catholic Register*; a February 23, 2008, article by Francis X. Rocca, published by Religion News Service; a non-bylined April 27, 2006, article published by the Catholic News Agency; a non-bylined March 2, 2007, article published by the Catholic News Service; a September 27, 2007, article by John Thavis, published by the Catholic News Service; an October 3, 2002, *USA Today* article by Cathy Lynn Grossman; a June 12, 2009, Associated Press article by Monika Scislowska and Nicole Winfield; a May 29, 2005, article by Monsignor Charles M. Mangan, published by *Catholic Online*; a two-part article by Frank M. Rega, published in December 2007 and January 2008 by *Catholic Digest*; a June 28, 2009, article by Jan Cienski, published by GlobalPost.com; a June 16, 2002, Associated Press article by Frances D'Emilio; a March 15, 2002, article by John L. Allen Jr., published by the *National Catholic Reporter*; a July 28, 2006, article by Cindy Wooden, published by the Catholic News Service; an October 26, 2007, article by John Thavis, published by the Catholic News Service; an article by Mike Sullivan, published in November/December 2004 by *Lay Witness Magazine*; an October 17, 2003, article by John L. Allen Jr., published by the *National Catholic Reporter*; an October 19, 2003, article by Paul Heinrichs, published by *The Age* (Australia); an October 10, 2002, article by Krittivas Mukherjee, published by Indio-Asian News Service; an October 20, 2003, article by Christopher Hitchens, published by Slate.com; a non-bylined April 2, 2007, article published by the Associated Press; a non-bylined April 3, 2006, article published by the Associated Press; an April 1, 2006, *Washington Post* article by Kristine M. Crane and Stacy Meichtry; an article on the Basilica of St. John Lateran, published by the *Catholic Encyclopedia*; a February 23, 2009, article retrieved from Zenit.org; an August 28, 2007, *New York Times* article by Nicola Clark; a June 23, 2005, article by Nicole Winfield, published by the Associated Press; a March 13, 2006, article by Nicole Winfield, published by the Associated Press; a March 19, 2006, article by Philip Pullella, published by Reuters; a June 12, 2005, article by Nigel Cawthorne, published by Reuters; a non-bylined December 7, 1999, article published by the *Daily Catholic*; a February 5, 2002, *Washington Post* article by Kevin Sullivan; an October 17, 2003, report by Satinder Bindra, broadcast by CNN; an October 5, 2007, *Time* magazine article by David Van Biema; an October 19, 2003, *New York Times* article by Alan Cowell; a non-bylined July 11, 2003, *Chicago Sun-Times* article; a non-bylined August 31, 2007, article in the *Hindustan Times*; information on the Fatima shrine from http://www.sacred-destinations.com/portugal/fatima-shrine-of-our-lady-of-fatima; *The Last Secret of Fatima*, by Cardinal Tarcisio Bertone; information on

Fatima financial troubles retrieved from a December 11, 2008, article at www
.eturbonews.com/6691/mayor-fatima-fatima-may-need-divine-intervention; a non-
bylined February 13, 2008, article published by the Associated Press; and an
April 3, 2007, *Chicago Sun-Times* article by Nicole Winfield.

CHAPTER TEN: THE TRIAL

My descriptions of the opening day of the Indianapolis Archdiocese tribunal
were drawn from my 2008 and 2009 interviews with Monsignor Fred Easton
and Father Jim Bonke, conducted in person as well as by telephone and e-mail.
I also used the trial transcript, my 2009 interview with Dr. John Barker, my
interview with Sister Jenny Howard, my interviews with Sister Marie Kevin
Tighe, and my interviews with Phil McCord. The day's weather was taken from
the archives at the Weather Underground, www.wunderground.com. My other
sources included *New Commentary on the Code of Canon Law*, edited by John P.
Beal, James A. Coriden, and Thomas J. Green; an October 13, 2006, article
by Sean Gallagher, published by the Indianapolis Archdiocese website, www
.Arch.Indy.org; an October 20, 2006, article by Sean Gallagher, published by
the Indianapolis Archdiocese website; a January 31, 2003, article written by
Jennifer Lindberg for the Indianapolis Archdiocese website; information on
the "Charter for the Protection of Children and Young People" from the U.S.
Conference of Catholic Bishops website, www.usccb.org/ocyp/charter.shtml.
Developments in 2010 regarding Pope John Paul II's cause were taken from
these sources: a non-bylined March 15, 2010, article published by the *Catholic
Herald*; a non-bylined March 5, 2010, article posted on the website Catholic-
Culture.org.

CHAPTER ELEVEN: THE DOCTORS

I relied on my interviews with Dr. Nick Rader, Dr. Jeffrey Jungers, Dr. John
Barker, and Phil McCord. I also used the transcript of the Indianapolis Archdiocese tribunal and the medical records of Phil McCord, which were collected
as evidence and reviewed by the tribunal. Other sources included a study by
the Bascom Palmer Eye Institute titled "Retained Nuclear Fragments in the
Anterior Chamber after Phacoemulsification with an Intact Posterior Capsule,"
published in 2006 by the American Academy of Ophthalmology and supplied

to me by Dr. Jungers; David Hume's estimated miracle odds from Massimo Pigliucci's Amazon blog; eye fluid flow information from the Glaucoma Research Foundation; the Consulta Medica rejection statistics approximation was taken from Franco de Rosa's interview with Kenneth L. Woodward, published by *Newsweek* on May 1, 2000. My sources for rejected miracle claims included a May 24, 2009, article by Ashley Kindergan in *The Record* (Bergen County, NJ); my 2009 interview with Brother Leo Wollenweber, who was a friar in Detroit, Michigan, and vice-postulator for the Father Solanus Casey beatification and canonization cause; an August 17, 2007, article by Robert Delaney, published by the *Michigan Catholic*; my 2008 interview with Archdiocese of Detroit priest Father Ken Kaucheck; a June 29, 2009, *Buffalo News* article by Charity Vogel; *The Day Donny Herbert Woke Up*, by Rich Blake; my two interviews with Father Kenneth J. Laverone, by phone and e-mail; a non-bylined June 14, 2007, *Rocky Mountain News* article; a July 3, 2007, *Denver Post* column by David Harsanyi; a June 13, 2007, *Rocky Mountain News* article by Jean Torkelson; a September 6, 2006, article by John Gleason in the *Denver Catholic Register*; a June 20, 2007, article by John Gleason, in the *Denver Catholic Register*; a non-bylined June 20, 2007, article published by the *California Catholic Daily*; a May 7, 2005, *New York Times* article by David Staba; a non-bylined November 27, 2000, United Press International article; my 2008 interview with Beth Donovan, director of public relations for Baker Victory Services in Buffalo, NY; a December 11, 2005, *Niagara Falls Reporter* article by David Staba; the *Catholic Encyclopedia* online and the *Baptist Observer* online for information on Baptists and Roman Catholics.

CHAPTER TWELVE: THE STAR WITNESS

My primary sources were my interviews with Phil and Debbie McCord, Monsignor Fred Easton, Father Jim Bonke, and Dr. John Barker. I also used the transcript of the Indianapolis tribunal. Additional sources for this chapter were the Arthur C. Clarke Foundation, a March 19, 2008, obituary of Arthur C. Clarke in *The Times* (London). Information on placebos came from a non-bylined October 24, 2008, *Chicago Tribune* article and from information at Skepdic.com. Information on the power of prayer was culled from a June 15, 2008, *St. Petersburg Times* article by John Barry; a July 25, 2005, *Boston Globe* article by Alice Dembner; *Why We Believe What We Believe: Uncovering Our*

Biological Need for Meaning, Spirituality and Truth, by Dr. Andrew Newberg; *How God Changes Your Brain*, by Dr. Andrew Newberg and Mark Robert Waldman; a March 31, 2006, *Chicago Tribune* article by Jeremy Manier; a March 31, 2006, *Los Angeles Times* article by Denise Gellene and Thomas H. Maugh II; and a May 4, 2009, *Albany Times Union* article by Diane Cameron. Additional information on brain science came from a February 26, 2008, article by Christen Brownlee, published by the Johns Hopkins School of Medicine.

CHAPTER THIRTEEN: THE JURY

The opening section of the chapter was based on my interviews with Monsignor Fred Easton and Father Jim Bonke, on the Indianapolis Archdiocese tribunal transcript, and on photographs of the packaging procedure supplied by the Sisters of Providence. The passage on the Consulta Medica was drawn from my 2009 interview with Consulta member Dr. Francesco Santori. Other sources for this section included an article by Stefania Falasca retrieved from the Italian website "30 Days," http://www.30giorni.it/us/articolo.asp?id=3664; a May 1, 2000, *Newsweek* article by Kenneth L. Woodward; an October 20, 2003, article by Richard Owen in *The Times* (London); an article featuring Dr. Raffaello Cortesini, retrieved from http://www.enlightened-spirituality.org; an October 18, 2003, *Los Angeles Times* article by Tracy Wilkinson; an article on the Consulta *Medica* retrieved from the Spanish website, http://amigosnet; an article from the website http://www.pobladores.com/channels/religion/Somos_cristianos/area/20; and *The Miracle Detective: An Investigation of Holy Visions*, by Randall Sullivan. The final section on the wait at the Woods was drawn from my interviews with Phil McCord, Sister Marie Kevin Tighe, Monsignor Fred Easton, Father Jim Bonke, Dr. Andrea Ambrosi, and Sister Denise Wilkinson. Other sources were the August 2004 edition of *The Founding Spirit*; a BBC report on February 1, 2005, about John Paul II's hospitalization; a non-bylined February 7, 2005, article published by the Associated Press; and a non-bylined February 24, 2005, article published by the Associated Press.

CHAPTER FOURTEEN: THE VERDICT

I relied on my interview with Sister Marie Kevin Tighe and on my two visits to the Woods, especially the Providence Hall dining room. I also used these sources: a June 20, 1999, *Chicago Sun-Times* article by Ernest Tucker; a July 29, 2004, *Religion News Service* article by David Briggs; a non-bylined July 28, 2002, article published by the Associated Press; a March 15, 2005, *Frederick News-Post* article by Nancy Hernandez; a July 10, 2004, *Syracuse Post-Standard* article by Renee K. Gadoua; a non-bylined September 22, 2006, article in the *Sun-Journal* (Lewiston, ME); a December 9, 2006, *Philadelphia Inquirer* article by Kristin E. Holmes; a non-bylined January 22, 2007, article published by *Waste News*; a non-bylined April 12, 2008, article published by the Associated Press; and the Sisters of Providence website. The passage on the illness and death of Pope John Paul II was based on these sources: a March 21, 2005, *Chicago Sun-Times* article by Victor L. Simpson; a March 28, 2005, *Washington Post* article by Daniel Williams; an April 1, 2005, *Chicago Tribune* article by Liz Sly; an April 6, 2005, article by Valentine Low in the *Evening Standard* (London); an April 3, 2005, article by Victor L. Simpson, published by the Associated Press. The section on selecting the next pope was based on these sources: an April, 2, 2005, *Chicago Tribune* article by Liz Sly and Tom Hundley; a non-bylined February 3, 2005, Associated Press article; an April 19, 2005, *Chicago Tribune* article by William J. Kole; an April 19, 2005, *Washington Times* article by John Phillips; and an April 20, 2005, Associated Press article by Nicole Winfield. The section of the chapter on the verdict was based on my interviews with Dr. Andrea Ambrosi, Sister Marie Kevin Tighe, Sister Ann Margaret O'Hara, and Sister Denise Wilkinson, and on Sister Ann Margaret's e-mails, which were provided by the Sisters of Providence archives. Other sources for this section included the March 2006 edition of the *Founding Spirit*; the Vatican website; the Sisters of Providence website entry on the bells; *A History of Key Characteristics in the Eighteenth and Early Nineteenth Centuries*, by Rita Steblin; a February 22, 2006, article by Sue Loughlin in the *Terre Haute Tribune-Star*; and a July 1, 2006, article by Robert L. Flott in the *Wabash Valley Journal of Business*.

CHAPTER FIFTEEN: THE THIRD MIRACLE

The bulk of the chapter was drawn from my interviews with Sister Marie Kevin Tighe, Phil and Debbie McCord, Kathy Fleming, Sister Ann Margaret O'Hara, Sister Dennis Wilkinson, Monsignor Fred Easton, Father Jim Bonke, Dr. Andrea Ambrosi, Sister Diane Ris, Sister Nancy Nolan, and Sister Jenny

Howard. My other sources were a BBC report titled "I Believe in Miracles," aired on May 8, 2007; an April 29, 2006, *Indianapolis Star* article by Robert King; an October 12, 2006, *Indianapolis Star* article by Robert King; an October 15, 2006, *Indianapolis Star* article by Robert King; an October 15, 2006, *Terre Haute Tribune-Star* article by Mark Bennett; an October 16, 2006, *Indianapolis Star* article by Robert King; a non-bylined October 22, 2006, Associated Press article; an October 23, 2006, Associated Press article by Ryan Lenz; an October 24, 2006, article by Esperanza Juarez, published by *University Wire*; the Vatican website. Information about the day of canonization was provided by the Sisters of Providence.

EPILOGUE: THE PARTING

Opening descriptions were drawn from my visits and tours of Saint Mary-of-the-Woods in 2008 and 2009. I also relied on my interviews with Phil and Debbie McCord, Sister Denise Wilkinson, Sister Marie Kevin Tighe, Brother Barry Donaghue, Father Jim Bonke, Monsignor Fred Easton, Sister Nancy Reynolds, and information pulled from the Sisters of Providence website and from a May, 4, 2007, BBC report about the Woods.

Bibliography

Abou-El-Haj, Barbara. *The Medieval Cult of Saints: Formations and Transformations*. New York: Cambridge University Press, 1997.

Allen, John L., Jr. *All the Pope's Men: The Inside Story of How the Vatican Really Thinks*. New York: Doubleday Image, 2004.

Andrea, Alfred J. *Contemporary Sources for the Fourth Crusade*. Leiden, Netherlands: Brill Academic Publishers, 2000.

Beal, John P., James Coriden, and Thomas J. Green, eds. *A New Commentary on the Code of Canon Law*. Mahwah, NJ: Paulist Press, 2000.

Bertone, Cardinal Tarcisio. *The Last Secret of Fatima*. New York: Doubleday, 2008.

Blake, Rich. *The Day Donny Herbert Woke Up*. New York: Three Rivers Press, 2008.

Block, Daniel, I., Kenneth A. Mathews, and David S. Dockery, eds. *The New American Commentary: An Exegetical and Theological Exposition of the Holy Scripture*. Nashville, TN: B&H Publishing Group, 1999.

Burns, Paul, and Alban Butler. *Butler's Lives of the Saints: The Third Millennium*. London: Continuum Books, 2005.

Burton, Katherine. *The Eighth American Saint: The Story of Saint Mother Théodore Guérin, Foundress of the Sisters of Providence of Saint Mary-of-the-Woods Indiana*. Skokie, IL: ACTA Publications, 2006.

Geary, Patrick J. *Furta sacra: Thefts of relics in the central Middle Ages*. Princeton, NJ: Princeton University Press, 1978.

Greeley, Andrew M., and Mary G. Durkin. *How to Save the Catholic Church*. New York: Viking, 1984.

Kant, Immanuel. *Religion within the Limits of Reason Alone*. New York: HarperOne, 1960.

Lockyer, Herbert. *All the Miracles of the Bible*. Grand Rapids, MI: Zondervan, 1988.

Madden, Sister Mary Roger, S.P. *The Path Marked Out: History of the Sisters of Saint Mary-of-the-Woods*. Saint Mary-of-the-Woods, IN: Sisters of Providence, 1991.

Matthews, Dale A., and Clark, Connie. *The Faith Factor: Proof of the Healing Power of Prayer*. New York: Penguin, 1999.

Mug, Sister Mary Theodosia, ed. *Mother Théodore Guérin: Journals and Letters*. Saint Mary-of-the-Woods, IN: Sisters of Providence, 1937, 1978.

Newberg, Dr. Andrew, and Mark Robert Waldman. *How God Changes Your Brain*. New York: Ballantine Books, 2009.

Newberg, Dr. Andrew, and Mark Robert Waldman. *Why We Believe What We Believe: Uncovering Our Biological Need for Meaning, Spirituality and Truth*. New York: Free Press, 2006.

The New Testament via http://scriptures.lds.org/nt/contents.

The Old Testament via http://scriptures.lds.org/ot/contents.

Schleich Beer, Kathryn. *Hollywood and Catholic Women: Virgins, Whores, Mothers and Other Images*. Bloomington, IN: iUniverse, Inc., 2003.

A member of the congregation of the Sisters of Providence. *Life and Life-work of Mother Théodore Guérin*. New York: Benziger Brothers, 1904.

Sloan, Richard P. *Blind Faith: The Unholy Alliance of Religion and Medicine*. New York: St. Martin's Press, 2006.

Steblin, Rita. *A History of Key Characteristics in the Eighteenth and Early Nineteenth Centuries*. Rochester, NY: University of Rochester Press, 1996.

Sullivan, Randall. *The Miracle Detective: An Investigation of Holy Visions*. New York: Atlantic Monthly Press, 2004.

Vincenti, Walter G. *What Engineers Know and How They Know It: Analytical Studies from Aeronautical History*. Baltimore: Johns Hopkins University Press, 1993.

Woestman, William H., ed. *Canonization: Theology, History, Process*. Ottawa: St. Paul University, 2002.

Woodward, Kenneth L. *Making Saints: How the Catholic Church Determines Who Becomes a Saint, Who Doesn't, and Why*. New York: Touchstone, 1990, 1996.

Bill Briggs is the coauthor of *Amped: A Soldier's Race for Gold in the Shadow of War* (Wiley, 2008). He earned seven national awards for the *Denver Post*, from investigative journalism to humor pieces. His articles ranged from an exposé on a sexual predator coaching youth basketball to a series revealing dysfunction and financial irregularities within the U.S. Olympic Committee. Briggs also has written for MSNBC.com, the *Financial Times*, the *Miami Herald*, and the *Nashville Banner*, covering business, sports, health, travel, and crime. A native of Lansing, New York, Briggs has lived in Nashville, Tennessee; and Hallandale Beach, Florida. Briggs has one daughter, Andrea, a college student. He lives in Denver, Colorado, with his wife, Nancy.

Printed in the United States
by Baker & Taylor Publisher Services